I0037543

Debt & Bankruptcy Terms

Financial Education Is Your Best Investment

Published February 29, 2020

Revision 2.2

Financial Terms Dictionary

Copyright And Trademark Notices

Limits of Liability and Disclaimer of Warranties

The materials in this book are provided "as is" and without warranties of any kind either express or implied. The Author disclaims all warranties, express or implied, including, but not limited to, implied warranties of merchantability and fitness for a particular purpose.

The Author does not warrant that defects will be corrected, or that that the site or the server that makes this eBook available are free of viruses or other harmful components. The Author does not warrant or make any representations regarding the use or the results of the use of the materials in this book in terms of their correctness, accuracy, reliability, or otherwise. Applicable law may not allow the exclusion of implied warranties, so the above exclusion may not apply to you.

Under no circumstances, including, but not limited to, negligence, shall the Author be liable for any special or consequential damages that result from the use of, or the inability to use this eBook, even if the Author or his authorized representative has been advised of the possibility of such damages.

Applicable law may not allow the limitation or exclusion of liability or incidental or consequential damages, so the above limitation or exclusion may not apply to you. In no event shall the Author's total liability to you for all damages, losses, and causes of action (whether in contract, tort, including but not limited to, negligence or otherwise) exceed the amount paid by you, if any, for this eBook.

Facts and information are believed to be accurate at the time they were placed in this book. All data provided in this book is to be used for information purposes only. The information contained within is not intended to provide specific legal, financial or tax advice, or any other advice whatsoever, for any individual or company and should not be relied upon in that regard. The services described are only offered in jurisdictions where they may be legally offered. Information provided is not all-inclusive and is limited to information that is made available and such information should not be relied upon as all-inclusive or accurate.

You are advised to do your own due diligence when it comes to making business decisions and should use caution and seek the advice of qualified professionals. You should check with your accountant, lawyer, or professional advisor, before acting on this or any information. You may not consider any examples, documents, or other content in this eBook or otherwise provided by the Author to be the equivalent of professional advice.

The Author assumes no responsibility for any losses or damages resulting from your use of any link, information, or opportunity contained in this book or within any other information disclosed by the author in any form whatsoever.

About the Author

Thomas Herold is a successful entrepreneur, mediator, author, and personal development coach. He published over 35 books with over 200,000 copies distributed worldwide and the founder of seven online businesses.

For over ten years Thomas Herold has studied the monetary system and has experienced some profound insights on how money and wealth are related. After three years of successful investing in silver, he released 'Building Wealth with Silver - How to Profit From The Biggest Wealth Transfer in History' in 2012. One of the first books that illustrate in a remarkable, simple way the monetary system and its consequences.

He is the founder and CEO of the 'Financial Terms Dictionary' book series and website, which explains in detail and comprehensive form over 1000 financial terms. In his financial book series, he informs in detail and with practical examples all aspects of the financial sector. His educational materials are designed to help people get started with financial education.

In his 2018 released book 'The Money Deception', Mr. Herold provides the most sophisticated insight and shocking details about the current monetary system. Never before has the massive manipulation of money caused so much economic inequality in the world. In spite of these frightening facts, 'The Money Deception' also provides remarkable and simple solutions to create abundance for all people, and it's a must-read if you want to survive the global monetary transformation that's underway right now.

In 2019 he released an entirely new financial book series explaining in detail and with practical examples over 1000 financial terms. The 'Herold Financial IQ Series' contains currently of 16 titles covering every category of the financial market.

His latest book "High Credit Score Secrets" offers the most effective strategies to boost the average credit score from as low as 450 points to over 810. It teaches the tactics to build excellent credit, repair credit, monitor credit and how to guard that good score for a lifetime. It reached bestseller status in 2020 in three categories.

For more information please visit the author's websites:

High Credit Score Secrets - The Smart Raise & Repair Guide to Excellent Credit
https://highcreditscoresecrets.com

The Money Deception - What Banks & Government Don't Want You to Know
https://www.moneydeception.com

The Herold Financial IQ Series - Financial Education Is Your Best Investment
https://www.financial-dictionary.com

The Online Financial Dictionary - Over 1000 Terms Explained
https://www.financial-dictionary.info

Please Leave Your Review on Amazon

This book and the Financial IQ Series are self-published and the author does not have a contract with one of the five largest publishers, which are able to support the author's work with advertising. If you like this book, please consider leaving a solid 4 or 5-star review on Amazon.

Herold Financial IQ Series on Amazon

Table Of Contents

Annual Percentage Rate (APR)

The annual percentage rate, or APR, is the actual interest rate that a loan charges each year. This single percentage number is truthfully used to represent the literal annual expense of using money over the life span of a given loan. Annual percentage rate not only covers interest charged, but can also be comprised of extra costs or fees that are attached to a given loan transaction.

Credit cards and loans commonly offer differing explanations for transaction fees, the structure of their interest rates, and any late fees that are assessed. The annual percentage rate provides an easy to understand formula for expressing to borrowers the real and actual percentage number of fees and interest so that they can measure these up against the rates that other possible lenders will charge them.

Annual percentage rate can include many different elements besides interest. With a nominal APR, it simply involves the rate of a given payment period multiplied out to the exact numbers of payment periods existing in a year. The effective APR is often referred to as the mathematically true rate of interest for a given year. Effective APR's are commonly the fees charged plus the rate of compound interest.

On a home mortgage, effective annual percentage rates could factor in Private Mortgage Insurance, discount points, and even processing costs. Some hidden fees do not make their ways into an effective APR number. Because of this, you should always read the fine print surrounding an APR and the costs associated with a mortgage or loan. As an example of how an effective APR can be deceptive with mortgages, the one time fees that are charged in the front of a mortgage are commonly assumed to be divided over a loan's long repayment period. If you only utilize the loan for a short time frame, then the APR number will be thrown off by this. An effective APR on a mortgage might look lower than it actually is when the loan will be paid off significantly earlier than the term of the loan.

The government created the concept of annual percentage rate to stop loan companies and credit cards issuers from deceiving consumers with fancy expressions of interest charges and fees. The law requires that all loan issuers and credit card companies have to demonstrate this annual percentage rate to all customers. This is so the consumers will obtain a fair comprehension of the true rates that are associated with their particular transactions. While credit card companies are in fact permitted to promote their monthly basis of interest rates, they still have to clearly show the actual annual percentage rate to their customers in advance of a contract or agreement being signed by the consumer.

Annual percentage rate is sometimes confused with annual percentage yield. This can be vastly different from the APR. Annual percentage yield includes calculations of compounded interest in its numbers.

Asset Protection

Asset Protection and planning refers to strategies and practices for protecting personal wealth. It happens through deliberate and involved planning processes that safeguard individuals' assets from the potential claims of any creditors. Both businesses and individuals alike can employ these specific techniques to reduce the ability of creditors to seize personal or business property within the legal boundaries of creditor debtor law.

What makes Asset Protection so powerful is that it is able to insulate a variety of assets and all legally. It does not require any of the shady or illegal activities inherent in concealing assets, illegal money transferring, bankruptcy fraud, or tax evasion. The asset experts will warn their clients that efficient protection of assets starts in advance of a liability, incident, or claim occurring. The reason is that it is generally over late to begin arranging such protection afterward. There are a wide variety of normal means for protecting such personal or business assets. Among the most popular are family limited partnerships, accounts receivable financing, and asset protection trusts.

In the heavily litigious society of the United States, Asset Protection involves protecting property from those who might win a judgment in court. There are a variety of lawsuits that could threaten a person's or business' assets. Among these are car accident claims, unintentional negligent acts, and even foreclosure on property lawsuits where the mortgage is no longer paid. The ultimate goal in Asset Protection is to take any nonexempt from creditors assets and move them to a position where they become exempt assets beyond the reach of any claims of the various creditors.

Asset Protection which an individual or business does when a lawsuit is already underway or even imminent to be filed will likely be reversed by the courts. This way they can seize the hidden assets that were deliberately transferred to protect them from an imminent court case judgment. This is the ultimate reason why effective protection of assets has to start well in advance of the first hints of litigious activity or creditor claims.

Two principal goals must be combined in order to effectively construct an efficient and ironclad Asset Protection plan. These include achieving both long term and short term goals and reaching estate planning goals. The financial goals component involves clearly understanding present and future income sources, the amount of resources needed for retirement, and any resources which will remain to leave to any heirs via estate planning. This helps people to come up with highly detailed financial plans.

After this has been done, individuals will want to examine carefully any present assets to decide if they are effectively exempted from any and all sundry creditors. The ones that are not should be clearly repositioned so that they are exempt. This also involves planning to position future assets so that they are similarly effectively protected.

The next step is to come up with a complete and all inclusive estate plan. It should encompass all forms of asset protection and relevant planning via advanced techniques of estate planning. Among these are irrevocable trusts for the individuals, their children, spouses, and beneficiaries as well as family limited liability companies.

The most common mistake that people or businesses make with this Asset Protection planning is waiting until it is too late to safeguard the assets. The other mistake is assuming that such planning can be done rapidly or as a short term fix for a longer term problem. Protecting assets is ultimately longer term planning that must be done carefully and ahead of potential creditor claims on assets or pending lawsuits.

Assumable Loan

An assumable loan is one that permits a home buyer to take over, or assume, a home seller's contract on their mortgage. This is not permitted by every mortgage lender in the place of a typical home purchase. Loans that do not have Due On Sale clauses, such as the majority of VA and FHA types of mortgages, can usually be assumed and are considered to be assumable loans.

Assumable home loans work in the following manner. A current home owner will simply transfer over his or her mortgage contract and obligations to a purchaser who is qualified to take over. In the past decades of the 1970's and 1980's, these types of mortgage note assumptions proved to be quite popular. Back then, they could be done without even having to obtain the mortgage lender's authorization. These days, the only types of mortgages that may be assumable loans without needing a lender's actual permission are those that are made by the FHA or VA.

Assumable loans provide opportunities for both buyers and sellers. It is often the case that a home buyer will not be able to secure a better rate for a new mortgage than that provided by an already existing mortgage. This could result from the negative credit history of the buyer in question or the conditions existing in the market place at the time. As existing interest rates rise, the appeal of non-existent lower rates on mortgages commonly pushes prospective home buyers to look out for assumable loans. Such a home buyer who secures an assumable loan then has the responsibility for the mortgage that the home seller previously carried.

The existing rates of the mortgage carry over for the buyer as if the person had made the original contract themselves. This assumable loan process also saves the buyer a number of the settlement costs that are incurred in making a new mortgage. This can be a substantial cost savings benefit.

Sellers similarly benefit from assumable loans. It is not uncommon for sellers to wish to be involved in the savings that buyers realize in the process of transferring over an assumable loan. Because of this, the two parties commonly share in the savings.

As an example, when the sale price of the home in question is greater than the amount owed on the mortgage itself, then the buyer will often have to put down a significant down payment, which goes straight to the home seller in this case. Otherwise, the buyer might have to get another mortgage to come up with the difference in amounts. A seller's principal benefit in participating in such an assumable loan transfer lies in having a good chance of getting a better price for the home.

Bad Credit

Bad Credit refers to the results of failing to stay current on credit agreements. In practice it leads to an incapability of being approved on new lines of personal (or business) credit. It usually results because the individuals or businesses in question have failed to pay prior credit obligations or loans in a timely fashion. It could also mean that the individuals (or companies) in question have failed to repay their credit obligations whatsoever.

Several major credit bureaus actually maintain a complete record of individuals' credit histories in files called personal credit reports. These credit reporting agencies gather all relevant credit information, including timely or delinquent payments or defaults on credit card obligations and outstanding loans. They place all of this good and bad information alike on the individuals' personal credit reports. Any accounts that had high balances, went out for collection, or led to vehicle or personal property repossession or the filing of bankruptcy protection will all be noted on the credit reports.

These episodes lead to seriously bad credit. It becomes most derogatory when there are many cases of such negative credit items which become filed by creditors in relatively short time spans. There are many negative credit events that can cause lenders to shun businesses and individuals when they only appear even once on a given credit report. Among these are repossessions, bankruptcies, and foreclosures.

Such information which collects in individual and business credit reports becomes the cornerstone for credit scores. These represent three digit numerical portraits of any individuals' or entities' credit history at a particular moment in time. For individuals, such credit scores typically run the gamut of from 300 to 850. While 850 would represent the ultimate in perfect, spotless credit, 300 refers to the worst possible or no credit history scenarios.

In point of fact, every lender makes its own determination for what is a negative or positive credit score. A range of breakdowns are more or less consensus with many firms however. Variations naturally exist on these ranges, as some companies are more credit averse and risk prone than others are. From 700 to 850 is typically regarded as excellent to very good credit. From 680 to 699 is commonly called a good credit rating, as the average American possesses a 682 score. From 620 to 679 they consider to be average credit.

Low credit kicks in ranging from 580 on up to 619 in general. Poor credit runs from 500 to 579. Outright bad credit ranges from 300 to 499. Obviously there are some variances of opinion on what is considered a low versus a poor or bad credit score. A massive number of lenders draw the line at 620. Under this represents significant credit risks, while above it is a score with which many of them will work.

Having bad credit means that the majority of lenders do not really want to extend credit to these individuals since they are likely to run behind on the agreed-upon repayment terms that come with the account. This leads to credit applications being rejected. For those who do manage to get approval despite their poor credit, they will typically find that they are receiving greater interest rates than those borrowers who maintain high to good credit scores. This is because the lender requires greater compensation in exchange for taking on a higher degree of risk in lending to credit-risky personal profiles.

For those who suffer from bad credit, there are other consequences beyond having loan, mortgage, and credit card applications rejected or receiving higher interest rates provided with successful applications. Insurance companies use deceptive variations on credit scores to come up with the insurance rates which they offer. Utility companies as well as cell phone carriers will commonly exact a security deposit from those applicants who boast negative credit. Landlords of properties will often demand a larger security deposit from those with poor credit. They could simply reject the rental application altogether over it.

Bad Debt

Bad debts are those accounts receivable that simply can not be collected. Once businesses make the determination that they are not likely to be able to collect on such sums, then they actually write these off as complete losses for the company. A debt is not typically deemed to be un-collectable until every effort within reason has been made to collect on the debt that is owed. This status is not typically reached on a debt until the person or firm owing the debt has filed for bankruptcy. Another reason for a debt to be declared a bad debt would be when the costs of continuing to collect on the debt are greater than is the amount of the debt in question.

Such bad debts commonly show up on a company income statement as an expense. This actually reduces the company's net income. At this point, bad debts have been completely written off via crediting the account of the debtor. This cancels out any remaining balance on the debtor's account. Such bad debts prove to be money that has been totally lost by a firm. Because of this, these kinds of bad debts are referred to as expenses for a business.

Companies attempt to estimate their expenses in the form of bad debts using records from similar past time frames. They look to figure out how many bad debts will show up in the current time frame based on what happened before so that they can attempt to estimate their actual earnings. The majority of corporations come up with an allowance for bad debts, as they understand that a percentage of their debtors will never repay them completely. Banks and credit card companies are especially concerned with bad debt allowances, since much of their entire business model revolves around the issuing of credit and repayment of debts from businesses and individuals.

The real difficulty with bad debts lies in determining if and when they are actually dead. When a debtor disappears, the collateral is destroyed, a lawsuit statute of limitations expires, bankruptcy is discharged, or significant pattern of a debtor abandoning debts is present, then a debt is finally determined to be bad debt. These can be subjective measurements in some cases.

Income tax laws contain a different definition for bad debts. These debts can be deducted against regular income on a 1040 C Form. These personal debts are also able to be deducted against short term types of capital gains. Debts that are owed for services which have been rendered to a person or business are not considered taxing purpose bad debts. This is because no income is present for such unpaid services that can be taxed.

Where individuals are concerned, bad debt can refer to credit card debt or any other form of high interest debt. These kinds of debts take away money from the individual in interest payments every month, creating a negative cash flow. Good debt for an individual would be debt that is used to properly leverage investments. Such leveraged investments that create positive cash flow prove to be the most desirable forms of debt.

Bailout

Bailouts prove to be the action of handing money or other capital to a company, individual, or nation that will likely go down without help. This is done in an effort to keep the entity from financial insolvency, bankruptcy, or total failure. Sometimes bankruptcies are pursued to permit an organization to fail without panic, so that fear and systemic failure does not become endemic, taking down other similar entities along the way.

Various different groups might qualify for urgent bailouts. Countries like Greece have been prime examples in the year 2010. Companies such as major banks and insurance outfits have been deemed too big to fail in the several years preceding 2010, during the height of the financial crisis and resulting Great Recession. Other industries have qualified as well, including car manufacturers, airlines, and vital transportation industries.

A good example of companies that receive preferential bailout treatment lies in the transportation industry. The Untied States government believes that transportation proves to be the underlying core of the nation's economic versatility, necessary to support the country's geopolitical power.

Because of this, the Federal Government works to safeguard the largest companies involved in transportation from failing with low interest rate loans and subsidies, which are a form of bailout. Oil companies, airlines, railroads, and trucking companies could all be considered to be a critical part of this industry. Such firms are considered to be too big and important to fail because their services prove to be nationally and constantly necessary to support the country's economy and thereby its eventual security.

Bailouts that are done in an emergency fashion typically prove to be full of controversy. In 2008 in the United States, intense and angry debates erupted regarding the failing banking and car manufacturing businesses. The camp standing against such bailouts looked at them as a means of passing the expensive bill for the failures over to the taxpayers.

Leaders of this group savagely denounced any monetary bailouts of the big three car makers and large banks, which they said all needed to be broken up as punishment for mismanagement. They criticized a new moral hazard that was being created by guaranteeing safety nets to other businesses. They similarly did not like the big central bureaucracy that arises from government agencies selecting the size and disposition of the bailouts. Finally, government bailouts of these groups were attacked as a form of corporate welfare that continues the cycle of more corporate irresponsibility.

The other camp argued that these bailouts were necessary evils, since the state of the American economy did not prove to be solid enough to suffer the failure of either the major banks or the car makers. With the car makers, fully three million jobs stood on the line. The banking industry had the argument of systemic failure of the financial system backing it up. No one on the side of the bailouts pretended to like having to engage in them, but they were said to be necessary nonetheless. In the end, such bailouts were issued to both major industries totaling in the trillions of dollars.

Balanced Budget

The phrase balanced budget refers to the scenario within the world of financial planning or a government budgeting in which the aggregate revenues prove to be greater than or at least equal to the total expenses. Government budgets are called balanced after the fact, once a complete year's expenses and revenues have been tallied up and reconciled. A firm's operating budget over a coming year might also be referred to as a balanced one assuming that the estimate and forecasts show it will be in practice.

Balanced budget is most often utilized to refer to the government's official budgets. As an example, a government might issue press releases which claim they will have a budget which is balanced in the pending fiscal year. Politicians on the campaign trail might similarly argue they will balance the federal budget if they are elected to office. One should realize that the term balanced budget may either refer to a scenario in which the expenses and revenues balance out or in which the final revenues surpass the ending expenses. This can never be the case if the final expenses are greater than the actual revenues.

The phrase balanced surplus is frequently employed alongside a balanced budget. With a budget surplus, the revenues are higher than the aggregate expenses. The difference between revenues minus expenses equals the amount of the surplus. Within the world of business, such surpluses might be reinvested into the corporation itself. They might plow this money into useful R&D research and development, as one example. They could also chose to provide shareholders of the company with extra dividends or take care of their hard working employees by issuing bonus checks.

Where the government is concerned, such a budget surplus occasionally happens as a calendar year's worth of tax revenues are higher than the actual expenditures of the government concerned. With the United States, this concept of a surplus is extremely rare. In all the years since 1970, the country has only managed to post a budget surplus on four occasions. These were within the Clinton presidency years of 1998-2001 consecutively.

Budget deficits are the opposite of budget surpluses and stand in marked contrast to balanced budgets. With a deficit, it means that the actual expenses are higher than the associated offsetting revenues. Deficits such as this practically always mean that higher government debts will be accrued. As an example, with the United States debt totaling in at more than $20 trillion as of 2017, this represents the total sum of numerous budget deficits accrued over at least five decades.

Those who are in favor of such balanced budgets claim that the deficits the country has run up over past decades are strapping an un-payable mountain of debt to the future American generations who have no say in the matter. One day eventually, there will have to be taxes levied or the money supply inflated away in order service the debt, not just to pay it. This would devalue the currency severely and finally ruin the savings and investments of countless millions of American retirees and workers.

There are still other economists who believe that these budget deficits do serve a useful end-result. In the government's quiver to address recessions, deficit spending is a key arrow. In times of contraction in the national economy, demand plunges and causes the GDP gross domestic product to fall. With unemployment declining in these times of recession, actual revenue from the taxes which the government levies and collects drops.

This means that they can not balance the budget unless they slash their spending in various areas in order to equal out with the reduced tax base and receipts. Such a move cuts demand further and pressures GDP even more. It could plunge the entire economy into a vicious negative spiral if pursued rigorously, as has happened in Greece with its creditors and their bailout requirements to slash spending year in and year out. Deficit spending then will help to prop up and eventually stimulate flagging demand in the economy by juicing it up with capital that is sorely needed at times like these.

Bank Run

A bank run is an event that happens when a bank or financial institution's customers choose to withdraw all of their deposits at the same time. This happens because of fears of the solvency of a particular bank. The effect is like a snowball. The more individuals who pull out their funds the greater the default probability becomes. This in turn leads still other customers to pull out their deposits. Severe bank run cases can create a scenario where the reserves of the bank are insufficient to meet all withdrawal demands.

Bank runs like these are not usually a result of actual insolvency of a financial institution. Rather they occur because of panic. Such fear can still evolve into a self fulfilling prophecy as a greater number of clients request their money. What starts as rumor and panic can transform into an actual ugly insolvency scenario. This means the fear of a default can actually cause a default in banking circles.

Banks run into these troubling situations sometimes because they generally only hold a tiny percentage of their actual deposits at hand. When withdrawal demands rise, it forces banks to boost their cash reserves. A common method for doing this is to sell assets, often at fire sale prices because they need funds immediately. The losses banks book for selling off assets at greatly reduced prices can lead them to actual insolvency. A bank run can become a full scale bank panic when a number of banks experience such runs on them all at once.

The best known example of a bank run occurred surrounding the infamous stock market crash in 1929. This led to numerous runs on financial institutions throughout the United States and finally to the Great Depression. The cascade of runs on the banks in the end of 1929 and the beginning of 1930 became like dominos falling. One bank's failure created fear and caused the panic of customers at neighboring banks that motivated them to take out their deposits as well. A failing bank in Nashville at the time created a number of bank runs throughout the Southeastern U.S.

Still other runs on banks occurred in the Great Depression because of the rumors begun by individual clients of the banks. The Bank of United States told a New York customer in December of 1930 he should not sell a certain stock he held. He departed from the branch and told other customers and individuals that the bank could not or would not sell his stock shares. Clients of the bank thought this meant the bank was insolvent. Thousands of them then lined up and withdrew more than $2 million out of the bank in only hours.

The developed nations' governments enacted a serious of steps to decrease the possibilities for future date bank runs as a result of the chaos in the 1930s. The most effective centered on minimum bank reserve requirements. These dictated what percent of aggregate deposits banks had to keep readily available in cash.

In 1933, the American Congress also created the FDIC Federal Deposit Insurance Corporation. They established it as a direct result of the numerous bank failures. The government agency has since then insured deposits in banks to a maximum account amount. It works to keep up public confidence and banking stability within the financial system of the United States.

Bank Stress Tests

Bank stress tests are special analyses that a government authority or company runs to determine the strength of a bank to resist difficult economic times. They conduct such tests using economic conditions that are unfavorable to learn if the banks possess sufficient capital to survive the effects of negative financial environments. In the United States, the law requires that banks which claim at least $50 billion worth of assets must perform their own internal stress tests. Their risk management department is responsible for overseeing these. The Federal Reserve conducts these stress tests on such banks as well.

The idea behind these bank stress tests is to look at several critical risks which can afflict the banks and banking system. They are supposed to evaluate the financial condition of the bank being tested in one or more crisis scenarios with regards to liquidity risk, market risk, and credit risk. The tests simulate fictitious potential crises using a number of different factors that the International Monetary Fund and Federal Reserve determine.

This mostly came about after the worldwide financial crisis and Great Recession of 2007-2009. As many banks had failed or nearly collapsed, government and international bodies became more concerned about checking on the financial strength of banks in potential crisis scenarios.

These bank stress tests were effectively set up and used on a widespread basis after this worst collapse since the Great Depression of the 1930s. The financial crisis had left in its wake a number of financial institutions, investment banks, and commercial banks that had insufficient capital. The stress tests were established to deal with this threat before it became severely problematic again.

There are two main types of bank stress tests that exist. The Federal Reserve runs its own yearly oversight stress tests of the U.S. banks that have at least $50 billion in assets on their balance sheets. The primary purpose of such a stress test is to learn if the banks possess sufficient capital to weather the storm of challenging economic conditions.

The company operated stress tests are done twice a year by law. They must be strictly reported according to the deadlines set by the Fed. Results must be turned in to the Federal Reserve board by no later than January 5th and July 5th.

In either of the stress tests, the banks receive a typical set of circumstances to evaluate their performance. It might be a 30% free fall in the prices of housing, a 5% to 10% decline in the stock market, and a 10% or higher unemployment rate. The banks must then take their future nine quarters of financial forecasts to ascertain if their capital levels are sufficient to endure the hypothetical crisis.

These bank stress tests have broader repercussions. Banks must make public their results by publishing them after they undergo the tests. The pubic and investors then learn how the bank in question would survive in a significant crisis situation. Laws and regulations passed since the financial crisis require that companies which are unable to pass the stress tests must cut their share buyback programs and dividend payments so that they can preserve the capital they have.

There are cases where banks receive a conditional passing grade on a stress test. This result states that the bank nearly failed its test. It puts them at risk of not being allowed to engage in more capital distributions going forward. Conditional passing means that a bank has to turn in a plan of action to address the capital shortfall.

These failures cause a bank to look bad to not only investors but the banking public. There have been a number of banks that failed such stress tests. Foreign banks like Germany's Deutsche Bank and Spain's Santander have failed to pass such tests on a number of occasions.

Bankruptcy

Bankruptcy is a term that refers to the elimination or restructuring of a person or company's debt. Three principal different types of bankruptcy filing are available. These are the personal bankruptcy options of Chapter 7 and Chapter 13 filings, and the business bankruptcy restructuring option of Chapter 11.

Individuals avail themselves of Chapter 7 or Chapter 13 bankruptcy filings when their financial situations warrant significant help. With a Chapter 7 filing, all of an individual's debt is erased through discharge. This provides a new start for the debtor. Due to changes in laws made back in October 2005, not every person is able to obtain this type of total debt relief any longer. As a result of this new bankruptcy law, a means test came into being that prospective bankruptcy filers must successfully pass if they are to prove eligibility for this kind of bankruptcy relief.

The net effect of this new test is that consumers find it much more difficult to qualify for total debt elimination under Chapter 7. Besides the means test, the cost of bankruptcy attorneys has now risen dramatically by upwards of a hundred percent as a result of the new laws. Before these laws went into effect, Chapter 7 filings represented around seventy percent of all personal filings for bankruptcy. Chapter 7 offered the individual the advantage of simply walking away from debts that they might be capable of paying back with sufficient time and some interest rate help.

Chapter 13 Bankruptcy filings prove to be much like debt restructuring procedures. In these proceedings, a person's creditors are made to agree to the repayment of principal and zero interest on debts over a longer span of time. The individual gets to keep all of her or his assets in this form of filing. The most common motivation for Chapter 13 proves to be a desire to stop a foreclosure on a home. Individuals are able to achieve this by halting foreclosure proceedings and catch up on back mortgage payments. Once a court examines the debtor's budget, it will sign off on the plan for repayment proposed by the person. Depending on the level of an individual's income, he or she may have no choice but to file a Chapter 13 filling, as a result to the 2005 law changes.

Companies and corporations that are in financial distress may avail themselves of bankruptcy protection as well. Chapter 11 allows for such businesses to have protection from their creditors while they restructure their debt. Some individuals who have a higher income level will take advantage of this form of filing as well, since it does not place income restrictions on the entity filing. It has been instrumental in saving many large and well known companies over the years, including K-Mart, that actually emerged strong enough from the Chapter 11 bankruptcy to buy out higher end rival Sears afterward.

Blanket Loans

Blanket loans are those which cover multiple properties or parcels of land. They handle the costs for or can be secured by more than a single piece of real estate. These are most typically employed by commercial land developers or investors. For individual consumers, they can be utilized as a type of bridge between new and old properties and mortgages. For these consumers, such a blanket loan will make it possible to pay for both mortgages until the owner reaches the point of selling the old property.

The feature that makes these mortgages most useful for developers is their release clause. These permit the borrowers to sell a single or even several pieces of real estate without the need of being forced to refinance the mortgage. This makes them significantly different from traditional mortgages. Normal mortgages make borrowers completely pay down their loan balance before they can sell the property which secures them.

For developers of residential properties, they find these blanket loans particularly helpful. They employ them to pay for large tracts of land on which they will build. When it is time for the loan to fund, it becomes secured by the full piece of property. The developer is allowed to subdivide his property and sell it in individual lots. For part of the security to be released, the developer must utilize some of the sale proceeds to pay down part of the loan.

This is helpful when builders are constructing subdivisions. Such a developer could put the blanket loan to use to buy the consecutive pieces of land while they are available. The developer would then be able to subdivide the total land into specific lots for building houses. With each home that he finishes and sells, the property becomes detached from the blanket loan without the financing having to be disrupted on the remainder of the development project.

Consumers also find these types of blanket loans helpful in making it possible to transition from the sale of their current home to the building or buying of the new house. This makes much more sense than having two concurrent mortgages or obtaining a more costly short term bridge loan. It can also help them so that they do not have to sell the property early and move into a rental while they look for a property to purchase.

These kinds of blanket loans are often governed by a contingency clause. These clauses detail that the newly purchased house and its mortgage will not close until the person is able to sell the existing home. The problem with such a contingency clause is that they have limited time frames on them. They may force a borrower into selling the home in a panic in order to meet the clause expiration date. This can lead to a lower selling price or disadvantageous terms on the sale.

Blanket loans get around such a dilemma by providing the borrowers with an extended period of time in the clause to sell their old house. Sometimes they are arranged as interest payment only loans for a full 12 months before amortizing starts. This gives the seller a sufficient time period to sell the house for a good price and reduces the overall burden of the mortgage at the same time.

The main downside to blanket loans for individuals is that they are significantly harder to find since the real estate crash and Great Recession of 2009. Their advantages include both flexibility and efficiency in financing. For an individual consumer, this means a single mortgage payment rather than two. Developers do not have to worry about constantly refinancing their property debt as they sell off parts of the property. Should a developer default on his loan, the bank simply assumes control of all remaining property which secures the loan.

C Corporation

C Corporations refers to the primary subchapter under which American businesses decide to incorporate themselves in order to restrict the total financial and legal liabilities of the owners. Such C Corporations prove to be the principle alternatives to S Corporations, whose profits are able to pass directly through to the owners and so only become taxable on the individual level. Limited liability companies are the other main choice to the C corporations. They deliver all of the legal safeties of corporations yet become tax treated as if they were sole proprietorships.

Unfortunately for C Corporations, they do suffer the effects of double taxation. Yet they do also permit the businesses to reinvest their profits back into the firm with a lower corporate tax rate penalty. The majority of incorporated companies within the United States turn out to be C Corporations.

Organizing a corporation starts with the new owners selecting the new entity's name (and in many states registering or reserving it with the secretary of state) of the new business enterprise. The owners must draft up the articles of incorporation and file them with the appropriate state business department. The first shareholders will then be issued their stock certificates once the business is established. Every C Corporation has to first file the Form SS-4 in order to get their EIN employer identification number. Every jurisdiction has its own varying requirements for these obligations, yet the corporations generally must file income, state, payroll, disability, and unemployment taxes for their employees.

Such C Corporations must hold minimally one meeting per year for the benefit of both the directors and the shareholders. These must have meeting minutes kept in order to transparently display the ways and means in which the business functions. There will have to be voting records maintained of the company directors as well as a full list of all owners' names and their ownership percentages in the firm. The company bylaws are required to be kept on the business headquarter premises at all times. Such enterprises also have to file all necessary financial disclosure reports, annual reports, and relevant financial statements with the SEC.

There are many benefits to such C Corporations. Most importantly for owners, they first limit the liability of all shareholders, directors, officers, and employees. It is not possible for the legal and debt obligations from the company to transfer over to one or more individuals under this type of corporate structuring. Even if each of the company owners become changed out, the corporation continues its existence. There is no limit to the numbers of shareholders and owners with this kind of corporation either as there would be with an S Corporation. Yet these must be registered properly with the SEC Securities and Exchange Commission once they reach a certain number of shareholders.

The primary downside to the C corporations centers on the idea of double taxation. As the firm generates its income, it will have to file a corporate tax return with the IRS Internal Revenue Service. Once the appropriate business expenses (including salaries) have been deducted from the gross income, the rest becomes subjected to corporate income taxes. Much of the remaining net income will then be distributed out to shareholders in what is called dividends. The income to the shareholders must be reported on the recipients' tax returns. This means that the C Corporation profits are being twice taxed, once at the corporate tax rate level and a second on the individuals' tax rate level. That income which is retained earnings will avoid double taxation only. It helps to explain why mega corporations like Apple hold on to billions of dollars in retained earnings routinely.

Cash Flow

Cash Flow is either an incoming revenue or outgoing expense stream that affects the value of any cash account over time. Inflows of cash, or positive cash flows, typically result from one of three possible activities, including operations, investing, or financing for businesses or individuals. Individuals are also able to realize positive cash flows from gifts or donations.

Negative cash flow is also called cash outflows. Outflows of cash happen because of either expenses or investments made. This is the case for both individuals' finances, as well as for those of businesses.

Where both individual finances and business corporate finances are concerned, positive cash flows are required to maintain solvency. Cash flows could be demonstrated because of a past transaction like selling a business product or a personal item or investment. They might also be projected into a future time for some consideration that a company or individual anticipates receiving and then possibly spending. No person or corporation can survive for long without cash flow.

Positive cash flow is essential for a variety of needs. Sufficient cash flow allows for money for you to pay your personal bills and creditors. It also allows a business to cover the costs of employee payroll, suppliers' bills, and creditors' payments in a timely fashion. When individuals and businesses lack sufficient cash on hand to maintain their budget or operations, then they are named insolvent. Lasting insolvency generally leads to personal or corporate bankruptcy.

For businesses, statements of cash flows are created by accountants. These demonstrate the quantity of cash that is created and utilized by a corporation in a certain time frame. Cash flows in this definition are calculated by totaling net income following taxes with non cash charges like depreciation. Cash flow is able to be assigned to either a business' entire operations or to one particular segment or project of the company. Cash flow is often considered to be an effective measurement of a business' ongoing financial strength.

Cash flows are also used by business and individuals to ascertain the value or return of a project or investment. The numbers of cash flows in to and out of such projects and investments are often utilized as inputs for indicators of performance like net present value and internal rate of return. A problem with a business' liquidity can also be determined by measuring the entire entity's cash flow.

Many individuals prefer investments that yield periodic positive cash flow over ones that pay only one time capital gains. High yielding dividend stocks, energy trusts, and real estate investment trusts are all examples of positive cash flow investments. Real estate properties can also be positive cash flow yielding investments when they provide greater amounts of rental income than their combined monthly mortgage payments, maintenance expenses, and property management upkeep costs and outflows total.

Cash Reserves

Cash reserves refer to money which an individual person, a company, or a corporation saves in order to be ready to cover any emergency funding or short term requirements. They can also be utilized to refer to a kind of extremely liquid, short term investment which usually garners a poor rate of return (under three percent in a year).

An example of this would be Fidelity Cash Reserves, one of the Fidelity mutual families of funds particular investments. Sometimes individuals will hold money they need rapid access to in such a fund which can be instantly liquidated on the same day they issue the order. Possessing a major amount in a cash reserve fund provides corporations, companies, individuals, families, or communities with the necessary capability to engage in a significant purchase right away.

There are various reasons why firms wish to maintain some cash reserves. They need to have sufficient money on hand in order to cover all of their costs which may be anticipated or even unanticipated over the short term time-frame. Besides this, they often prefer to have enough cash readily available for such interesting possible investments which could arise with little to no warning.

Though cash is always considered to be the most liquid type of wealth and assets, there are also short term kinds of assets like three month U.S. Treasury bills which investors also deem to be a type of a cash reserve because of the ease and frequency with which they can exchange them and their close proximity to maturity date. Major corporations like Alphabet (Google), General Electric, IBM, and Apple keep enormous cash reserves available. These typically range from fifty billion dollars to one hundred and fifty billion dollars.

At the beginning of 2016, Apple boasted such cash reserve ranging from fifty billion to one hundred fifty billion dollars. At the same time, Alphabet (Google) counted $75.3 billion in their immediate cash on hand reserves. This permitted Google to buy out major corporate purchases like their acquisition of Nest, which they bought for a hefty $3 billion price tag back in 2014.

With banks, governmental oversight agencies require that they maintain a minimum quantity of cash reserves on hand. This is because their operations are critical for the functioning of any economy. In the United States, it is the American Federal Reserve that determines these cash reserve amounts for the banks. In other countries, it is often the national central bank or some other governmental oversight regulator who makes the call.

Banking cash reserves will typically be set as a certain percentage of the banks' liabilities or net transaction accounts. With those banks which contain in excess of $110.2 million in their net transaction accounts, this amount within the U.S. proves to be 10 percent of such liabilities. This amount became effective on January 1st of 2016. Such bank reserves have to be kept in either deposits at a Federal Reserve Bank or in their own vaults as cash on hand. With euro currency liabilities or time deposits of a non-personal nature, these liabilities are not subjected to such a cash reserve requirement.

Economists and personal finance gurus generally state that individuals are wise to keep minimally sufficient cash on hand to cover from three to six months of expenses in the event they suffer a family emergency. Such an emergency fund is a form of a cash reserve. These reserves would be kept in either their local bank accounts or otherwise in a stable and short term time frame investment which will maintain its value regardless of what happens in the markets. In this way, individuals are able to draw on their own emergency funds or alternatively to sell such investments at a moment's notice without taking a financial loss. This needs to be the case no matter how the financial investment markets are performing.

Other forms of personal cash reserves could be held in a savings account, checking account, money market account, money market fund, or even CDs and Treasury Bills. For those businesses or individuals who do not plan ahead with enough cash reserves, they may have to instead to fall back on credit, loans, or in some drastic cases, declaring bankruptcy.

Chapter 11 Bankruptcy

Chapter 11 Bankruptcy proves to be a specific type of bankruptcy. This kind has to do with the business assets, debts, and affairs being reorganized. The business reorganization filing was named for the Section 11 of the United States' Bankruptcy Code. Corporations commonly file it that need some time to rearrange the terms of their debts and their business operations. It gives them a fresh start on repaying their debt obligations. Naturally the indebted company will have to stick to the terms of the reorganization plan. This proves to be the most highly complex type of bankruptcy filing possible. Companies have been advised to only entertain it once they have contemplated their other options and analyzed the repercussions of such a filing.

This Chapter 11 bankruptcy rarely makes the news unless it is a nationally known or famous corporation which is filing. Among the major corporations that have filed such a Chapter 11 bankruptcy are United Airlines, General Motors, K-Mart, and Lehman Brothers. The first three successfully emerged from it and became as great or stronger than they were before falling into hard times financially. In reality, the vast majority of these cases are unknown to the general public. As an example, in the year 2010, nearly 14,000 separate corporations filed for Chapter 11.

The point of this Chapter 11 Bankruptcy is to assist a corporation in restructuring both obligations and debts. The goal is not to close down the business. In fact it rarely leads to the corporation closing. Instead, corporations like K-mart, General Motors, and tens of thousands of others were able to survive and once again thrive thanks to the useful process of protection from creditors and reorganization of business debts.

It is typically LLCs Limited Liability Companies, partnerships, and corporations that make application for Chapter 11 Bankruptcy. There are cases where individuals who are positively saddled with debt and who are not able to be approved for a Chapter 13 or Chapter 7 filing can be qualified for Chapter 11 instead. The time table for successfully completing Chapter 11 bankruptcy ranges from several months to as long as two years.

Businesses that are in the middle of their Chapter 11 cases are encouraged to keep operating. The debtor in possession will typically run the business normally. Where there are cases that have gross incompetence, dishonest dealings, or even fraud involved, typically trustees come in to take over the business and its daily operations while the bankruptcy proceedings are ongoing.

Corporations in the midst of these filings will not be permitted to engage in specific decisions without first having to consult with the courts to proceed. They may not terminate or sign rental agreements, sell any assets beyond regular inventory, or expand existing business operations or alternatively cease them. The bankruptcy court retains full control regarding any hiring and paying of lawyers as well as signing contracts with either unions or vendors. Lastly, such indebted organizations and entities may not sign for a loan that will pay once the bankruptcy process finishes.

After the business or person files their chapter 11 bankruptcy, it gains the right to offer a first reorganization plan. Such plans often include renegotiating owed debts and reducing the company size in order to slash expenses. There are some scenarios where the plan will require every asset to be liquidated in order to pay off the creditors, as with Lehman Brothers.

When plans are fair and workable, courts will approve them. This moves the reorganization process ahead. For plans to be accepted, they also have to maintain the creditors' best interests for the future repayment of debts owed to them. When the debtor can not or will not put forward a plan of their own for reorganization, then the creditors are invited to offer one in the indebted company or person's place.

Chapter 7 Bankruptcy

Chapter 7 bankruptcy is a form of protection from creditors. Unlike Chapter 13 bankruptcy, it does not have any repayment plan. In the Chapter 7 a bankruptcy trustee determines what eligible assets the debtor individual or company has. The trustee then collects these available assets, sells them, and distributes proceeds to the creditors against their debts. This is all done under the rules of the Bankruptcy Code.

Debtors are permitted to keep specific property that is exempt, such as their house. Other property that the debtor holds will be mortgaged or have liens put against it to pledge it to the various creditors until it is liquidated. Debtors who file chapter 7 will likely forfeit property in partial payment of debts.

Chapter 7 bankruptcy is available to corporations, partnerships, and individuals who pass a means test. The relief can be granted whether or not the debtor is ruled to be insolvent.

Chapter 7 bankruptcy cases start when debtors file their petitions with their particular area's bankruptcy court. For businesses, they use the address where the main office is located. Debtors are required to give the court information that includes schedules of current expenditures and income and liabilities and assets.

They are also required to furnish a financial affairs statement and a schedule of contracts and leases which are not expired. The debtors will also have to deliver the trustee tax return copies from the most current tax year along with any tax returns which they file while the case is ongoing.

Debtors who are individuals also have to furnish their court with other documents. They are required to file a credit counseling certificate and any repayment plan created there. They must also file proof of income from employers 60 days before their original filing, a monthly income statement along with expected increases in either, and notice of interest they have in tuition or state education accounts. Husbands and wives are allowed to file individually or jointly. They must abide by the requirements for individual debtors either way.

The courts are required to charge debtors who file $335 in filing, administrative, and trustee fees. Debtors typically pay these when they file to the clerk of court. The court can give permission for individuals to pay by installments instead. When the income of debtor's proves to be less than 150% of the amount of the poverty level, the court can choose to drop the fee requirements.

Debtors will have to provide a great amount of information in order to complete their Chapter 7 filing and receive a discharge of debts. They have to list out each of their creditors along with the amounts they owe then and the type of claim. Debtors have to furnish a list of all property the own. They must also give the information on the amount, source, and frequency of income they have to the court.

Finally, they will be required to provide an in depth list of all monthly living expenses that includes housing, utilities, food, transportation, clothing, medicine, and taxes. This helps the court to determine if the debtor is able to set up a repayment plan instead of discharging the debts.

From 21 to 40 days after the debtor files the petition with the courts, the trustee hosts a creditors' meeting. The debtor will have to cooperate with the trustee on any requests for additional financial documents or records. At this meeting, the trustee will ask questions to make sure the debtor is fully aware of the consequences of debt discharge by the bankruptcy court. Sometimes trustees will deliver this in written form to the debtor before or at the meeting. Assuming the trustee makes the recommendation for discharge, the Federal bankruptcy court judge will discharge the debts when the process is completed.

Collateral

Collateral refers to an asset or piece of Real Estate which borrowers provide as security to lenders in exchange for a loan. This property actually secures the mortgage or other form of loan. In the event that the borrowers do not continue to make the agreed upon payments on the loan according to the laid out schedule, the financial institution has the right to seize this property in order to recover the principal losses.

Because such collateral provides at least nominal security to the lending institution in the scenarios where the borrower refuses to or is unable repay the loan, these forms of loans are commonly provided with lower interest rates as compared to those loans which are unsecured entirely. When such a lender has interest in the underlying property provided by the borrower then this is referred to as a lien.

In the end there are several arrangements with such collateral. The type of loan often determines which form will be required within the contract. With car loans or mortgages, the loans are secured by the property upon which the financial institution issues the loan. Other forms of loans have more flexible security, as with collateralized personal loans. In order for any loan to be called secured, the backing security has to be at least equal to or greater than the balance that remains on the loan in question.

Such secured loans entail far less risk for lenders because the underlying property serves as an incentive for the borrower to keep paying back the loan. Borrowers know all too well that if they do not complete the required payments then the financial institution which holds the loan may legally possess (or repossess) this collateral in order to recoup the money it is owed on the rest of the loan.

With mortgages, the collateral in question will always be the home that the borrower buys using the loan in the first place. If and when they fail to pay the debts, then the lender may seize possession of the property by utilizing a procedure called foreclosure. After the lender completes the necessary court process and has the property back in its possession, it is allowed to sell off the home to someone else. This will permit the bank to cover the principal which remains on the original loan along with their costs for the foreclosure.

Houses also can also be utilized for second mortgage collateral, or against HELOC's (Home Equity Lines of Credit). In such scenarios, the credit delivered by the financial institution may not be greater than the equity which exists within the home itself. As a tangible example, a home could have a market value of $300,000. At the same time, it might be that $175,000 of the original mortgage balance remains to pay. This would mean that the majority of HELOC's or even second mortgages would not exceed the available equity of $125,000.

Collateral is also utilized in margin accounts' trading of stocks, commodities, and futures. In this case, it is the securities themselves that become the property which secures the brokerage loan. In the event that a margin call has to be issued and the account holder will not or can not pay it on demand, then the securities' value ultimately makes certain that the brokerage will get back its loaned money.

Sometimes financial institutions will require additional collateral be put up for a given existing loan, if the contract allows such a scenario. This will reduce increasing risks for the lending institution. A creditor could give notice that without such additional security, they will be forced to raise the interest rate on the loan. Additionally accepted security could be certificates of deposit, cash, equipment, letters of credit, or even shares of stock.

Compound Interest

Compound interest represents interest which calculates on both the original principal amount as well as the interest that was accumulated previously during the loan or investment. Economists have called this miraculous phenomenon an interest on interest. It causes loans or invested deposits to increase at a significantly faster pace than only simple interest, the opposite of compound interest. Simple interest proves to be interest that calculates on just the principal amount of money.

Compound interest accrues at an interest rate which determines how often the compounding occurs. The higher the compound interest rate turns out to be, the faster the principal will compound and the more compounding periods will occur. Consider an example of how effective compounding truly is. $100 that is compounded at a rate of 10% per year will turn out to be less than $100 which is compounded at only 5% but semi annually during the same length of time.

Compound interest is important to individuals as it is able to take a few dollars worth of savings now and transform them into significant money throughout lifetimes. Investors do not need an MBA or a Wall Street background in order to benefit from this principle. Practically all investments earn compounding interest if the owners leave these earnings in the investment account over the long term.

This form of interest cuts both ways on the receiving and paying sides. When individuals are saving and investing money, it helps them grow the amount faster. When they are borrowing and paying the same interest on the debt, it grows against them faster. Individuals who are saving wish their money to compound as often as they can. Individuals who are borrowing wish it to compound as infrequently as possible. Savers are better off if they are able to compound quarterly instead of annually while just the opposite is true for borrowers.

For people who are compounding their investments, time works on their side. Money that grows at a rate of 6% each year doubles every 12 years. This means that it increases to four times as much as the original amount in only 24 years. For individuals paying compound interest, time is similarly working against them. Credit card companies utilize this principle to keep their card owners in debt forever by encouraging them to only make minimum monthly payments on the bills.

Thanks to compounding, a smaller amount of money that a person adds to an account upfront is more valuable than a larger sum of money he or she adds decades later. This cuts both ways. By paying down principal on a credit card with an extra $5 per month, the amount of compound interest individuals pay on a 14% interest rate credit card decreases by $1,315 over ten years. This is true even though they have paid only $600 in extra payments over this amount of time.

Anyone can make the miracle of compounding work for them. The idea works the same whether individuals are investing $100 or $100 million instead. Millionaires have greater ranges of investment choices. Even relatively poor people can compound their interest to increase their original amount and double their money as often as possible.

Compounding interest means that participants have to give up using some dollars today in order to obtain a greater benefit from them in the future. The little money may be missed now, but the rewards for the more significant amounts in the future will more than make up for the little sacrifice the individual makes now. Financial planners have claimed that the difference between poverty and financial comfort in the future amounts to even a few dollars in savings each week invested now rather than later.

Compounding of Money

The compounding of money has everything to do with compound interest. Compounding of money through such compounding interest can become among the most potent of weapons in your investing arsenal. Compound interest allows your money to grow at a faster rate as a result of the way that the interest is added to your money's balance. Various types of compound interest are available for compounding your money.

Compounding your money with compound interest works through taking the interest that your money has earned over a time frame and adding it back to the initial amount of money. Then when the next period is figured up, this total dollar value is calculated in the next portion of interest that you will earn. Simply put, every time frame's interest is placed directly back in to the entire sum of money on which the interest will be earned. Every time the interest is figured up, your money will earn a greater amount of interest like this.

A variety of different forms of compound interest exist. These always relate to the time frame over which the interest and money compounds. Such time frames of compounding of money are comprised of yearly, monthly, and daily compounding interest. With yearly compounding interest, the interest rate is figured up each year. In monthly compounding of interest, this rate is applied to the new principal balance each month. Daily compounding of interest involves an every day accounting of the interest and new principal.

Compounding of money involves several factors. These are periodic rates of compound interest, which are the rates actually applied to your balance, and compounding periods, which are the amount of the time frame before such interest is literally applied on to your total balance. As an example, if you invested $10,000 in a .1% daily periodic rate money market form of account, then on the second day, your balance would be $10,010. The next day, this rate would then be applied to the new balance of $10,010. Figuring out the actual annual effective rate entails you taking the whole year's interest and dividing it by the amount of the investment that you started with at the beginning of the year, or $10,000 in this case.

Compounding of money through such compound interest proves to be an extremely potent weapon. This is because the interest earned is immediately added on to the account balance to be counted as principal for the next time period. Each time frame the interest rate applies to the greater balance. Accounts grow faster through the compounding of money as the interest is not held back.

This compounding of money effect multiplies when you use it with accounts that are tax deferred, such as municipal bond funds and annuities. As no penalties of taxes are paid in a given year, your money increases quicker and quicker since greater amounts are constantly in the account to receive interest.

An example of how effective compounding of money using compound interest can be is illuminating. If you put $10,000 into a simple interest account that does not compound but receives twelve percent interest, then it will increase to $46,000 over thirty years. The same money that is compounded annually will rise to about $300,000, and to as much as $347,000 if the money is compounded quarterly. Money that is compounded over a daily time frame would naturally earn the greatest amount of interest and highest principal over a period of time.

Constructive Eviction

Constructive eviction is a backdoor way of evicting a tenant. It is not done through legal means because of a tenant failing to pay rent or seriously breaking the property rules. It is instead the process of a landlord making a rental uninhabitable for the tenant. Though the term sounds positive, it is quite the opposite. Landlords who engage in this type of eviction are failing to carry out their legal obligations.

For constructive eviction to take place, a residential rental property must deteriorate into enough disrepair that it becomes very difficult or near impossible to live in the property. It could also be that the landlord allows a condition to exist that makes inhabiting the home or apartment intolerable. As the condition becomes so severe that the property is no longer fit to live in, the tenant is forced to leave. An uninhabitable property exists in a state that compels the renter to move away, or to be constructively evicted. Because the renter is incapable of completely utilizing and possessing the property, he or she has been evicted technically.

There are a number of way in which a tenant could be a victim of constructive eviction. The landlord might turn off the electricity, gas, or water utilities. The owner might disregard an environmental problem such as toxic mold or flaking off lead paint and not properly clean it. He or she could also not fix leaking roofs. This causes water damage to walls and eventually leads to mold. The owners could block the unit entrance or change the locks. They might do something extreme such as take out sinks or toilets from the property as well. When the conditions deteriorate to the point that tenants abandon the rental then constructive eviction has occurred.

A landlord might engage in this type of unethical behavior because of rental controls. Many cities limit the amount by which rent can be increased. They may also allow the tenant to remain in the rental with an automatically renewing lease so long as they fulfill the contract obligations.

Tenants have the ability to fight back against this type of eviction. This starts with providing the owner a notice in writing of the constructive eviction. The landlord must be given a fair amount of time to address the issue. This may not translate to an instant repair that happens in 24 hours. Many repairs require more time to have completed. Water and gas leaks are examples of these. Still the repairs have to be done in a time frame that is reasonable.

Renters who find themselves in living conditions that are poor should take pictures. They also should invite independent inspectors to examine the property. These types of inspectors come from the permit or building department, as well as from the area health department.

When landlords are unwilling to address the uninhabitable living conditions in a reasonable time frame after having been given fair written notice, renters have rights. They are usually allowed to leave the property without having to pay rent that would still be owed according to the rental or lease agreement. In general, tenants have to move away from the property while they begin the legal process of terminating the lease and suing the owner for damages.

It is often better to compel the owner to make the necessary repairs or to address the issues that are creating the uninhabitable living conditions on the property in the first place. This is easier in cities and states that have strong legal enforcement of the landlord obligations. New York City and state are an example of places in the United States that make it difficult for owners to practice constructive eviction by requiring that they fulfill their maintenance duties.

Consumer Debt

Consumer debt refers to debts which individuals owe because of goods they have purchased. These goods must be consumable forms which do not appreciate in value to qualify for the designation. Having huge amounts of consumer debts is generally considered to be negative for individuals since it raises the burden on their resources to keep up with the debt servicing. It also makes it harder to remit the installment payments which are often laden with interest. When these types of debts are not well managed, they can cause a consumer to be forced into bankruptcy.

There are cases where some analysts and economists feel that a little consumer debt can benefit the individual. These scenarios mostly center on instances where the debt is run up in purchasing an asset that will increase the earning power of the individual. Several examples of this are useful to consider. One of them surrounds buying a car with financing in order to reach a job which pays more. Another might be incurring student debt to obtain a higher degree that will make it possible to secure a promotion or better job.

There are differences between this consumer debt and those that governments or businesses owe. Consumer debt is also referred to as consumer credit. This type of debt can be obtained from credit unions, commercial banks, and sometimes the United States federal government. Among the two categories of consumer debt are revolving debt and non-revolving debt.

Revolving debt is represented by credit cards. These debts are called revolving as they were originally intended to be repaid every month when the bill comes due. In practice this does not often happen, as consumers carry balances forward much of the time. Non-revolving debts are fixed installment payment loans. They are not paid off fully in a typical given month. They are more commonly held against the underlying asset's useful life. Mortgages on homes are not considered to be consumer debt. Rather they are counted as personal forms of investment in real estate under the category of personal residential.

As of January 2017, the total debt of American consumers increased to

$3.77 trillion. This represented a 2.8 percent increase over the prior month. Around $2.78 trillion of this consumer debt was comprised of non-revolving loans. It had grown by 5.5 percent. Debts on credit cards represented $995 billion at this point. This had dropped by 4.6 percent in January versus December of 2016.

There are three reasons why Americans find themselves so deeply in debt today. These are school loans, car loans, and credit cards. School loans commonly last for ten years. They can also be pushed to an over 25 year repayment schedule by extension. The federal government guarantees most of these loans since there are no assets with which to back a college degree. The rates are low to encourage higher education. During the Great Recession, these loan defaults skyrocketed as the loans increased massively with many people who were unemployed "going back to school" to improve their prospects. The Affordable Care Act gave the Federal government authority to take over this national student loan program from Sallie Mae, the private company which previously administered it.

Car loans typically run from three to five years, which is considered to be the safe collateral life of the new vehicle. After this point, the value of these cars depreciates so highly that they are no longer considered to be valuable collateral. Banks simply repossess the vehicle if the borrowers default on the payment schedule. There are more of these loans now thanks to the low interest rates which encourage borrowing to buy vehicles.

Finally, credit card debt soared because of the Bankruptcy Protection Act of 2005. People could no longer easily declare bankruptcy, so they were forced to run up their credit cards in an effort to pay bills, especially healthcare. In July of 2008, the credit card debt peaked at its historic high of $1.028 trillion. This amounted to a per household average of $8,640.

Consumer Financial Protection Bureau (CFPB)

The CFPB is the Consumer Financial Protection Bureau. Congress created this government agency in 2008 as one of the reactions it took to the devastating financial crisis and Great Recession, the worst financial shocks to the system since the end of the 1930s era Great Depression.

The idea was to erect an organization that would protect consumers from risks and predatory practices of Wall Street and the mega banks which already had been determined as "too big to fail." The Dodd-Frank Wall Street Reform and Consumer Protection Act actually set up this new entity the CFPB.

The role of this new twenty-first century organization is to assist consumers in the financial markets through creating rules that are more efficient and fair, by continuously and equitably enforcing the rules, and by helping consumers to be able to gain additional command over their own economic futures and affairs.

The Consumer Financial Protection Bureau's goal is to ensure that the various financial markets function fairly and appropriately for providers, consumers, and the all around national economy. To this effect they strive to safeguard consumers from deceptive, predatory, abusive, and unfair activities in the marketplaces. They enforce action on any companies which break the laws. The CFPB provides people with the tools and information they require to make decisions that are smart for their own situations.

The Consumer Financial Protection Bureau believes in and labors towards a financial market that works fairly. This means that the terms, risks, and prices of any deals must be transparent and obvious in advance so that all consumers are able to know their choices and fairly and effectively comparison shop. They work to see that all corporations abide by the identical consumer protection rules. Each company must fairly compete to provide high quality goods and services.

To see this vision become reality, the Consumer Financial Protection Bureau strives to empower, enforce, and educate. Empowering means that they develop tools, answer commonly posed queries, and offer helpful tips for consumers who are interested in making their way through the various financial options to shop around for the deal that best meets their needs. They pride themselves on their effective enforcement of the rules against predatory operations and actions that break the law.

The CFPB has obtained and returned literally billions of dollars in damages to customers who were wronged. Education means that the CFPB fosters consumer abilities and educational opportunities from a young age extending on to retirement. They inform financial companies of their legal and ethical responsibilities and publish research to help out consumers.

The Consumer Financial Protection Bureau operates in several core functions. They acknowledge that the government created them to offer one accountability agency to enforce the laws for federal consumer finance and to safeguard consumers in the financial arena. This used to be the purview of a number of different agencies. Among the CFPB's core functions are receiving complaints from consumers, enforcing the discrimination laws in consumer finance, and creating and enforcing rules to rid the market of abusive, deceptive, and predatory actions by companies.

They also foster financial education among consumers, regulate and oversee the financial markets for upcoming risks for consumers, and do research on consumer's experiences in utilizing financial services and products. They do this to try to locate problems lurking in the financial marketplace so that more fair ultimate outcomes can be achieved for American consumers everywhere.

As of 2016, Richard Cordray is the Consumer Financial Protection Bureau's first director. Before he assumed this important responsibility, he served in the role as head of the Bureau's Office of Enforcement.

Consumer Price Index (CPI)

The Consumer Price Index, also known by its acronym of CPI, actually measures changes that take place over time in the level of the pricing of various consumer goods and services that American households buy. The Bureau of Labor Statistics in the U.S. says that the Consumer Price Index is a measurement of the over time change in the prices that urban consumers actually pay for a certain grouping of consumer goods and services.

This consumer price index is not literal in the sense of what inflation really turns out to be. Instead, it is a statistical estimate that is built utilizing the costs of a basket of sample items that are supposed to be representative for the entire economy. These goods and services' prices are ascertained from time to time. In actual practice, both sub indices such as clothing, and even sub-sub indices, such as men's dress shirts, are calculated for varying sub-categories of services and goods. These are then taken and added together to create the total index. The different goods are assigned varying weights as shares of the total amount of the expenditures of consumers that the index covers.

Two essential pieces of information are necessary to build the consumer price index. These are the weighting data and the pricing data. Weighting data comes from estimates of differing kinds of expenditure shares as a percentage of the entire expenditure that the index covers. Sample household expenditure surveys are sourced to figure what the weightings should be. Otherwise, the National Income and Product Accounts estimates of expenditures on consumption are utilized. Pricing data is gathered from a sampling of goods and services taken from a sample range of sales outlets in varying locations and at a sampling of times.

The consumer price index is figured up monthly in the United States. Some other countries determine their CPI's on a quarterly basis. The different components of the consumer price index include food, clothing, and housing, all of which are weighted averages of the sub-sub indices. The CPI index literally compares the prices of one month with the prices in the reference month.

Consumer Price Index is only one of a few different pricing indices that the majority of national statistical agencies calculate. Inflation is figured up using the yearly percentage changes in the underlying consume price index. Uses of this CPI can include adjusting real values of pensions, salaries, and wages for inflation's effects, as well as for monitoring costs, and showing alterations in actual values through deflating the monetary magnitudes. The CPI and US National Income and Product Accounts prove to be among the most carefully followed of economic indicators.

Cost of living index is another measurement that is generated based on the consumer price index. It demonstrates how much consumer expenditures need to adjust to compensate for changes in prices. This details how much consumers need to keep up a constant standard of living.

Core CPI

Core CPI refers to the Consumer Price Index. This term revolves around the idea of core inflation. It reveals the longer term price trend in a given item or economy. Core CPI is a means of measuring inflation which leaves out some specific items, particularly those that experience volatility in their pricing. There is a reason for excluding these items. To learn what long term inflation actually is, volatility in prices over the short term and temporary price changes have to be eliminated.

Core inflation is most typically figured up by using the core CPI. This takes out some products like food and energy items, especially oil and gas. Both of these categories may experience short term price changes. Such short term shocks often differ from the bigger picture trend in inflation and provide a false reading of it.

There is another way of calculating core CPI. This is called the outlier method. This way of figuring core inflation takes away products that show the biggest price movements. Many of these items' prices fluctuate rapidly in commodity markets when speculators trade them for profit. Since their prices do not reflect actual alterations of supply and demand, it can make sense to exclude them.

The government is very concerned about which method of measuring inflation it uses. The Federal Reserve decided to switch from CPI to the PCE Index back in January of 2012. They prefer PCE because it offers trends in inflation which are less dramatically impacted by changes in short term prices. Different agencies find other ways to get to what they believe are more accurate means of measuring inflation.

The BEA Bureau of Economic Administration is concerned with eliminating those short term price changes that speculators and traders cause. To get around this, the BEA works with the gross domestic product numbers that already exist and calculates price changes from it. It then takes the monthly release of Retail Survey numbers and measures them against the CPI data-provided consumer prices. The BEA eliminates irregular fluctuations in the inflation data this way and gains more accurate long term trend information.

Determining core CPI inflation is important. It reveals the correlations between goods and services with their prices and the purchasing value of the general income of consumers. Should the costs of goods and services go up in a given time frame while the consumers' parallel income levels do not rise, the buying power of consumers is weakening. This is because their money's actual value is declining when measured against the costs of critical goods and services.

The process could be virtuous as well. Sometimes inflation occurs only on the income of consumers while the costs of goods and services remain constant. In this case, consumers gain greater purchasing power. This means that they will be able to buy an additional amount of the identical services and goods. Asset inflation can also benefit consumers. If the price of their house or the value of their investment portfolio goes up, the consumer has additional buying power also.

Core Inflation

Core Inflation refers to the change in the cost of goods and services without calculating the important categories of food and energy. The U.S. federal government believes this to be the most accurate means of figuring up true inflationary trends. They claim that both energy products and food components are priced too volatilely to be a part of the core inflation calculation and figure. This is because they constantly change so rapidly that they interfere with inflation readings.

The reason for this is that they are subject to the whims of the traders on the various commodity market exchanges. The majority of core food products like beef, pork, wheat, orange juice, and more and energy products such as oil, natural gas, and gasoline trade each and every week day all throughout the day.

As an example, traders of commodities will likely bid up the prices of oil and its derivative products when they believe its supplies will diminish or if they feel that demand will outpace supplies. It could be that a strike will interrupt production and oil supplies from Nigeria, Venezuela, or Angola. Because of this fear, traders will purchase oil at the prices today and hope to sell it for a higher amount at the anticipated greater prices tomorrow or next week.

That is all that it really takes to radically increase the price of oil. Should the strike wrap up quickly, then the oil prices will plunge when traders suddenly all sell out of their positions. This is why both energy and food prices depend on rapidly changing human emotions rather than real changes to underlying forces of supply and demand. Between this and the inelastic demand of food and energy which people simply have to possess in order to live, these commodities rise and fall crazily sometimes.

Consider how gasoline prices will change when their primary input oil does. Yet as people require gas to travel to school and work, they cannot delay their purchases and wait for prices to decline. Food prices also vary according to gasoline and oil prices as they are shipped by truck throughout the United States. In truth, most foods on your dinner plate have more frequent flyer miles than you ever dreamed of acquiring.

The Fed has a few tools to deal with higher than desired core inflation. The problem comes with their tools needing time to take effect on the broader economy. This might mean as much as from six to 18 months before changes to the Fed Funds rate will show a meaningful impact on the inflation rate in the U.S. As the Fed Funds rate goes higher, so will the bank loans and mortgage rates. Credit will tighten and slow economic growth. Corporations find themselves lowering their core prices in order to keep selling merchandise. This lowers inflation as it finally all feeds through to the economy.

The Federal Reserve targets inflation with their policies. They promise to not take action when the core inflation rate remains at two percent or lower. Consider a real world example. Inflation has a tendency to creep higher throughout the summer as people go on vacations. The Fed does not wish to raise rates each summer though, which would force them to proportionally lower them again in the fall.

Rather, they wait and see if such summer increases boost the prices of the goods and services ex food and energy permanently. Yet ultimately higher food and gas prices force up the prices of all other goods and services if they remain elevated for long. This is why the Federal Reserve will also consider the headline inflation rate, which is the opposite of the core inflation rate. This broader measure of inflation considers food and energy prices alongside all other goods and services.

The core inflation rate can be measured via the Core Price Index, or core CPI, as well as the core Personal Consumption Expenditures price index, or core PCE price index.

Cost of Living

Cost of living refers to the sum of money individuals require in order to maintain a given standard of living. The two concepts of standard of living and cost of living are therefore closely related. Expenses included in such a concept include all necessary costs for sustaining life, such as food, housing, health care, and taxes. This living cost frequently finds use in comparing the expenses to live between one city and another one. It is similarly closely connected with salaries and wages. This is because the levels for salaries are commonly measured up against the costs which individuals must pay in order to sustain their typical living standard in a given geographical area. Such living costs can and often do vary substantially from one part of the United States to the next.

The real Cost of living proves to be an important element in how successful an individual is in accumulating money and wealth. Even lower salaries will stretch longer in cities that are inexpensive places to live. At the same time, earning a big salary will hardly be enough to live decently in a costly city like New York City or London.

Mercer publishes its annual Cost of Living Survey that proves to be most illuminating on the differences in living costs from one major city to the next around the world. For their 2015 survey, they found the cities with the most expensive living costs to be Tokyo, Osaka (Japan), Moscow, Geneva, Hong Kong, Zurich, Copenhagen, and New York City. Among the American cities that boasted expensive living costs in 2015 were Honolulu, New York City, Los Angeles, Washington D.C., and San Francisco.

This leads to the Cost of living Index. Such an important index allows for comparisons between one significant city and another comparable one. To come up with a meaningful metric, the index takes into consideration elements that make up the basic living needs of people. It then compiles these into a total measurement that allows workers to reference and utilize when negotiating salaries in various towns and cities. This is particularly important for recent college graduates. They need to consider carefully their entry level jobs into their career and where they will work. For those already employed who are contemplating relocation for work, this index delivers a useful one-stop snapshot of food, rental, and transportation expenses in a prospective place of employment.

For the year 2016, the Cost of Living Index relied on New York City as its United States' and North American cities benchmark. With this as the base for that year, San Francisco boasted the most expensive living costs in all of the Americas. This meant that at least in that particular year, the rent costs for San Francisco proved to be around three percent greater than those of New York City. Food prices were an eye watering 22 percent higher than compatible levels of New York. On the other side of the spectrum, Reno in Nevada offered its residents a living cost which equated to roughly 43 percent less than the one in New York City.

This Cost of living figure also can be extrapolated to standard sized families. In the year 2015, the average living costs for the typical American family of four (two adults and two children) stood at $65,000. Keep in mind that this amount did not include any optional discretionary categories of spending for those goods and services deemed to be nonessential. This would include dinners out, entertainment, leisure activities, vacations, and also luxury goods.

The living costs figure presents policymakers with a challenge and ongoing debate in the highest levels of government. It centers on the national federal minimum wage. There is a significant shortfall between the government's minimally allowed wage and the income which families need to sustain a basic cost of living. This has grown progressively worse since the late 1960's and early 1970's to the point where no family can live decently on either one or even two minimum wage incomes any longer.

Cost of Living Index

The Cost of Living Index refers to a price index that was created so that businesses and individuals are able to compare and contrast the cost of living relative to other cities, regions, countries, and times. This theoretical index takes the measure of variations in the costs of different key goods and services. It also permits substitutions with other similar goods when prices fluctuate.

One thing that is interesting regarding this Cost of Living Index is that there is not only a single methodology and index that reveals the national (or international) cost of living. One of the most widely used systems for these indices is known as the Konüs Index. These formats utilize an expenditure function like those employed in considering anticipated compensating variation.

In the United States, the most widely recognized and cited version of the Cost of Living Index was developed and is continuously maintained by the C2ER Council for Community and Economic Research. It first appeared in 1968. This version has proven to be the most consistent index for sourcing city to city cost-based comparisons in the United States. Their COLI data is widely recognized by such American governmental organizations as the U.S. Bureau of Labor Statistics and the U.S. Census Bureau. Similarly the President's Council of Economic Advisors utilizes it routinely. Private national media outlets including CNN Money, U.S. News and World Report, Forbes, Kiplinger's, ABC News, and countless others reference this index for the cost of living purposes. This makes it the closest possible thing to a nationally recognized and utilized COLI.

The reason for the C2ER COLI success centers on their entirely transparent methodology for creating and their locally sourcing of data. Users of the index know precisely how they compile it. They have an Advisory Board made up of government officials and academic researchers which reviews their methodology and data continuously. This helps to explain why this COLI finds reference use within the Census Bureau Statistical Abstract of the United States. As the C2ER publishes it quarterly and collects data on local levels from more than 300 different independent researchers, this represents the only locally-based and –sourced Cost of

Living Index compiled on the United States.

The firm employs more than 60 goods and services within the index's underlying data. They precisely select these different representative goods and services in order to take into consideration the various consumer categories of spending. They assign weights for the various costs utilizing data from government surveys citing executive and professional households' spending habits. Each item becomes priced at a fixed point in time for every locality utilizing specifications which are standardized.

A number of characteristics set this particular renowned COLI apart from its various inferior competitors. The data is provided for both county and large city MSA metropolitan statistical areas. They organize it by six different categories. These include housing, food, utilities, health care, transportation, and miscellaneous services and goods. Naturally C2ER offer the composite index as their primary one. The data comes out quarterly, no later than three months following its collection, so it is both fresh and relevant. Besides all of the government organizations which rely on their data and COLI in general, the Brookings Institution and Bankrate.com also cite their well-regarded methodology.

All of the various mainstream cost of living indexes rely on the theory which the Russian economist A. A. Konüs developed. The theory is only somewhat hampered by the assumption that the consumers act as optimizers to receive the maximum utility possible out of the money which they possess and can spend. The weakness is that this standard baseline assertion does not always work out to be the case in practice.

Cost Push Inflation

Cost-push inflation is a scenario where all around price levels go up, creating inflation. This happens because of rising prices in the important inputs of raw materials as well as higher wages for labor. This type of inflation appears because of rising production factors costs. This leads to a lower amount of total supply and production in the economy. With a smaller quantity of good being produced as the supply weakens while demand for such goods remains constant, the final cost for the finished products goes higher. This creates the inflation.

Cost-push inflation most typically begins when the costs of production rise. This is many times an unexpected cost increase. It could come as a result of higher prices in input raw materials, an unforeseen shutdown of or damage to a key production facility (like with natural disasters or fire), or forced higher wages for the employees in production. The higher wages could result from an increase in the minimum wage that automatically boosts the salaries of the workers who were making less than the new legally accepted minimum standard.

In order for such cost-push inflation to occur, the associated demand of the product in question has to stay constant while the changes in costs of production are actually happening. Producers then feel they have no choice but to compensate for the rising production expenses. They raise their end prices for their consumers so that they can hold their profit margins as they attempt to keep up production with anticipated demand for the products.

There can be several unanticipated causes of this cost-push inflation. Natural disasters are a common example. There might be earthquakes, floods, tornadoes, hurricanes, or other kinds of large "acts of God" events that interfere with some component in the production chain. These create higher costs of production. Natural disasters that do not lead to higher costs of production do not qualify as an example of this type of inflation.

There are other actions that can eventually cause rising costs of production as well. It might be a strike of the plant workers that happens because of failed negotiations in contracts. It could also result from a rapid change in government as often happens in developing countries. This might create an inability for the country to keep up its prior levels of production output.

There are similarly cost-push inflation causes that may be anticipated but are still unavoidable. Present regulations and laws can change. These changes may be foreseen. Despite this, there could still be no practical means of offsetting the resulting higher costs that come along with the changes.

Cost-push inflation is one of the two main types of inflation. The other kind is demand-pull inflation. This is the opposite form. In demand-pull, higher production costs force up the price of an individual service or good. With demand-pull inflation, the increase in demand happens even when production may not be boosted to cover the rising needs. In such cases, the costs of the product will go up because of the resulting imbalance that is created in the natural demand and supply model.

Credit Analysis

Credit analysis refers to a kind of detailed consideration of a corporation or similar agency which issues debt. It is performed by managers of bond portfolios and investors. They seek to determine the ability of the borrower to cover their obligations of debt with this type of analysis. The ultimate goal is to discern the correct amount of default risk which investing in that specific agency or company will entail.

There are a number of different considerations in performing this credit analysis. Some of these are fixed expenses, operating margins, cash flows, and overhead costs. These are also considered in equity analysis, yet with a different emphasis. It is true that stronger credit ratings do not equate to any guarantee of impressive share price performance. Yet when investors grasp a company's credit ratings and the implications, they are able to better assess both the debt and equity results for a given corporation.

Financial elements of a particular company are extremely important in credit analysis. Analysts will consider incoming revenues as well as costs and expenses of the corporation. These will be assessed both as stand-alone values and versus the competitors in the industry. For a firm to be considered strong where credit is concerned, its overhead must permit it to attain better than average profit levels in all points of the business life cycle. Even in a downturn in the economy, stronger companies can deliver results which are higher than average for the industry. Stronger firms also can demonstrate pricing power. This represents the capability of passing on cost increases for inputs and raw materials to the customers via higher prices.

Competitive position is also important in a thorough credit analysis. Only companies which are strong competitively will be capable of maintaining their financial performances in the future. Companies which are highly competitive show long-running positive trends and abilities with quality of service, development of new products, and customer retention and satisfaction levels. It also helps a company's competitive position when there are effective barriers to competition. These can be in the form of protective regulations, substantial copyright and/or patent protections, or agreements on licensing, permits, and franchising.

The business environment is a third area of consideration for those performing credit analyses. This refers to three primary areas known as country risk, currency risk, and industry risk. Country risk relates to the ways in which the business activities of the enterprise can be negatively impacted by changes in the tax, regulatory, social, legal, and political regimes in those nations where they have a significant business presence.

Currency risk simply refers to the effects of drastic foreign exchange movements on both the corporate balance sheet and the company's capabilities of sourcing raw materials and other inputs or of selling their goods and products abroad. Industry risk pertains to the dynamics of the business, regulatory regime, and legal and market elements within the industry. These considerations can impact not only the industry but a particular company being evaluated by credit analysis.

Looking at some examples of this can help to better understand the concept. Where there are currency exposures throughout the supply chain, the company could hedge these appropriately in the futures markets. Another example is that the company may know its earnings will not change much even as their industry segment progresses along a change in technology.

There are many parallels between credit ratings of even different borrowing entities. This is why though the risk profile on an AAA-rated state government is less than that of an AAA-rated corporation, triple A rated borrowers in either scenario will always be far safer and less risky than the comparable B- and especially C-rated borrowers in each field. As an example, the A-rated S&P 500 companies boasted an average return of 10.74% in the period ending August 30th of 2013. For those same S&P companies with BB or lower credit ratings, their average return over the identical time period proved to be only 6.53%.

Credit Bureaus

Credit bureaus are agencies that collect financial information. They go by different names in various countries around the world. In the United Kingdom they are known as credit reference agencies. In Australia, the bureaus are called credit reporting bodies. India knows their credit agencies as credit information companies.

Within the United States, these organizations are called consumer reporting agencies. Whatever name they go by, they all serve the same function. The bureaus gather information from banks and other financial sources to deliver consumer credit information about individual consumers.

The U.S. consumer reporting agencies are governed by the Fair Credit Reporting Act. Other laws that regulate the activities of the bureaus are the Fair and Accurate Credit Transactions Act, the Fair Credit Billing Act, the Fair Credit Reporting Act, and Regulation B. These acts attempt to safeguard consumers against unfair practices and mistakes made by the data providers and the credit reporting agencies themselves.

The U.S. has two separate government organizations who oversee the credit bureaus and their data suppliers. These are the FTC and the OCC. Primary oversight of the credit reporting agencies as they deal with consumers belongs to the Federal Trade Commission. The banks are monitored for all of the information that they provide the reporting agencies by the Office of the Controller of the Currency. This government agency supervises, regulates, and charters all of the national banks and any information they turn over to the consumer credit reporting agencies.

Three main credit reporting bureaus dominate nearly all credit reporting in the U.S. These are Experian, Equifax, and TransUnion. None of these three agencies are owned by government entities. All of them exist as companies seeking to make a profit and are traded publically. They are carefully monitored for fairness by the government provided oversight organizations.

The consumer reporting agencies operate through a vast network with the credit card issuing companies, banks, and other financial entities with which individuals have accounts. All of these ties ensure that credit account information and histories show up on the credit reports of one, two, or even all of the bureaus.

The credit bureaus compile all of this information into a consumer credit report. They each then utilize proprietary trade secret formulas to determine every individual's FICO credit score. Each of the three bureaus formulates its own score that is different from that of its competitors. They also come up with educational credit score numbers which are often vastly different from the official scores.

Consumers do not have to settle for educational credit scores. They have the rights to see what is on their credit reports. Each and every year, individuals are able to obtain an official credit report from each of the three credit bureaus. This can be done by going to the government mandated website AnnualCreditReport.com.

Besides this, consumers are allowed to go to the websites of the three main consumer reporting agencies and order credit reports and scores from them directly. The only way to get the official credit score is to pay for and order it from the credit bureaus themselves. These are not provided in the annual free reports. Experian and Equifax offer all three credit reports in a single convenient to view document.

Sometimes the credit bureaus will make mistakes with individuals' credit reports. When this happens, it is important to get in touch with the credit bureau itself in order to dispute any information that is inaccurate. These organizations also should be contacted directly if there is concern about fraud so that they can place a security alert or fraud alert on the person's credit report.

Credit Ratings Agencies

Credit Ratings Agencies are those companies whose purpose is to consider and report on the financial strength which firms and government agencies demonstrate. They report on national as well as international corporations and agencies in this capacity. Their reports are most interested in the ability of the entities in question to fulfill their obligations for both principal and interest repayments of their bonds and other kinds of debts. Besides this, the various ratings agencies carefully examine and review the conditions and terms on every debt issue.

The end result of the agencies' work is to release a credit rating on both the debt issues in particular and the debt issuers more generally. When they agencies have high confidence that the issuer will be able to meet their debt servicing of principal and interest as promised, they will issue a high credit rating. When the opposite is true, the credit rating will be lower. It is entirely possible for a particular issue of debt to receive a differing credit rating from the issuer. This heavily depends on the particular terms of the issuer.

The impacts of these debt issue ratings are enormous in the industry and for the specific issuers in question. Those debt issues that obtain the best credit ratings will receive the most attractive interest rates from the credit markets. This is because the confidence of investors in an entity's capability of making their various payment obligations comes down to the credit ratings agencies review, analyses and especially ratings. Since the interest rates which investors demand for a specific debt issue will be inversely correlated to the borrower's particular creditworthiness, weaker borrowers will have to pay more while the stronger ones will enjoy paying less.

In this way, the credit ratings agencies act on behalf of businesses in much the same capacity as the consumer credit bureaus do for individual consumers. Such credit scores which the credit bureaus develop for individual people will greatly impact the interest rates at which individuals are able to borrow money.

The downside to these credit ratings agencies and their work is that they have been made the scapegoat for company and government defaults in recent years. Their research quality in particular has been the target of heavy criticism from observers and analysts who point out companies which they rated highly suddenly collapsed. Governments in Europe on which they provided high credit ratings defaulted or almost defaulted on their debts, as with Greece in particular.

This caused third party observers to argue that the various credit ratings agencies are actually poor at financial forecasting, at uncovering growing and negative trends for the debt issuers they follow, and also are overly late in revising down their ratings. Besides this, critics point to the many conflicts of interest of the ratings agencies. This is because the debt issuers are able to pick out and pay the ratings agencies for the reviews of their bonds. In a survey conducted in 2008, 11 percent of the various investment professionals surveyed by the CFA Institute responded that they had observed personally instances where the major ratings agencies had actually upgraded their given ratings on bonds when they were pressured by the debt issuers in question.

There are only three firms today which dominate the space, and this is part of the problem. The Wall Street Journal provided the ratings shares of the big 3 agencies in their 2011 report. Of the 2.8 million ratings they issue collectively (with the other seven minor agencies), S&P 500 controls the greatest market share with 42.2 percent. Moody's holds 36.9 percent of the market. Fitch rounds out the top three with 17.9 percent.

The article claimed that fully 95 percent of all revenues in this industry were earned by the big three. Only 2.9 percent of the ratings issued came from the other seven firms. The other seven credit ratings agencies were A.M. Best, DBRS, Japan Credit Rating Agency, Rating and Investment Info., Egan-Jones Ratings, Morningstar Credit Ratings, and Kroll Bond Rating Agency.

Between the top two issuers Moody's and Standard & Poor's, they provide ratings for roughly 80 percent of all municipal and corporate bond issues. They are typically regarded as a level higher than Fitch. One particular example speaks volumes. While Egan-Jones had downgraded the U.S. Federal government debt to the second highest rating years earlier, it was ignored largely by the markets and world. When Standard & Poor's took the same action by downgrading the Federal government of the United States debt to AA+ on August 5th of 2011, this shook the world bond, currency, and stock markets. It demonstrates the clout S&P and Moody's especially enjoy over all of their various credit ratings agencies rivals.

Credit Repair Organizations

Credit repair organizations are those which offer to assist individuals with clearing up their credit report and improving their credit scores. While a number of them are legitimate operations, others can be scams. Such credit repair clinics often charge exorbitant prices to perform services that individuals can do for themselves. There were enough problems with fraud or unfulfilled promises from these organizations that Congress created a law to reduce abuse. This is known as the Credit Repair Organizations Act.

Many credit repair organizations will offer to have incorrect information removed from the credit file of an individual. Consumers can do this themselves according to the provisions of the Fair Credit Reporting Act. Others will promise to take off information that is negative but correct from the files. Generally this takes seven years or longer for such information to go away if it is accurate.

The credit repair clinics have a strategy to challenge all items in a customer's file. These could be neutral, negative, or positive. They do this hoping that they can overwhelm the credit bureaus so that they will simply take off information rather than verify it first. The problem with this tactic is that credit bureaus are allowed under the Fair Credit Reporting Act to dismiss frivolous challenges. There are cases where the credit bureau may remove such information. The problem is that correct information often shows up again in one to two months as the original creditors will report negative information again.

Credit repair organizations also offer to have court judgments and existing debt balances taken off of credit files. They can do this by negotiating partial or whole payments with the creditors in exchange for taking negative information away from the credit report. While these are legitimate negotiation tactics, individuals can do this without having to pay credit repair clinics for the service.

Another suggestion that such credit repair organizations may make to consumer clients is to obtain a secured credit card from a bank which offers them. These are simply credit cards that individuals use after putting a deposit in an account at their bank. These secured credit card lists that the credit repair clinics offer are not proprietary. Individuals can find the same information for free or very little online.

Congress attempted to curb abuses from credit repair clinics with their Credit Repair Organizations Act. It regulates these clinics that are for profit. The law states that these credit repair outfits must provide individuals with written statements of rights provided by the FCR Act. They must correctly present what they are and are not able to accomplish. They are not allowed to charge and collect fees until they render all services which they promised.

The credit repair clinic must provide a contract in writing. They have to allow consumers to cancel the contracts within three days of signing them. Consumers must provide such cancellations in writing. All contracts that do not follow the Credit Repair Organizations Act become void. Consumers can not sign away any of their rights.

There are unethical credit repair clinics which have found a means to get around the law. They incorporate themselves as not for profit organizations. This makes it easier for them to offer poor or limited results and to take customers' money. They also find it simpler to perform the same services that consumers can do for themselves this way.

Credit Report

A credit report is an individual or business' credit history. This includes their record of borrowing and repaying money in the past. It similarly covers data pertaining to any late payments made or bankruptcies that have been declared. In some countries, credit reports are also referred to as credit reputations.

When an American like you completes a credit application for a bank, a credit card company, or a retail store, this information is directly sent on to one of the three main credit bureaus. These are Experian, Trans Union, and Equifax. These credit bureaus then match up your name, identification, address, and phone number on the application for such credit with the data that they keep in their bureau's files. Because of this match up process, it is essential that lenders, creditors, and other parties always provide exactly correct information to the credit bureaus.

Such information in these files at the three major credit bureaus is then utilized by lenders like credit card companies in order to decide if you are deserving of having credit issued to you by the creditor. Another way of putting this is that they decide how likely that you will be to pay back these debts. Such willingness to pay back a debt is usually indicated by the timeliness of prior payments to other lenders. Such lenders will prefer to see the debt obligations of individual consumers, such as yourself, paid on time every month.

The second element considered in a lender offering loans or credit to individuals like you is based on your actual income. Higher incomes generally lead to greater amounts of credit being accessible. Still, lenders look at both willingness, as shown in the credit report and prior payment history, along with ability, as shown by income, in deciding whether or not to extend you credit.

Credit reports have become even more significant in light of risk based pricing. Practically all lenders of the financial services industry rely on credit reports to determine what the annual percentage rate and grace period of repayment of a loan or offer of credit will be. Other obligations of the contract are similarly based on this credit report.

In the past, a great deal of discussion has gone on considering the information contained in the credit reports. Scientific studies done on the issue have determined that for the most part, this credit report information is extremely accurate. Such credit bureaus also have their own authorized studies of fifty-two million credit reports that show that the information contained therein is right a vast majority of the time.

Congress has heard testimony from the Consumer Data Industry Association that in fewer than two percent of credit report issue cases have there been data which had to be erased because it was wrong. In the few cases where these did exist, more than seventy percent of such disputes are handled in fourteen days or less. More than ninety-five percent of consumers with disputes report being satisfied with the resolution.

Credit Score

Credit Score refers to a number generated by the credit bureaus to represent the creditworthiness of an individual. The credit bureaus possess literally from hundreds to thousands of distinct lines worth of information on each person with a credit profile. This makes it extremely difficult for lending institutions to go through it all. Since they lack the man hours to carefully peruse each applicant's credit reports personally, the majority of financial institutions which lend money employ these credit scores rather than tediously read through credit reports on applicants.

These Credit Scores are actually numbers that a computer program generates after crawling through an individual's credit report. Such programs seek out certain fundamentals, patterns, and so-called warning flags in any credit report and history. They then generate a credit score based on what they find. Lenders love these scores since they can be basically interpreted by a consistent set of comparative rules.

Consider the following examples. Lending institutions might automatically approve any application that comes with an associated 720 credit score or higher. Those profiles with 650 to 720 would likely be approved but with a greater interest rate. Applications with credit scores below 650 might simply be rejected. The computer is consistent and fair using these standards, so no one is treated in a discriminatory way relative to any other applicant.

Federal laws require that each individual be granted a free credit report annually from every one of the big three credit bureaus Experian, Trans Union, and Equifax. This does not mean that anyone is required to hand out free credit scores. In fact there is no such thing as a truly free credit score offer. There are scores provided in exchange for signing up for trial membership services in things like credit monitoring services. In general though, individuals pay for their credit scores from each of the major credit bureaus.

The particulars of a Credit Score are interesting. It is always a three digit formatted number that ranges from 300 to 850. These become created using one of a variety of mathematical algorithms that work off of both the individuals' credit profiles and their credit report's particular information.

This score is crafted with the intention of predicting risk to the lenders, not to benefit the person it covers. It is particularly concerned with the chances of an individual going delinquent on any credit obligations within the next 24 months after the score has been issued.

It is a common misnomer among many individuals that there is only one credit scoring model in the country. There are countless models that exist. It is only the FICO credit score that matters in nearly all cases though. This is because fully 90 percent of financial institutions within the United States rely on FICO credit scores in making their decisions on to whom they will extend credit and at what interest rate.

The higher the FICO score these algorithms generate, the lower the risk is to the various lenders. What makes matters more confusing is that there is not only one FICO credit score in existence for every adult American. Each of the three major bureaus generates its own particular score. Since 2009, consumers are only able to view two of their credit scores, those from both Trans Union and Equifax. This is because Experian chose to terminate its myFICO.com arrangements in 2009. Experian does not share their proprietary credit scores with consumers any longer.

Five different significant categories make up the FICO Credit Score. These are payment history (35 percent of the total component), Amounts owed (30 percent), length of credit history (15 percent), types of credit used (10 percent), and new credit inquiries and accounts opened (10 percent).

Debasing the Currency

Debasing the currency refers to the all too common historical process of lowering a currency's actual value. In the past, this phrase commonly came to be associated with commodity money made principally from either silver or gold. Should the sum total of silver, gold, nickel, or copper be reduced, then the physical money is called debased. Even venerable institutions like the Roman Empire, with a thousand year history of growth and stability, have stooped to such debasing of the currency.

Reasons that a government chooses to debase the currency in this way center around the financial benefits that the government is able to reap. These are done at the citizenry's expense though. Governments that lowered the quantity of gold and silver in their coinage found that they could quietly mint more coins from a given fixed quantity of metal on hand.

The downside to this for the general population centers on the inflation that this in turn causes. Such inflation is yet another benefit for the currency debasing government that then finds that it can pay off government debt or repudiate government bonds easier. The populace's purchasing power is significantly reduced as a result of this, along with their then lowered standard of living.

Debasing a currency lowers the value of the currency in question. Given enough time and abuse by the governing authorities, this debasing can even lead to a collapse in the existing currency that causes a newer currency or coinage to be created and launched for the nation or state.

In present day times, debasing the currency is accomplished in more subtle means. Since currencies these days are made of only paper, involving no metal, debasing the currency simply involves printing additional paper dollars. With the advent of electronic banking, even this printing press operation is no longer required. The government simply creates money on a computer screen, literally conjuring it out of thin air.

They are able to accomplish this in one of two ways. One way that they do this is via the Federal Reserve, which buys treasury securities by simply crediting the receivers' bank accounts with electronically created money.

The Federal Reserve then has tangible assets in Treasury bills that is it able to trade or sell when it wishes.

Another way that this creation of money that debases the currency is able to be performed is through the Fractional Reserve Banking System. Since the Federal Reserve only requires banks to keep a ten percent reserve ratio of deposits on hand, these banks when they are credited funds from the Federal Reserve are able to loan this new money out in multiples that are equivalent to the leverage created by this ten percent only reserve ratio. In both of these ways, the Federal Reserve is able to create more money quietly and at will. This is how modern day debasing of the currency is effectively accomplished.

Debit Card

Debit cards are plastic cards that function like a check and are easily utilized like a credit card. Debit cards are commonly one of two types, either branded Visa or Master Card. When you use such a debit card to pay for a purchase, then this amount is deducted immediately from your checking account. Both convenience and security features are included in the use of a debit card.

Debit cards provide tremendous convenience in their ease of use. No longer do you have to make sure that you are carrying enough money on you, or to take the time to write out a physical check while the long line waits impatiently behind you. Besides this ease of use, debit cards are accepted at literally millions of places around the country and the world.

Nowadays, they can be used for almost any purchase, such as lunches or dinners at restaurants, monthly bill payments, merchandise in retail stores, groceries, prescriptions, gas, online purchases, over the phone orders, and even fast food.

Debit cards' spending is easy to keep track of as well. The majority of such transactions are both deducted and posted to a checking account in twenty-four hours or less. This allows for you to conveniently monitor your constantly updated transaction record and balance either over the phone or the bank or card issuer's website. Besides this, debit cards also offer statements, much like credit cards, that outline all purchases made, with details on the name of the merchant, date, location, and amount of transaction.

Debit cards offer another benefit in their security provisions. These cards include free fraud monitoring that helps to find and stop activity that is suspicious with your debit card. They also come with policies of zero liability that protect you from charges that you did not make or authorize. Fraudulently taken out funds are guaranteed to be returned to your account. The vast majority of debit cards also come with the security feature of three digit security codes that allow you to confirm your identity for both phone and Internet orders and purchases.

Debit cards allow two ways for completing in person transactions. One of these is through swiping the card and then signing the receipt issued by the merchant representative. The other is via using a pad with your PIN, or personal identification code, after the card is swiped.

A final benefit that you gain from a debit card is that most of them provide rewards that are earned simply by utilizing them. These are earned in one of two ways. With Visa Debit cards, you are able to receive discounts from some merchants who provide these special price breaks for the holders of Visa cards.

Other debit cards provide extras rewards programs. These rewards programs pay you back with some type of reward for every purchase that you make. These can be cash rebates or more commonly awards that are earned through the collection of such points.

Debt Ceiling

The Debt Ceiling refers to an American budgetary and financial constraint which the nation self imposed beginning in 1917. Congress mandates this limit for the maximum amount of debt the Federal government may have at any point in time. Back on November 2nd of 2015, the U.S. Congress suspended the debt ceiling with the Bipartisan Budget Act of 2015. The ceiling remained suspended through March 15th of 2017, after the Presidential election. They did this deliberately to allow time for the new President (Trump) and his (Republican) Congress to establish themselves before they have to address the continuous debt crisis of the United States.

The prior debt ceiling was a whopping $18.113 trillion. Because the country was about to surpass this level on March 15th of 2015, then American Treasury Secretary Jacob Lew ordered a suspension to the debt issuance of the U.S. He began engaging in what analysts call "extraordinary measures" in order to stop the debt from breaking through the artificially created limit. To do this, he quit paying Federal government staff as well as the retirement fund contributions for U.S. Post Office employees. He began to sell the investments which these funds held as well.

The debt limit also covers a significant quantity of debt which the Federal government must repay itself. This includes the massive creditor the Social Security Trust Fund. Money owed to everyone outside of the U.S. government they call the American public debt. This amount represents approximately 70 percent of the aggregate Federal debt.

It was actually the Second Liberty Bond Act of 1917 which first saw Congress establish the initial debt ceiling. This law permitted the U.S. Treasury Department to sell Liberty bonds in order to pay for the then-vast costs of the U.S. military involvement in the First World War. By such an action, Congress gained the upper hand in overseeing total government spending for the first moment in U.S. history. Up to this point, the Congress had only held authority to approve particular debts, such as short term notes or for the Panama Canal.

By 1974, Congress found a way to gain absolute control over the budget process and effective spending in the United States. They called this new law the Budget Control Act of 1974. This new procedure for the budget envisioned Congress working closely in concert with the U.S. President to agree on what amount of money the country's government will actually spend. This all made the debt ceiling need irrelevant, since all it does is permit the Federal government to borrow necessary funds to pay for spending it previously approved anyway.

The reason this debt ceiling still matters is because Congress intentionally limits the amount of money which the U.S. Treasury may effectively borrow with it. If they do not continuously raise this artificially imposed limit, then the United States will default on its outstanding debt obligations. In general, the Congress has experienced no remorse for raising it. They raised it around ten times over the last decade, of which four of those times occurred in only 2008 and 2009.

This debt ceiling becomes a crisis in the event that both Congress and the American President are unable to come to an agreement on the country's fiscal policy. This has happened with alarmingly increasing frequency over the last few decades. It was an issue in 1985, 1995/1996, 2002, 2003, 2011, 2013, and 2015. The ceiling and associated government spending becomes an issue when the debt versus GDP ratio becomes excessively high.

The International Monetary Fund states that the maximum safe level for developed nations is 77 percent. After this point, holders of government debts then feel justifiable concerns that the nation will be unable to create sufficient revenues to repay the total debts.

Debt Consolidation

Debt consolidation is combining all of an individual's personal debts into a single larger debt. When people go though debt consolidation, they obtain one loan which they then use to pay down all smaller loans or outstanding debts. The idea is that this provides consumers with only a single payment that they make once per month. This is supposed to be simpler for consumers to pay and manage.

A main goal with debt consolidation is to obtain a lower interest rate. The monthly payment generally becomes lower through the process as well. Despite the fact that the payment is lower, the debt can be repaid faster. The lower interest rate makes this possible.

Debt consolidation is different from debt settlement. In debt settlement, higher outstanding bills are negotiated to lower more manageable amounts. In debt consolidation, individuals fully pay off all of their bills. There are no bad impacts on credit history and reports as a result of the consolidation process.

Consumers pursue debt consolidation through either an unsecured or a secured loan. An unsecured loan does not involve any collateral. This means that no personal assets back the loan. The lender extends the loan because the individual pledges to repay it. A credit card is a prime example of an unsecured loan. Many credit cards offer debt consolidation with a lower promotional interest rate to their customers. In general, the rates are higher on unsecured loans. This is because the risk is greater for the lender with an unsecured loan than with a secured loan.

With a secured loan, individuals receive the debt consolidation funds because they pledge an asset. These assets that secure the loan are usually a car or a home. Car loans and mortgages are both secured forms of loans. The downside to a secured loan is that a lender can seize the asset if consumers fall behind on the loan.

Debt consolidation with a secured loan happens through a variety of different types of loans. Among the more popular secured debt consolidation loans is a second mortgage home loan or a home equity line of credit. It is also possible to obtain a debt consolidation loan with a 401k. In this type of loan, retirement funds are the asset that underlies the loan. Insurance policies allow owners to take loans against the value in the policy as well.

Annuities are another vehicle that can sometimes be borrowed against. A number of special financing companies also issue loans against lottery winnings or lawsuit claims. In each of these cases, the element in common is that the asset secures the debt consolidation loan.

There are both pros and cons to consolidating bills with an unsecured loan. The biggest difficulty with these types of loans is obtaining them. Unsecured loans require fantastic credit in order to qualify. The interest rates are typically higher than those on secured loans as well. Still the rates are often lower than the ones charged by high interest credit cards. If these consolidation rates are not substantially lower than those of the bills on the debt consolidation loan, then it may not make a difference in the payments and payoff time-frame.

Debt consolidation loans that rely on credit card balance transfers can present problems. It is important to be aware of what happens after the promotional balance expires. The new interest rate may be so high that the loan does not provide any benefits over the terms of the old debts. There are commonly transfer fees with these credit card balance transfers. These can eat up a part of the savings that the debt consolidation should provide.

Debt Coverage Ratio (DCR)

Debt coverage ratio has different meanings dependent on what entity is using it. In the world of corporate finance, it is the amount of cash flow that a company has to service its current debts. This ratio utilizes the net operating income divided by the debt payments due in a year or less. This includes principal, interest, lease payments, and the sinking fund.

It has a different meaning with governments and individuals. For finances of a national government, debt coverage ratio refers to the export earnings required for the country to make its yearly principal and interest payments with the external debts of the nation. With individual finance, banks and their loan officers utilize this ratio to decide on income property loans.

Debt coverage ratios must be higher than one in order for the government, company, or individual to prove enough income to satisfy its present debt obligations. With a DCR under 1, it lacks the means to do so. This ratio is determined by dividing Net Operating Income by the Total Debt Service.

The net operating income turns out to be the revenue of a company less its operating expenses. This does not cover interest payments or taxes. The NOI can also equate to the EBIT Earnings Before Interest and Tax. Investors and lenders which are evaluating the creditworthiness of corporations and companies should use criteria that is consistent when they figure out the DCR.

Total debt service is the term that concerns the present debt obligations. This will include principal, interest, lease payments, and sinking fund all owed in the next year. Balance sheets also include both the long term debt current portion and the short term debt.

When a debt coverage ratio is lower than one, it says that the entity cash flow is negative. With a DCR of .90, the company would only possess sufficient NOI to handle 90% of their yearly debt payments. With personal finance this would mean that the borrower had to access some outside funds each month in order to cover the payments. Lenders usually discourage loans with negative cash flow. They may permit them when the borrower can show a strong outside income.

Lenders almost always consider the debt coverage ratio of borrowers before they extend loans to them. They do not want to loan money to entities with lower than one. Such groups will have to draw on sources outside of their traditional income or borrow more in order to make their debt payments. When the DCR is dangerously close to one, then the borrower is considered to be vulnerable to a slowdown in income. Only a minor setback to its cash flow would mean it would not be able to service the debts. Some lenders will actually insist that the borrowers keep minimum levels of debt coverage ratios while they have a loan balance. In these cases, borrowers whose ratios decline below this minimum level are in technical default.

Lenders can be more lenient on debt coverage ratios when the economy is booming. An expanding economy means that credit is available more easily. This often causes lenders to work with companies and individuals on their lower ratios. The problem is that borrowers which are under qualified can impact the stability of the economy.

In the 2008 financial crisis, subprime borrowers received credit in the form of mortgages without proper consideration of their finances. As such borrowers defaulted in large numbers, the lenders that had made loans to them failed. The largest savings and loan institution Washington Mutual turned out to be the most egregious example of this scenario.

Debt Deflation

Debt Deflation refers to the scenario where the loan collateral (or any other type of debt) sees a decrease in value. This is generally a negative end result. It often causes the loan issuer to insist on a restructure of the loan agreement. In other cases, they may be able to demand that the loan itself be completely restructured. Other phrases that describe this concept are collateral deflation and worst deflation.

Mortgages are a great example of this to consider. They are a traditional type of secured debt. If an individual takes out a mortgage to buy a house with, then the house itself proves to be the securing underlying collateral on this mortgage loan. This means that if the buyer later subsequently defaults on the payments which he or she make to the bank each month, then the bank would begin the tedious process to repossesses the house. A problem arises when the value of the house diminishes in value at the same time that the buyer is still caught up in the process of making the payments owed to the bank. This would create a potentially devastating debt deflation downward spiral and uncomfortable situation. In severe cases, this can be enough to cause a home owner to completely despair and simply walk away from the house and its associated mortgage come what may.

This actually happened back in the Subprime Mortgage Meltdown, Great Recession, and Global Financial Crisis of 2007-2009. So many homes had been purchased in the boom period of the early 2000's that when prices began to plunge on a breath taking national and regional scale, many buyers found themselves severely underwater on their mortgage loan collateral. The houses in many cases became worth significantly less than the principal balance on the loan which purchased them. Defaults went through the proverbial roof as many buyers realized that they had no realistic hope of seeing the value of the house rise back up.

It helps to look at an example of the despair this subprime mortgage crisis meltdown caused countless Americans, many of whom had been irresponsible, it is true. If a person had purchased a $300,000 priced house with a mortgage for $270,000 before 2006 peak pricing in the national housing market, then he or she might have sat helplessly by as the value of this same house subsequently plummeted by even 25 percent. It would meant that the $300,000 dream home was then only worth $225,000. Now in order for the house to again be worth just what the buyer owed on it, it would have to rise back up to the $270,000 mortgage total balance amount. This meant that the value had to increase by $45,000, or a staggering 20 percent, just to get back to even on the mortgage balance amount owed. In order for the house to be worth the actual $300,000 the buyer had originally paid out, it would have to rise by an even steeper $75,000, representing a whopping 33.3 percent. This would take years once the market actually bottomed out, itself a hopeless-looking procedure that require literally years before rock bottom was finally hit.

Nationally, home values that began to crash and burn in 2007 did not start to slowly crawl back up until 2011 to 2012, four to five long years later. A decade after the original crash period began many of the homes that lost 25 percent (or even far more in many cases and in overinflated-valued regions around the country) have still not recovered or just barely recovered.

It helps to explain why so many people quickly despaired and chose to default on their mortgages and to simply give the house back to the bank lender and then to walk away free and clear. Ironically in many cases, their shattered credit history and associated credit rating would actually recover faster than the value of their severely underwater home and mortgage finally did.

Debt Forgiveness

Debt Forgiveness refers to the action of writing off all or some of a debt which a debtor has outstanding and usually simply cannot hope to repay. This act of forgiving debt can occur for the purpose of reducing the total sum of loss which the lender will otherwise incur because of defaults. From time to time, this idea has been pursued to strengthen the national economy in countries that would rather write down their debt against resources they borrowed on in prior years.

There are definite advantages for a lender or creditor in choosing to pursue debt forgiveness with their borrowers. When they grant this forgiveness of debt, they can save huge amounts of resources and wasted time trying to collect on a bad debt. This means that such resources are then freed up for more productive activities going forward. In a number of countries, the regulations and laws concerning credit and debt permit the creditor to claim an associated tax deduction for at least some if not all of the debt which they forgive. This enables them to additionally reduce the revenue loss from the anticipated income stream of the borrower's payments.

In these scenarios, debtors receive the opportunity to escape from part of even all of the debt in question. This can significantly help them to ease their financial case especially after they have suffered from various dramatic financial setbacks and can no longer honor the previously negotiated debts. One downside is that many sovereign governments choose to tax any and all debt forgiveness as real income. This means that while the debtor may enjoy a temporary form of relief from the burdensome debts, they may become categorized according to a higher tax bracket at least for that particular year. This could lead to a hefty tax bill which they cannot settle with the taxing authorities. It can create a whole host of new problems in place of the older and now forgiven ones.

The process of debt forgiveness even happens between one nation and another creditor country. It always helps to consider concrete examples of these concepts to better understand them. Nations which are recovering form devastating natural disasters could not be able to pay debts or even interest owed on them for a few years after such a disaster occurs. Instead of destroy the nation's fragile economy at that point and time, creditor nations will often decide instead to simply write off the loan. This is not an atypical event when it is clear that the economy of the nation will collapse otherwise, especially as this often impacts the entire global economy should it occur.

It is not important as to whether such debt forgiveness is actually applied to individuals, companies, or nations. The process is generally the same. It is also rarely pursued before all other potential avenues are fully explored. Usually what will happen is that debt will not be written down or off if there is any practical possibility that the financial condition for the debtor in question will improve in an acceptable to the creditor time frame. Yet in the end, this debt forgiveness will typically prove to be the most intelligent and ultimately practical form of action if the debtor's financial condition does not look like it will improve any time soon so that the debtor can actually resume their debt and interest payments in an reasonable time frame going forward.

Debt Fund

A Debt Fund refers to an investment pool. This might be either an exchange traded fund or a mutual fund. In it the core assets will be various types of fixed income investments. They could choose to invest in longer term bonds or shorter term ones, money market instruments, securitized products, or even floating rate debt. The debt funds feature lower fee ratios on average than do the comparable equity funds. This is in part because the total management costs prove to be significantly lower for the debt funds than for the equity funds.

The primary objectives for investing in a debt fund will commonly be the generation of income as well as preservation of the original capital. They often consider their performance against a comparable major benchmark as a means of measuring success and judging absolute returns with these debt funds. As such, they will invest in as many promising opportunities as they can find. This might include MIP's monthly income plans, liquid funds, STP's short term plans, Gilt funds, and FMP's fixed maturity plans.

In general, these debt funds will be preferred by those investors who do not want to experience scary high volatility which investing in the stock market easily often can present. It means that such a debt fund will deliver low but steady income as compared to equity funds. Yet the volatility is minor by comparison. Debt funds like these provide a number of advantages.

The tax rules have changed to favor them. Investors will have to stay invested for minimally three years in order to enjoy the advantage of lower taxed longer term capital gains. Those which are redeemed in under three years will be treated as ordinary income for taxable purposes. Debt funds thus become far more tax efficient than even fixed deposits when investors hold them for at least three years. Debt funds will only be taxed at the rate of 20 percent once they are indexed, which is often considerably lower than many investors' otherwise earned income tax rate.

There is also no tax deduction for debt funds at the source, known as TDS on any and all gains which they realize. The returns also are linked to the market performance though they do not offer corresponding returns. When interest rates rise, they can lose, though it is a remote chance of them losing. The maturity of the various holdings defines the actual volatility of the debt fund. Those funds which mostly hold shorter term bonds will not demonstrate much volatility and will still provide returns that are approximately equal to the prevailing interest rates.

Debt funds also allow individuals to invest in SIP's. These are the smartest ways to purchase equity or debt funds. With large sums, they can be sunk into a debt fund that will make systematic transfers into the plan or any fund for which an individual opts. Each month, a fixed and predetermined sum will move from the debt fund over to the other funds that the investors selected.

There will also be an exit load on debt funds. This is the tradeoff for vastly greater liquidity than with many competing investments. Individuals are able to withdraw at any point with only a day's notice. Some of the funds do assess a penalty for leaving in under a preset minimum period. Exit loads range from a reasonable .5 percent on up to a steeper two percent penalty. The minimum holding period is often anywhere from six months on out to as long as two years.

Debt Ratio

Debt Ratio refers to a highly favored financial ratio. This one measures the consumer or company's debt leverage. This ratio is best explained as the ratio for all of the longer-term and shorter-term debt divided by all assets of the individual or enterprise. It is then expressed out in percentage or decimal format. Another way of stating it is the proportion of a firm's assets financed by outright debt. The debt ratio is sometimes called the debt to assets ratio as well.

All else being equal, as this debt ratio is higher it means that the firm has a higher degree of leverage. This generally implies a higher amount of financial risk. Yet simultaneously it is true that such leverage is a critical tool which many corporations employ to expand. Countless firms have discovered many sustainable uses of such debt.

Naturally, acceptable and average debt ratios will range drastically from one industry to the next. Utilities and pipelines are capital-intensive firms. They will necessarily possess far greater debt ratios than do companies in such industries as technology. Consider a clear example to help understand this term better. When corporations have assets of $200 million and aggregate debts of $50 million, then the debt ratio would amount to 25 percent or .25 alternatively. This company would therefore be in a stronger financial position than a comparable one with a 35 percent debt to asset ratio, but not always.

This is because 25 percent debt to asset ratios can be excessive in an industry that boasts unstable cash flows. These businesses simply cannot assume too much debt. Such a firm that possessed an overly high debt ratio as measured up against its rivals would discover how costly additional borrowing would become. This means that it might fall into a cash crunch in shifting circumstances. The fracking industry starting in summer 2014 found itself in dire straits thanks to its huge debt levels and plunging energy prices.

At the same time, debt levels that amount to 35 percent could be easy to manage for those firms which are in an industry like utilities. The cash flows in these businesses are far stronger and more stable. Higher debt to assets ratios are not only acceptable in this business, they are expected. For those firms that find themselves with an over 100 percent debt ratio, you know that its debt levels actually exceed its amount of assets. Conversely, when firms possess a ratio under 100 percent, the firm possesses more assets than debt. Alongside other metrics for determining financial soundness, this ratio will allow investors to ascertain how high the risk level is for a given business.

Debt ratios do not take into account all money that a firm owes necessarily. While they will always count longer- and shorter-term debts, they will leave out liabilities. Some of these liabilities that do not figure into the calculations are negative goodwill, accounts payable, and "other" items.

Consider a real-world example of how this works out in practice. Starbucks possesses a debt ratio of around 22.5 percent. Morningstar considers that the typical ratio for the industry is more like 40 percent on average. This means that the Starbucks Corporation can easily borrow money on the markets. Creditors understand that its finances are solid as a rock. They anticipate receiving full repayment on time. The non-callable and fixed rate Starbucks' bonds that mature in 2045 possess coupon rates of only 4.3 percent.

Contrast this with a basic materials firm like Arch Coal Incorporated. The industry of coal mining is regarded as highly capital intensive. This is why the industry forgives utilizing leverage to operate effectively. The average debt to assets ratio proves to be 47 percent. Yet Arch Coal Inc. has a 64 percent ratio. This makes it costly for them to borrow money. In fact their non-callable, fixed rate bonds that mature in 2023 come with a painful interest coupon rate amounting to 12 percent.

Debt Relief

Debt relief refers to the effective reorganizing of any form of debt so that the indebted party experiences at least some debt forgiveness. This could be complete or partial relief of debt from a large or even overwhelming burden. It is possible for it to take a wide range of scenarios. Relief might be offered in the form of lowering the aggregate principal in whole or in part. It might also be accomplished through lengthening the loan term or reducing the total interest rate and payments of loans which are due.

Debt relief also relates to debt forgiveness in order to stop the growth of the principal or at least to slow it down. This can be done for groups ranging from individual people to companies or multinational corporations to entire nations. From the days of the ancient world up to the 1800s, it primarily pertained to individual and household debt. This especially meant freeing of slaves from indebtedness or forgiving agriculture debts.

In the last years of the 1900s, the use of the phrase changed to cover mostly debt of the Third World. This began with the skyrocketing debt from the Latin American Debt Crisis that included such countries as Mexico and Argentina. By the early years of the 2000s, the phrase had greater application to individuals in wealthy countries that had been ravaged by housing and credit bubbles.

Debt relief in the 20th century came to apply to nations after the devastating effects of the First World War. Those debt payments from the allies of the United states were suspended in the dark depths of the Great Depression from 1931. Finland was the only country to repay these debts in full. Germany also received debt relief of its war reparation burdens from the United States, Britain, and France with the Agreement on German External Debts in 1953. This represented one of the first large scale applications of debt relief on an international scale.

By the 1990s, debt relief had become an urgent need for those under-developed nations which were heavily in debt. This became a mission in the 1990s for a number of Christian organizations, Non Governmental Organizations focused on development, and others partners who worked in an enormous coalition which called itself Jubilee 2000. As part of the campaign to push for debt forgiveness and relief, there were demonstrations at meetings like the G8 Summit in Birmingham, England in 1998. This helped the agenda for debt relief to reach the radar of international organizations like the World Bank and IMF International Monetary Fund as well as Western developed nations' governments.

It actually became public policy through an initiative called the HIPC Heavily Indebted Poor Countries program. This initiative started out in order to offer consistent help in the form of debt relief to those most impoverished nations of the world. It worked strenuously to make certain that the money donated went for reduction of poverty and did not get siphoned off to infrastructure or military buildup programs.

This World Bank-supervised project involved conditions which were much like those accompanying loans from the World Bank and IMF International Monetary Fund. They mandated strict structural reforms that often involved privatizing public utilities including electricity and water. The prospective nations had to institute Poverty Reduction Strategies and demonstrate substantial macroeconomic stability for minimally a year.

In order to cut inflation, there were nations goaded into reducing their expenditures on important sectors such as education and health. The World Bank may have deemed the HIPC protocols a triumph for the twin goals of poverty and debt reduction, but many scholars and analysts offered significant criticisms of the program.

Despite critiques though, the HIPC became extended through the MDRI Multilateral Debt Relief Initiative. After the Gleneagles G8 meeting of 2005 in July, the wealthy creditor nations signed on to the MDRI. This provided full, complete elimination of all HIPC countries' multilateral debts which they owed to the IMF, World Bank, and African Development Bank.

Debt Relief Order

A Debt Relief Order (also known by their acronym DRO) refers to a British legal system type of insolvency method which is relatively new. It was Chapter 4 from the Tribunals, Courts, and Enforcement Act 2007 that actually created these new orders. The advantage that such DROs offer is a less expensive, faster, and simpler means of receiving bankruptcy styled relief in Great Britain.

The DRO works well for those indebted individuals who possess no or very few assets (under 1,000 British pounds without owning a home), and who count tiny disposable income levels (which have to be under 50 pounds sterling each month). Individuals who meet these criteria and several others may pay only a 90 pounds one time fee and then make application for the Debt Relief Order without a court appearance. Participants can even pay this fairly reasonable fee in a period of installments before they file the application for the order. Such DROs took the full force of law for both England and Wales on April 6th of 2009.

There are a range of specific requirements that individuals must meet in order to qualify for such a Debt Relief Order. It must be clear the persons can not pay their debts. They must not owe more than 20,000 pounds in total unsecured bills. Homeowners do not qualify, nor do those who have over 1,000 pounds in total gross assets. They can only keep their car if its value is under 1,000 pounds. The debt holder has to live in Wales or England or at least have been resident or engaged in business in either place within the past three years. They also may not have been issued a DRO in the prior six years.

Besides this the indebted individuals may not be part of any other kind of insolvency proceedings. These include bankruptcies which are not yet discharged, voluntary individual arrangements, present debt relief restrictions, present bankruptcy restrictions, a bankruptcy petition, or an interim order. It is true that these Debt Relief Orders are still insolvency forms that will be publicly listed in the insolvency services website.

In order for Debt Relief Orders to be successfully implemented, there must be a government approved intermediary who handles the event with the relevant authorities. For intermediaries to be approved, they generally have to be debt advice organization personnel which have experience as debt advisors. Some of these approved organizations include the Consumer Credit Counseling Service, one of the Citizens Advice Bureaus, Baines and Ernst National Debtline, Think Money, Payplan, the Institute of Money Advisers, and members of the entity Advice UK. Any of these approved intermediaries are able to consider the information of the persons applying, discern if they are DRO eligible, and finally make an online application on their behalf. These intermediaries who are approved do not charge fees to submit such applications.

The Official Receivers are able to issue the Debt Relief Orders after they obtain both the fee and the application. No court involvement is necessary if the applicant is eligible. Otherwise they will reject the application out of hand. These Official Receivers also have the authority to rescind these DROs if more relevant information on the debtors' financial conditions appears after the order has been granted. There are also criminal charges and penalties allowed by the British law if the applicants knowingly perjure themselves or provide deliberately misleading information on their financial conditions, assets, debts, and other personal financial costs.

Back in November of 2014, the New Policy Institute released data (research funded by the Trust for London) on the quantities of debt relief orders throughout different parts of the United Kingdom. Unsurprisingly, the total numbers of these DROs for London in the years of 2009 to 2013 proved to be vastly less than the rest of England's average.

Debt Restructuring

Debt restructuring refers to a means which corporations or countries with overwhelming debt loads utilize to change the terms of their outstanding debt arrangements so they can gain advantage in repayment. Corporations will often utilize a form of debt restructuring so that they can sidestep defaulting on their already existing debt levels. They might also wish to gain the benefits of lower interest rates that may be available to them on the markets.

One way that companies accomplish this is by issuing a series of callable bonds. These permit them to easily and rapidly restructure their new debts at a given point in the future. In this case, the firms' existing debts will be called. They will then replace them with a newer issued debt for the lower, more advantageous interest rate. Another way that corporations are able to restructure their debt lies in changing the provisions and terms of the current debt issue.

With corporate debt restructuring, a company will typically reorganize its actual obligations by lowering the debt burdens on their firm. They can do this by reducing the payable rates on the debt or by extending the amount of time they have until they repay the debt obligations. By doing either of these, the company ensures it is able to service its relevant debt burdens. There are other cases where the creditors will opt to forgive a part of the debt in exchange for obtaining an equity stake in the firm.

A need for this type of corporate debt restructuring most often occurs when corporations or companies are experiencing financial difficulties. These make it most difficult to keep up with their full range of financial obligations. Sometimes such troubles can be sufficient to create a significant risk of the company declaring bankruptcy. In these cases, they have the ability to engage in a structured negotiation with the creditors to lower the burdens so that they can avoid entering bankruptcy-led defaults.

Within the United States, there is a provision of the corporate bankruptcy code known as Chapter 11. These protocols permit corporations to obtain effective protection from their creditors so that they are able to try to rearrange the debt terms to continue on as a reorganized, ongoing, viable concern. Thanks to federal bankruptcy courts becoming involved in this process, even when the creditors refuse to accept such a settlement and reorganization, the courts can mandate that the creditors accept the plan if they deem it to be reasonable and fair.

It is not only corporations and companies which can avail themselves of such debt restructuring. Governments also have needs for help with their debts when they finally become unsustainable. This is not a new phenomenon. It stretches back to the first historically recorded sovereign debt default of the fourth century B.C. At this time, ten different Greek city-states defaulted on loans they had taken from the sacred temple of Delos. Despite the fact that this has occurred for at least 2,300 years, today no clear and mutually understood rules exist to structure the process for what will occur if a sovereign state can not pay their debts.

The most recent classic example of this dates back to the huge default by Argentina. Their enormous debt default in 2001 was among the largest in modern history. The rules are unclear as to who has jurisdiction and who can set restructuring terms. For years Argentina refused to negotiate terms with the eight percent of its bondholders who would not agree to the terms the country set in 2001. Then a court ruling from the U.S. Supreme Court confused the issue by ordering Argentina to settle with the remaining holdouts at full value plus interest before they could pay the agreed-upon settled amount to the other 92 percent of debt holders.

Argentina then came back to the table for the eight percent of mostly opportunistic hedge funds which had bought their defaulted debt for pennies on the dollar. Grudgingly under duress they paid the hedge fund eight percent claimants. This was an unusual case study that only worked out because the debt had been issued under American debt law. In other cases and scenarios, it is only the IMF International Monetary Fund that is attempting to create some sort of rules on situations like these.

Yet in the end, no one can force a country to pay its debts back to creditors short of going to war with them to seize their physical assets or by freezing assets of the offending country in the banks or vaults of the debt holders' countries.

Debt Service

Debt service refers to the cash that is necessary to be paid over a certain period of time in order to repay both principal and interest on a given debt. For individuals, monthly mortgage payments, or credit card bill payments, prove to be good examples of personal debt service. For businesses, payments on lines of credit, business loans, or coupon payments of bonds represent samples of corporate debt service.

Where businesses or personal debt service is concerned, this is used to calculate the DSCR, or debt service coverage ratio. This ratio is that of the cash that is on hand for servicing the debt's principal, interest, and lease payments. This measurement is a much utilized benchmark that helps to determine a company or an individual's capability of generating sufficient money to cover the payments on their debt. With a higher debt service coverage ratio, loans are easier to get for both companies and people.

The commercial banking industry also employs this phrase. Here, it can refer to the minimally acceptable ratio that a given lender will accept. This might turn out to be a condition of making the entity such a loan in the end. When this type of a condition is part of the loan covenant, then violating the debt service coverage ratio can sometimes be considered an action of default.

Debt service coverage ratios are similarly used in the world of corporate finance. Here, they describe the sum of available cash flow that is usable for covering yearly principal and interest payments on any and all debts. This includes payments for sinking funds.

Commercial real estate finance similarly utilizes debt service and debt service coverage ratios as the main means of discovering if a given property is capable of maintaining its level of debt using only its own cash flow. In the past ten or so years, banks would look for a minimum debt service coverage ratio of minimally 1.2. Banks that proved to be more aggressive were willing to work with lower ratios.

This practice led to greater risk in the system that helped to bring on the financial meltdown and resulting crisis that stretched from 2007 to 2010.

When an entity has more than a ratio of one debt service coverage ratio, it is theoretically capable of covering its debt requirements with cash flow. Similarly, if this ratio is less than one, then the statistics claim that an insufficient amount of cash flow exists to meet the required loan payments.

Debt to Equity

Debt to Equity refers to a ratio that is extremely important and often scrutinized in the world of business. It is the amount of longer term debt on the balance sheet of a corporation as related to and divided by the company equity. Long term debt for a company means money that it will not be expected to pay back in the coming 12 months. Both are critical factors in effective balance sheet analysis.

This ratio tells an analyst or investor a great deal about a company and the amount of debt it is carrying compared to its true net worth. This is accomplished by gathering together all of the company liabilities and then dividing this amount up by the shareholder equity. The end result which comes back in dividing the total debt by the equity proves to be the percentage of the firm which is leveraged (or more accurately stated--- indebted).

Over time, the acceptable and average amount of debt to equity has varied significantly in the corporate world. Today it heavily depends on both the state of the economy, the industry in which the company operates, and the all-around feelings of society concerning credit and debt. If all else is equal, any firm with a debt to equity ratio in excess of 40 percent to 50 percent should be more careful about the risk hidden within its balance sheet and books. These could lead to a liquidity crisis at some point in the future.

When analysts consider the working capital of the company and find that both it and the current ratios of the firm are dramatically low, then this is a glaring sign of significant financial weakness in a corporation. This is why an analyst or investor truly needs to adjust any current profitability numbers to the economic cycle at hand. Many investors have lost fortunes over the years because the plugged in peak earnings at the height of an economic boom as their base case scenario metric for a firm's ability to pay back its various debt obligations.

There is no good reason to fall for this age old trap after all. All that is required to avoid it is to predict that the economy may fall off a proverbial cliff at any point and time. Then consider if the cash flow would be sufficient to cover the liabilities without the corporation being hurt and hampered by a lack of money for critical daily, monthly, and yearly expenses on items such as plant, property, and equipment.

The truth is that debt and elevated debt to equity ratios is not necessarily a bad thing. Many businesses are quite adept at earning a greater return on their capital than the cost of the interest which they incur in borrowing the money. This would make it extremely profitable to borrow money in such cases. It allows such firms to boost their earnings and profitability for one thing. The real key element is that the company management clearly understands the level of debt which will represent a danger level for smart and forward thinking stewardship of their company. Leverage cuts both ways. It dramatically boosts returns when it is working well for a firm, and it similarly can even totally wipe out a company if things turn on the firm in an economic recession or even economic depression.

Investors especially need to be careful in buying corporate bonds in such environments. Bonds issued in the lower interest rate environments of today will suffer drastically when the interest rates invariably rise higher, especially if this is quick and unexpected. This will lead to less profitability for the firm when the bonds have to be financed again. If the management did not wisely prepare for such an issue well in advance, then the company will truly have been mismanaged during the golden boom days and will suffer needlessly during the inevitable bust economic times.

Deed in Lieu of Foreclosure

A deed in lieu of foreclosure represents an alternative option to a standard foreclosure on a house. In this deed in lieu arrangement, the owner of the property decides to hand over the property in question to the lender on a completely voluntary basis. In exchange for agreeing to this, the lender cancels out the mortgage loan. The deed to the house becomes transferred from the owner to the lender. As part of this conciliatory arrangement, the mortgage lender guarantees that it will not start the foreclosure process on the owner. If there are any foreclosure actions that have already begun, the lender will also terminate these. It is up to the lender to decide if they will forgive any extra balance that the sale of the home does not cover.

There are some tax issues that can arise with a deed in lieu of foreclosure deal. One potential downside to this type of debt forgiveness involves the consequences of it with the IRS. Federal law in the United States requires creditors to file 1099C forms for tax purposes when they choose to forgive any loan balance that amounts to more than $600. This debt forgiveness is then considered to be income and it becomes a tax liability for the home owner.

Fortunately for many home owners during the financial crisis, Congress passed the Mortgage Forgiveness Debt Relief Act of 2007. This delivered tax relief on a number of loans that banks forgave in the years starting from 2007 till the end of 2013.

The main issue and advantage that a deed in lieu of foreclosure offers centers around this excess balance debt forgiveness. Anyone who enters into such a voluntary agreement should carefully review the contract to learn how the deficiency balance topic will be addressed. Sometimes the documents are not clear on this point.

In this case, the homeowner should take the deed in lieu document to a lawyer who specializes in property law. It is not inexpensive to have a lawyer review such a contract document. The money it can save the home owner in the future for signing a contract he or she does not understand and may suffer significantly from will make the fees seem reasonable by comparison.

There are a number of requirements in order for a deed in lieu of foreclosure to be accepted. First the house would have to be on the seller market for a minimum number of days. Ninety days is usual. There also may not be any liens on the house. The property typically could not be in the process of foreclosure already. Finally, the deed in lieu offer has to be voluntary on the part of the home owner.

Another option that can be pursued in place of this deed in lieu of foreclosure is a short sale. Short sales have the same requirements as do the deed in lieu arrangements with several additional stipulations. The home seller must be suffering from financial hardship. The home itself has to be offered at a reasonable price.

In an alternative short sale, the mortgage lender will consent to receiving a lesser amount from the sale than the remaining mortgage balance that the owner still owes. It is up to the bank and the contract if any additional balance which exists will be forgiven or not. The same tax issues apply if the lender agrees to forgive more than $600.

Deed of Priority

Deed of Priority refers to a deed or other form of contract where two or more creditors concur between themselves on the order that their security for a debtor in common will rank. In other words, they set out the rights which each of them will have pertaining to recovering the debts which the specific debtor in question owes them all should said debtor choose to default.

Many times in practice this phrase is interchanged with the similar term inter-creditor agreement. It is true that both kinds of documents look to arrange the order of precedence rank between a group of creditors. There are important differences between these two types of documents though. For one, the inter-creditor agreement is usually a more complicated document. It tends to detail equity and debt provider rights as well as the rights to obtain payments in advance of a debtor going insolvent and the rights to seize security.

Deeds of Priority are also referred to as Waiver Arrangements in Britain, and as Ranking Arrangements in Scotland. Both businesses and consumers have opportunities to source finance from multiple sources. Each lender will want some form of security with which to back the loan naturally. This might amount to any business assets or only specific ones. The second lender will also wish to obtain security in the form of some of the business assets regarding the loan they are issuing.

It is critical for every lender involved in the project, both original ones and new ones, to be aware of the different security arrangements which have already been made between the customer and earlier lenders. In other words, the various lenders will need someone to act as liaison between them so that each lender is able to ascertain and confirm its part of the secured assets, as well as its ranking for them. They will require such assurances before they actually issue the funds in the agreed upon loan.

There are a means by which they could attempt to effectively do this. One of them is the waiver arrangement. Another is using the deed of priority discussed in this article. The deed of priority is usually preferable since it spells out clearly and concisely the terms which pertain between each and every lender in the case of this specific borrower. It helps them all to understand how the various company or personal assets will be fairly and equitably distributed and shared out in the case of a default on one or more of their repayment agreements with the borrowing customer.

These scenarios will most commonly arise when a business already had a financing arrangement in place with a traditional bank. The business may then open negotiations with what is known as an alternative lender to borrow additional capital. Naturally this alternative lender will then want an arrangement hammered out with the other lender so that it can be sure of obtaining some level of collateral security over assets which are already pledged in part or whole to the original lender.

They will then sit down to fine tune the priority ranking of the various securities of the business, or to establish a release of assets from the existing security in play with the original lender. Paperwork must be drawn up, legalized, and signed off on by all lenders involved typically as swiftly as possible.

Fortunately for British- based businesses, there is a protocol in place to handle these matters. The British Bankers Association (or BBA) has compiled a PDF document called the "Deeds of Priority and Waivers: What You Need to Know as a Small or Medium Sized Business and What the Major Banks Are Committed to."

All of the major British banks have signed on to the terms of this protocol, making it far easier for British businesses to work out the deeds of priority arrangements so that they can obtain their supplementary financing from the second institutions.

Defeasance Clause

A defeasance clause refers to a mortgage contract. It is the statement in a mortgage loan that explains what will happen once a borrower has repaid all of the outstanding loan amounts. At that point, the lender usually will be required by law to hand over the title of the property to the owner. These defeasance clauses are not utilized in every part of the country. Instead they are a part of mortgages where they are not issued on a lien basis. When such liens are used instead, lenders keep their interest in the house. This gives them the right and ability to foreclose on the property in case the borrower does not make the payments according to the loan terms and agreement.

When a loan contains a defeasance clause, borrowers should carefully read through it. They must be certain that the lender interest in the house will come to an end after the loan is fully paid off including principle, interest, and other costs. This is the standard and accepted practice in the industry.

As mortgages are set up using a defeasance clause, lenders keep a special form of title called a defeasible title. These conditional titles may be revoked in specific scenarios. It is the defeasance clause itself found in the mortgage contract that determines when the lender will give up the title to the property after the borrower has fulfilled all of the loan obligations. The clause may also detail additional information. This can include penalties for prepayment should the loan come with them.

After the home buyers have completely repaid their loan, they can redeem their property's title. The one time borrower then becomes the home owner with title. Having the title is important for many reasons. It allows owners to refinance the home, sell it, rent it out, pledge it for a line of credit, or keep and live in it indefinitely. These titles are supposed to be free and clear after the interest of the lender terminates. An exception to this might be if the title had other issues hanging over it that had nothing to do with the mortgage loan with which the buyer purchased it. This might be from a tax lien or other problem.

It is the paperwork associated with the mortgage which usually spells out such things as defeasance clauses. Such paperwork should come with terms and conditions that are spelled out in great detail. For example, this contract contains all of the relevant information that pertains to the forecast repayment date, total amount to be paid back throughout the loan, and other issues. Buyers should carefully review all of this for accuracy. If any of it does not appear to be as expected by the borrowers, then they need to talk with the lender before signing any contracts.

There are several different ways that titles can be released by the lender. A defeasance clause may stipulate that the lender needs to release the title at once to the borrower after the loan has been completely paid. In other cases, the borrower might need to file paperwork for the release before the title comes back. The title should be cleared when the loan is paid off in full. Should any problems with this title arise, it can be a serious issue in the future when the owner wants to sell or refinance the house. Clearing up issues and mistakes on a title can take time, so these should be addressed as soon as possible.

Deflation

Deflation is simply the prices of goods and services going down in a given time frame. Deflation is the opposite of inflation, which is the rising cost of goods and services over a period of time. This does not make deflation a good thing in the long run.

Another way of defining deflation is the increasing value of money versus various economic goods over a span of time. With inflation, money is becoming less valuable versus goods over time. Deflation happens as a result of the interaction of four factors. On the one hand, the supply of money in circulation might decline. At the same time, supplies of available goods might increase. The need for goods could drop as well. Finally, the demand for money could go up. If any of these four things happen either separately or in concert, deflation is commonly the result.

The easiest way for deflation to occur is as the supply of goods available on the market goes up at a more rapid pace than does the supply of money. The combination of these elements explains how some goods' costs go up while the costs of others go down at the same time. Despite this, deflation can pose certain problems.

The majority of economists today concur that deflation proves to be both a symptom of economic problems as well as a malaise in and of itself. Some buy into the concepts of good and bad deflation. Good deflation happens as companies are consistently capable of manufacturing goods for cheaper and lower prices because of gains in productivity and other ways of reducing costs. This type of deflation permits a strong and growing GDP growth, with lower unemployment, and rising profits.

Bad deflation is more challenging to grasp. Bad deflation rises as a result of the central bank, or the Federal Reserve, choosing to revalue the country's currency. Or, you could say that the supply of money declining results in this negative form of deflation.

The actual problem that deflation causes is that it creates uncertainty for businesses and their relationships. As a rule, business thrives on confidence and falters on the unknown. Borrowers have to make loan payments that turn out to be greater and greater amounts of purchasing power in deflationary time periods. All the while, the value of the asset that you purchased with the loan is declining. In these circumstances, many borrowers elect to default on the loan and its payments.

A declining spiral similarly exists in deflationary periods. Since businesses begin to enjoy fewer profits, they decide to reduce their employment roles. Individuals do not spend as much money as a result. Businesses then realize smaller profits and again cut back. This degenerates into a vicious cycle down before long, as it becomes self reinforcing. Consumers learn that larger ticket items such as houses and cars will actually cost less in the future and then delay their purchases.

Though deflation has been discussed as a potential problem for the U.S. economy with the economic downturn, the reality is far different. At the same time, from 2006 to 2009, the Federal Reserve massively increased the money supply by more than three hundred percent. This argues not for deflation in the United States' future, but for inflation instead.

Deflationary Bias

Deflationary Bias refers to a government approach to managing inflation versus deflation. Inflation means that prices are rising, whereas deflation signifies that the prices of goods and services are decreasing. It is helpful to consider a real example of these two opposing concepts in order to understand them and the problems deflation can quickly cause.

If individuals go to their local grocery store and discover that bread has increased to $2.50 instead of the previous price of $2.00, they will not be happy. This is inflation and represents inflationary bias. On the other hand if the individuals went down to the car lot and discovered that a car which sold for $25,000 before is now selling for $23,000, they would be ecstatic. This is deflation and represents a deflationary bias. In general, consumers will always prefer deflation to inflation, at least on the surface.

The picture becomes more complicated when debt is considered. On a consumer level, as home prices decline, the home owners suddenly find themselves holding a mortgage that may be higher than the house's actual value proves to be. As this becomes a severe problem, individuals who own the house and are paying down the mortgage little by little (over likely 30 years) will not be able to sell and move simply because the mortgage is so much greater than the value of the house. The debt laden homeowners become unwitting victims of deflation in these cases. As a result, they are unable to move to expand their job hunting possibilities and will likely cut back on spending as they realize that they are upside down in the home thanks to the ravages of deflation.

This logic similarly applies to business as well. Because contracts exist in fixed terms not real terms, as real prices rise or fall, losers and winners emerge every time. As inflation occurs, sellers in a contract prove to be the winners, along with debtors whose debt is priced less in real terms. When deflation happens, prices fall and the sellers and debtors become the all around losers as their debt now costs more to repay in real terms. The buyers and creditors are the winners in this deflationary scenario. Ultimately this means that regardless of accounting tricks and confusing statistics, both deflation and inflation create income transfers with zero sum game losers and winners.

Governments attempt to smooth out the precarious extremes of either deflation or inflation utilizing monetary policy. The problem occurs as some prices rise at the same time as others fall. Gas prices may be declining at the same time as new cars are becoming more expensive. This is where the various monetary policies of governments meet their match. As these policies are effectively massive but blunt instruments, it is impossible for them to flexibly address the two extreme scenarios simultaneously.

This leaves policy makers with one of two unappealing choices. They will have to show one bias or another in their approach to managing an economy. Will they pursue an inflationary bias or instead a deflationary bias? With the inflationary bias they will be favoring greater employment levels and higher growth over the shorter term time frame. With a deflationary bias they will be favoring lower employment and less growth over the short term. The problem is that these biases similarly impact both sellers and buyers of any assets as they cause the assets to be less or more valuable in real terms as the debt in which they hold them is constant.

The reason that central banks and policy makers hate deflation so much is because of the real world effects on holders of debt. They are in terror of deflation since it alters consumer and business psychology and spending. With the Western societies that are so heavily indebted, deflation is the greatest possible enemy. This is true for the consumers, businesses, and especially the debt-ridden sovereign governments alike.

It is why the policy makers around Europe and the U.S. are desperate to re-inflate their respective economies. Japan has been caught in a deflationary spiral for decades now. The terrifying result has been a long period of economic stagnation and malaise from which they have never escaped since the end of the 1980s.

Delinquency

Delinquency refers to primarily an individual (but also conceivably an entity or business) failing to make good on what was expected of them according to their duty or the law. It often pertains to failing to affect the minimum due payment or carry out a fiduciary responsibility. An individual who practices Delinquency is called a delinquent. These persons have contractually undertaken obligations to turn in payments on loan accounts according to a pre-arranged routine deadline.

This might include minimum monthly amounts of money owed on a car payment, a credit card payment, or a mortgage payment. As the individuals do not make these payments on time, they become delinquent. When mortgage holders become delinquent, the financial institutions holding the loans are able to start working through foreclosure processes. They will do this when the mortgage account stays unpaid for a specific length of time.

There are many different types of accounts on which people fall into Delinquency. This could be retail account payments, income taxes, mortgages, lines of credit, and more. Individuals who become delinquent suffer the consequences for these financial actions. Such impacts vary with the kind of Delinquency, cause, and length of time it has continued in this unfortunate state. As individuals become late on credit card bills, they can be charged late fees. Those who do not make their required tax payments can have their wages garnered or even their bank account levied by the Internal Revenue Service.

Besides these financial Delinquencies, there are responsibilities which when they are not carried out can be labeled delinquent. By not carrying out one's fiduciary duties, professional responsibilities, or other contractual obligations as set forth by custom or the law, individuals can be called delinquents as well. Police officers who do not professionally carry out their responsibilities to protect ordinary citizens in the line of duty can be found to be delinquent.

It is important not to confuse Delinquency with default. Individuals are officially delinquent at the point when they miss making a required payment of some sort in a timely fashion. By contrast, loan defaults happen as borrowers do not pay back a loan according to the terms on which they agreed to in their original contract. Loans can stay in the delinquent stage without being treated as in default for an unspecified amount of time. The amount of time this remains delinquent rather than in default varies considerably from one creditor and financial institution to another. For example, with student loans, the United States' Federal Government permits these to be fully delinquent for as long as 270 consecutive days before they become considered to be in default.

The U.S. keeps track of its various national Delinquency rates. Per the year 2016 in the fourth quarter, such Delinquencies amounted to 4.15 percent for real estate loans on residential loans, 2.15 percent on loans for consumer credit cards, and .85 percent for real estate loans on commercial loans. The government also maintains official statistics for these rates by year of loan issued. For 2016, this amounted to 2.04 percent, which was near the historically typical average.

The devastating global financial crisis and U.S. mortgage crisis which erupted in 2007 caused the rates to spike to a high in the Great Recession years which reached fully 7.4 percent in the year 2010 in its first quarter. For residential real estate, the rate topped out at 11.26 percent for these specific types of loans. Up to the year 2008 in its second quarter these Delinquencies had not been higher than three percent all the way back to the year 1994 in its first quarter.

Delinquent Rent

Delinquent Rent refers to rent that tenants pay their landlords late. This is called one of the two greatest frustrations for landlords in the renting process. The other one is handling tenants who vandalize a place. Making good on late or unpaid rent is a hassle for landlords that is almost always an expensive and time consuming process. There are various processes available to landlords for them to obtain their unpaid or late rents. These vary widely based on the state where the property lies, as each state has its own laws pertaining to rentals. The rental agreement also plays its part based on the provisions it contains.

Rental relationships were once arranged with mere handshakes, but that simpler time is now long gone forever. In today's complicated and litigious world, such business arrangements become specified by the law and in contracts instead of on a trust basis. In today's rental arrangements, the rental agreement governs the means of obtaining Delinquent Rent or unpaid balances. This is why it is so important to obtain a solid rent contract template before individuals become landlords and execute rental agreements for the first time.

Oral arrangements are never a good idea in these scenarios. This is because courts frown on enforcing them and they may even doubt their existence or validity. Well-defined lease contracts spell out each provision of the rental arrangements. This includes the amount of rent that has to be furnished and at what point said rent must be paid. Landlords who are unable to specify the precise date on which the rent must be paid will find they are often stymied in their subsequent late and unpaid rent collection endeavors.

It is similarly important for landlords to never agree to verbal alterations to a written out and executed contract. Verbal changes become hotly contested and debatable in law courts. They often will diminish the ability to collect on late rents which the written contract adequately specified. This is why instead the landlords must focus on writing in the maximum number of self help (for rental collection) avenues as the laws in a given state will permit.

In the majority of cases, the state laws provide for two different forms of dealing with unpaid and Delinquent Rent. The ones mentioned above are called self help remedies. These involve any methods a landlord may enforce without needing to make court appearances, file lawsuits, and involve judges. They can only include the relevant property code and state rental law provision allowances. Some of these so-called self help remedies include the ability to enforce liens on the personal property of the renter, to post a notice of eviction, and to physically engage in a lockout of the tenant by changing the locks on the property.

There are states that restrict the kinds of personal property that landlords may seize against Delinquent Rent or back rent. State contract law usually has provisions governing lockouts and eviction notices too. Landlords have to obey the contractual and state law requirements for both methods carefully. For example, shutting off electricity, water, and gas is typically not permitted by most states among the procedures for collecting late rent.

Eviction notices are often the most effective means of dealing with back rent. This is because the majority of tenants do not actually wish to be evicted forcefully by the sheriff from the property. The will generally respond to such a notice by paying any and all rent which they owe at this point.

When self help remedies do not resolve the situation, the small claims court is the place that handles the majority of landlord-tenant disputes. The landlord will have to pay filing fees in order to lodge a rent collection lawsuit. Tenants must be notified of the opening of such a rental dispute lawsuit. Every jurisdiction has its own regulations for the format of the notice which the landlord must provide to the tenant. Among these are in person notification, by fax, by mail, or other means of notification. Once a hearing is held before the judge, a judgment will typically be awarded for the rent that remains unpaid or delinquent.

Distressed Assets

Distressed assets are assets that a company or individual has been forced to place for sale at a significant discount to the acquired or actual value. This usually happens as the owner has no choice but to sell the asset to raise cash. Several different reasons might exist for why this is the case. These include excessive debt levels, bankruptcy, and regulatory requirements. Even debt can be put on sale at an amount that is lower than its face value. When this happens, it is known as distressed debt.

Although there are various types of distressed assets offered for sale, among the most common in the wake of 2007-2010's financial crisis and Great Recession are non performing loans on houses or foreclosures on mortgaged properties. Investors of all sizes are able to take advantage of such distressed assets in property by availing themselves of a homeowner's lack of ability to meet the mandatory mortgage payments or of his or her critical requirements for cash. In situations like this, such homeowners will consent much of the time to selling the property for a substantial discount in order to achieve a fast sale.

In the past, banks dealt with such distressed asset mortgages almost entirely themselves. As a result of the American banks still repairing their heavily damaged balance sheets from the countless write offs and over leveraging that they engaged in over the past five to ten years, they can not keep up any longer with the enormous number of foreclosures on their books. This leaves them with little choice but to have to sell some of their mortgage property asserts at massive discounts to actual value in order to be able to create quick cash flow.

The end result is that distressed assets can present a potentially profitable investment opportunity for you. The still ongoing crisis in global liquidity and credit has banks selling mortgages to individual, as well as to large, investors at significant discounts. Such discounts to perceived value would never occur in the days of normalized conditions in the mortgage and credit market place.

This means that investors are currently able to purchase distressed home assets with discounts amounting to as much as 72.5%. With as little as

$100,000, smaller investors are able to get involved with this efficient and potentially lucrative investment strategy. Professional management teams are available to help small investors realize appropriate exit strategies whose goal is to generate an impressive 20% return on investment per year.

Purchasing distressed assets such as homes in mortgage payment trouble can offer ethical options and benefits as well. Investors are able to restructure the debt and payments of the home owner in such a way that distressed home owners are able to afford the new payments. This lets the troubled home owners stay in their houses so long as the investor owns the mortgage and the home owner is able to work with the newly arranged payment schedule.

Distressed assets of companies include many different types of assets. These might be commercial office buildings, commercial jets, and even factories and equipment sold at substantial discounts to real value. Many times, other corporations are able to acquire these distressed assets for their own uses at fantastic prices.

Distressed Securities

Distressed Securities refer to a corporation's financial instruments when the underlying companies are nearing or actually undergoing bankruptcy presently. Because such a firm is unable to cover all of its various financial responsibilities, its financial instruments will have undergone a dramatic decline in value. Yet thanks to the implied volatility that comes along with such inherent risk, the instruments actually provide investors with the very real possibilities of enormous returns. Such securities might be comprised of corporate bonds, trade claims, bank debt preferred stock, or common stock shares.

In the challenging investing climate of today, there are often many investors competing for opportunities which are bargain priced that might come with higher risk in the form of such Distressed Securities. There are scenarios where investors will carefully study up on the company plight and determine that it is not actually so serious as the market and public perceive it to be.

Because of this, they believe that their investments bought at a steep discount may increase dramatically in value as the situation of the company's finances becomes finally resolved. There are other cases where the investors agree with analysts that the firm may fall into bankruptcy. Yet they might be confident at the same time that the liquidation proceeds will be sufficient to cover the value of the securities which they obtain at a drastic discount to face value.

Individual investors should be extremely familiar with what will happen to such Distressed Securities should the company slide into either Chapter 7 or Chapter 11 bankruptcy. With the overwhelming majority of these bankruptcies, the common share equity will be completely wiped out. This means that investing in distressed stocks is highly risky. Yet many of the senior-most debt instruments like bonds, trade claims, and bank debts can provide some amount of payout after liquidation.

This is particularly the case when businesses elect to file a case of Chapter 7 bankruptcy. This halts operations and forces liquidation. The resulting funds will then be collected and dispersed out to the creditors according to their various degrees of seniority. With Chapter 11 bankruptcy, the corporation will restructure and resume its business operations. Assuming that such reorganization becomes a success, the distressed securities in the form of either corporate bonds or company stock could return incredible profit percentages as they stage a massive recovery alongside the company's improving fortunes and future prospects.

The trick is to understand at what stage such securities become Distressed Securities. Analysts will commonly label them as such when the firm that issues them cannot effectively meet a great number of its financial obligations. In the overwhelming majority of such scenarios, these securities will have been previously downgraded to junk credit rating status, as in CCC or lower by the major credit ratings arms of the debt rating agencies like Moody's Investor Services or Standard and Poor's.

Distressed securities are not necessarily always junk bonds though and should not be confused as such. Junk bonds only need to feature a credit rating of BBB or lower in order to be classified as junk. The underlying firm of the bonds is not in bankruptcy nor imminent to go there just because its bond issues carry the junk bond rating and label.

It is worth noting that the expected rate of return for distressed securities will be greater than 1,000 basis points (ten percent) over the rates of return for risk-free assets. This would include U.S. government bonds or Treasury bills' effective rates of return. It means that when the yield on five-year Treasury bonds amounts to one percent, then the Distressed Securities corporate bond should offer a rate of return of at least 11 percent.

Economic Inequality

Economic Inequality concerns disparity financially between various groups of individuals. There are no societies in the world where all people fall into precisely the identical class economically. In other words, all individuals do not have the same amount of material or financial resources. Unfortunately, just the opposite is more common.

In many nations, some people have such vast income and wealth differences from others who live in dire poverty. On the other extreme, the wealthy live ultra luxuriously. This causes great and intense debate as the effects of economic inequality spill over into other parts of life that would normally not be determined by one's economic standing.

In most economies and countries, there are poor people, rich people, and then many medium classed ones which live in the middle. This is most clearly demonstrated in respect to the richest class. They earn and possess substantially greater resources than all of the other classes, particularly versus the bottom one. It is this whole scenario that economists call economic inequality.

Two different focuses surface as analysts consider such economic inequalities. Wealth is the first of these. This refers to the quantifiable amount of money and possessions that people have. Such wealth massively affects the lifestyle of individuals as it is almost exclusively the determining factor of what people can buy and what choices they have in their daily lives and when making longer-term plans. The wealthy naturally have higher standards of living than the rest of the classes.

The other critical financial indicator for measuring the level of economic inequality has to do with income. There are a number of individuals who possess no or little wealth as they have next to no meaningful income. In most cases, the people who command the greatest amount of wealth and so enjoy the highest standards of living are similarly the ones who enjoy the most significant levels of income.

It is interesting to realize that this kind of inequality economically is more severe in some nations and regions than it is in other ones. Nations that do not have sufficient social services find that the disparities are greatest and painfully obvious. In some of these countries, some individuals are extravagantly wealthy while others on the other extreme live in appalling conditions or suffer from starvation or at least severe malnutrition. Other countries have adequate social service networks and find that the gap between the richest and the poorest proves to be less severe. This still will not stop significant differences from appearing between the different groups and their actual lifestyles.

The debate rages on regarding economic inequality because of a variety of reasons. One strong argument against wealth and income disparities is that these dramatically impact the ability of citizens to obtain core services and basic items that ought to be easily available to all people. This includes such things as food, clean drinking water, legal representation, and adequate health care. Another complaint regarding inequality concerns the unfair access to impacting the political environment that the rich enjoy.

In recent years, the United States has been ranked among the most unequal of all developed nation rivals. In fact the OECD ranks the U.S. as second highest in inequality levels once it takes market incomes and adjusts them for the redistribution impacts of income transfer programs and tax policies (like unemployment compensation and Social Security payouts). According to their measurements, only Chile has a greater level of economic inequality from all 31 developed nations.

Similarly, the U.S. economic inequality has become the highest since 1928 in recent years. As of 2012, the highest earning one percent in the U.S obtained 22.5 percent of all pretax income. The bottom earning 90 percent enjoyed only 49.6 percent of the national income share.

Enron Bankruptcy

The Enron bankruptcy turned out to be among the largest corporate failures in American history. When the company filed for protection from its creditors, it showed assets amounting to $49.8 billion and debts that equaled $31.2 billion. These debt totals left out a number of items that were not properly listed on the company's financial statements.

The Enron bankruptcy was subsequently massively eclipsed by Lehman Brothers and it's over $600 billion in assets and bad debts when it filed. At the time Enron failed, it represented the seventh largest company in America by revenues. The failure cost around 20,000 employees their jobs and made worthless the company share retirement holdings of many employees and the stock holdings of countless investors.

The Enron corporation arose in 1985 because of a merger of Houston Natural Gas and InterNorth. The two were regional American corporations that were fairly small. Before the Enron bankruptcy happened, the company grew by 2001 to become the largest energy trader in the world which stood as among the biggest natural gas, electricity, paper and pulp, and communications companies on earth. It permanently changed the way that companies bought and sold electricity, energy, and natural gas. The company's revenues for the year 2000 were almost $111 billion. Fortune had awarded the company the prestigious designation of "America's Most Innovative Company" for six years in a row.

In the end of December 2001, the ugly truth emerged. The company had sustained its existence through cleverly disguised accounting fraud. This creatively orchestrated and systemic corruption became known as the Enron scandal. One of the major five accounting firms in the U.S., Arthur Andersen, became dissolved as a result of its complicit role in auditing the company books. Enron's stock went from $90 per share to worthless in a period of under a year.

The scandal significantly rocked the business and political world. A great number of corporations around the U.S. had their business activities and accounting practices questioned as a result of the attention Enron brought to bear. It encouraged Congress to pass the Sarbanes-Oxley Act of 2002.

Before the company failed, Houston based Dynegy attempted to rescue it from imminent bankruptcy. Negotiations broke down as Dynegy backed out after uncovering the extent of the misrepresentations and deterioration of Enron. The company sued Dynegy for taking control of its largest and most lucrative natural gas pipeline when the deal collapsed. Enron also attempted to secure $1 billion in loans and the financial backstopping of JP Morgan Chase and Citibank, but this fell through as well.

The complexity of the company ensured that the Enron bankruptcy would be a long, drawn out process. Weil, Gotshal, & Manges served as bankruptcy attorneys for the company's Southern District of New York court filing at the end of 2001. The bankruptcy did not end until November of 2004, nearly three years later. The court sanctioned a reorganization plan to distribute assets to creditors.

The new board of directors altered the company's name from Enron. They changed it to Enron Creditors Recovery Corp. The main endeavors of the new outfit were restricted to regrouping and selling off assets and operations the company had held before it went into bankruptcy.

With pipelines and 12 business units, this process went on for another two years. It was not until September 7 in 2006 that the company sold its last energy business. Ashmore Energy International Limited (AEI) acquired Enron's Prisma Energy International and ended the saga of one of America's most spectacular business collapses.

Equal Credit Opportunity Act (ECOA)

The Equal Credit Opportunity Act is also known as the ECOA. Congress created this regulation in order to provide all legal American residents with a fair and reasonable opportunity to obtain loans from banks or other financial institutions that make loans.

The act clearly states that such organizations may not discriminate against individual people for any reason that does not directly pertain to their credit history and file. It makes it illegal for lenders and creditors alike to take into consideration such factors as the consumer's color, race, ethnicity, nation of origin, religion, sex, or marital status when they are determining whether or not they will accept the credit or loan application.

Besides this, the law prohibits denying any credit application because of the age of the applicant. This assumes that the person applying has attained the legal minimum age and demonstrates the mental abilities necessary to execute such a contract. Finally, companies making loans may not reject an applicant because he or she receives public assistance funds from the government.

The governmental agency responsible for enforcing this Equal Credit Opportunity Act turns out to be the FTC Federal Trade Commission. As the consumer protection agency for the country, the FTC monitors lending organizations to make sure that they are not in violation of any of these discriminatory rules. Creditors are allowed to ask applicants for such information as their color, race, religion, sex, ethnicity, nation of origin, age, or marital status.

They are not allowed to consider any of these factors when determining whether or not to extend credit or even when deciding the terms of the credit which they are offering. The fact remains that not all people applying for credit will receive it or will obtain it on equal terms. Many factors are taken into consideration by lenders in ascertaining a person's creditworthiness, such as expenses, income, credit history, and levels of debts.

This Equal Credit Opportunity Act specifically protects consumers when they transact with investors or organizations that routinely offer credit. This includes loan and finance companies, banks, department or retail stores, credit unions, and credit card companies. Every party who is a part of the credit granting or terms setting decisions has to abide by the rules of the ECOA. This includes even the finance arrangers such as real estate brokers.

As a person applies for a mortgage, lenders will routinely inquire about some of the elements of information that are forbidden to be considered in the ultimate application decision. Because of this, applicants do not have to respond to these questions. The only considerations which they are allowed to employ in judging the merits of the individual must be information that is financially relevant, like the person's income, credit score, and present debt levels.

The Equal Credit Opportunity Act will not allow lenders to make approval decisions because of an individual's present or past marital status. They will require that applicants inform them of any child support or alimony payments which they are making. Persons receiving such substantial payments as part of their income should also disclose this so that they can obtain the loan. Companies may refuse to provide a loan because the individual's financial obligations along with child support payments are too high to pay back the loan under the required terms. This does not mean that a person can be turned down for a loan because he or she is or has been divorced.

The penalties for violating the Equal Credit Opportunity Act are severe. Class action lawsuits can be brought against them. Organizations found guilty of ignoring this act can be made to pay damages that amount to either $500,000 or a percent of the applicant's net worth, whichever is less.

Equifax

Equifax today is an agency that reports consumer credit within the U.S. Analysts number it among the big three American credit bureau agencies alongside rivals Trans Union and Experian. The company proves to be the oldest of the three main credit bureaus in the country as it became established back in 1899.

The firm gathers and keeps information on more than 800 million consumers and over 88 million businesses around the globe. They are headquartered in Atlanta, Georgia and remain a worldwide data services provider that has annual revenues of $2.7 billion. They have over 7,000 staff operating in 14 different countries. The company is listed on the NYSE New York Stock Exchange. One of their many divisions (Equifax Workforce Solutions) is among the 55 national contractors which the United States Department of Health and Human Services hired to help develop the federal government's HealthCare.gov website.

The original company which later became Equifax was Retail Credit Company founded in 1899. The firm rapidly expanded and already counted offices around both the United States and Canada by 1920. In the 1960s, this Retail Credit Company represented among the largest of the credit bureaus. It contained files for millions of American and Canadian citizens.

While the firm engaged in some credit reporting at the time, the main part of their business came from providing reports to the many insurance companies throughout the U.S. and Canada as consumers applied for insurance policies such as auto, life, medical, and fire insurance lines. Back in the day, every one of the significant insurance firms relied on Retail Credit Company to gather their information on health, morals, habits, finances, and the utilization of cars and vehicles. Besides this, the firm investigated various insurance claims and also gave employment reports out to companies as consumers sought new jobs. The majority of their credit reporting work at that time they delegated to a subsidiary company called Retailers Commercial Agency.

In 1975, the company changed its name to be Equifax because of image problems they had earned by keeping shady and intimate personal details on all American's lives and selling them to anyone willing to pay. It was after this that the new company Equifax expanded its operations into commercial credit reporting on firms located in the United States, the United Kingdom, and Canada. Here it engaged in competition against such firms as Experian and Dun & Bradstreet. In the 1990s, they began to phase out their insurance reporting operations and spun off their division which gathered and sold specialist credit information to insurance companies. Among this was the CLUE Comprehensive Loss Underwriting Exchange database they had developed, which they included in the Choice Point spinoff back in 1997.

Throughout the vast majority of its company history, the firm engaged mostly in the B2B sector. They sold insurance and consumer credit reports and associated analytics to businesses which operated in a variety of industries and segments. Among these were insurance firms, retailers, utilities, healthcare providers, banks, credit unions, government agencies, specialty finance companies, personal finance operations, and various other kinds of financial institutions.

Since they divested from their insurance reporting primary operation, the company sells information which includes business credit and consumer credit reports, demographic information, analytics, and software. Their credit reports offer a wide and detailed profile on the payment history and personal creditworthiness of individuals and businesses. This reveals how well these groups have honored their various financial obligations, including paying back loans and bills.

Starting in 1999, Equifax started offering its vast services into the consumer credit sector. They also began consumer operations with such important services as protection from identity theft and from credit fraud. The company along with its other two main rivals is required to offer American residents a single free credit file report once per year. The data from the U.S. Equifax credit records becomes incorporated into the Annual Credit Report.com website.

European Debt Crisis

The European Debt Crisis refers to the ongoing European sovereign government struggle to repay various national debts the countries ran up over the past several decades. There were five of the peripheral EU states in particular that were unable to create sufficient economic growth in order to make possible their repaying of the national bondholders as they promised to originally.

These countries included especially Greece, Portugal, and Ireland, but also enmeshed were Spain and Italy to one degree or another. Though only these five nations showed signs of potential default during the crisis peak in the years 2010 to 2011, the crisis had broad and dangerous consequences that impacted not only the rest of the European Union, but also the world in general. The governor of the Bank of England called this the "most serious financial crisis at least since the 1930s, if not ever," back in October of 2011.

The European Debt Crisis did not suddenly appear overnight, but was years and even decades in the making. Slower growth from the time of the American based financial crisis and Great Recession from 2007 to 2009 demonstrated that many spending policies in Europe and the world at large were truly unsustainable any more. Greece became the poster child for the effects of reckless overspending in the following years. The Greeks had spent with great largesse for seemingly endless years and avoided painful but urgently needed financial and fiscal reforms. They were the first to feel the negative effects of weaker ongoing growth as it so happened.

As growth slows down, tax revenues also decrease apace. This means that greater budget deficits become impossible to sustain. The Greeks had been hiding the amounts of their large and increasing national deficits for years, but by the end of 2009, it was no longer possible to keep them from world markets and the enraged Greek populace any longer. The Greek debts had become so vast that they substantially exceeded the entire economy of the smaller nation.

Investors in their sovereign debt naturally retaliated by insisting on larger yields on their Greek national bonds. The unfortunate side effect of this action was that the interest payments on the Greek debt also skyrocketed, causing their debt burden to become so onerous that they could not manage it any longer. The EU and European Central Bank had to come riding to the rescue of the Greek government and economy in consequence. This did not stop investors and markets from pushing up the yields of bonds in other similarly indebted nations throughout Europe, where they expected similar crises and potential collapse as had already tragically occurred in Greece.

The vicious cycle of higher demand yields leading to greater borrowing costs for the nations in crisis led to greater fiscal strain which caused investors to require still higher interest yields on the troubled European sovereign bonds. This gradual erosion of investor confidence did not stay focused on Greece, but impacted the other shaky economies of Portugal, Ireland, Cyprus, Spain, and even G7 trillion-plus dollar economy Italy. This became known as financial crisis contagion. Portugal, Ireland, Cyprus, and Spain were forced to seek out bailouts either for their embattled sovereign government finances, their national primary banks, or in the cases of Portugal and Ireland, both.

The problems were exacerbated by the fact that the European Union moved so slowly to address the severe problems. This is because their actions required the approval of all 28 countries in the economic and political union. Bailouts were offered to the troubled governments via the European Stabilization Mechanism or ESM. The European Central Bank acted in a substitute capacity by cutting interest rates and providing unlimited loans to European national banks which were in trouble in exchange for assets (which were highly questionable at best) as collateral.

The problems of the European Debt Crisis are far from over fully five long years later. Italy's banks have not yet addressed their over $360 billion in bad loans to this day. Their third largest and oldest bank Monte Dei Paschi Di Sienna has 28 billion Euros in bad debts it has been trying unsuccessfully to offload as it sought out 5 billion Euros in fresh capital from skeptical investors. Greece is on its third consecutive bailout program from the EU so far in only five years. Portugal, Ireland, and Cyprus have all emerged successfully from their bailout and bank recapitalization programs, while Spain is on the right track and making measurable and material progress in escaping from theirs.

European Sovereign Debt Crisis

The European sovereign debt crisis threatened to overthrow financial institutions, sovereign countries' bonds, and even the Euro currency at several points. This crisis erupted in 2008 when Iceland saw its entire banking system collapse.

From here it spread to other peripheral European nations including Greece, Portugal, and Ireland throughout the subsequent year 2009. A number of peripheral EU countries like Spain and their financial institutions faced default as government debt and sovereign bond yields rose dangerously. The ensuing crisis in debt created a cascading confidence crisis for European economies, businesses, and consumers.

In the end it took financial backstop guarantees from European Union countries and the IMF International Monetary Fund to bring the crisis under control. EU member states became concerned that financial contagion would spread enough that even the Euro itself might collapse.

While the crisis raged, a few of the Eurozone countries suffered from repeated agency downgrading of their sovereign debt. Greece in particular experienced a debt rating of junk status at the low point of its crisis. Bailouts were issued to a number of the countries on the EU periphery, including Greece, Spain, Portugal, Cyprus, and Ireland. These loan deals involved austerity measures that were intended to reduce the growing public debts of the countries.

The sovereign debt crisis in Europe reached its climax in 2009-2010. At this point, nations ranging from Greece, Ireland, and Spain to Portugal and Cyprus could no longer pay their debt payments, refinance government debts, or save their struggling banks without recourse to third party help.

At this point, these countries turned to international financial institutions such as the International Monetary Fund, the European Central Bank, and the EFSF European Financial Stability Facility to provide financial assistance. The Eurozone 17 member countries created the EFSF itself in 2010 to combat the problems created by the sovereign debt crisis.

Other situations combined to contribute to this long lasting sovereign debt crisis. The financial crisis of 2007 and 2008, ensuing Great Recession of 2008 to 2012, and several nations' real estate crises all worked together to exacerbate the situation. A few EU members had also violated their government budget deficit limits and created a more serious crisis of confidence.

In 2009 Greece revealed that its prior government had intentionally under-stated its budget deficits. This violated policies of the European Union and led to fears that the Euro itself might collapse because of the ensuing financial contagion. Suspicions mounted that both the amounts of debt and financial positions of a variety of Eurozone countries were drastically and unsustainably overextended.

By 2010 this agitated level of fear of too much sovereign debt caused the lenders to insist on greater interest rates from the countries in the EZ that possessed both high deficit and debt amounts. This meant that such nations were struggling to finance their deficits because they suffered from a small level of economic growth.

Portugal and Ireland joined Greece in having their sovereign debt cut to humiliating junk levels by the major credit ratings agencies. Ireland had to obtain a bailout by November of 2010 while Portugal required one by May of 2011. Even Spain and also Cyprus needed help to save their ailing banking sectors by June of 2012.

In or by 2014 Ireland, Spain, and Portugal had made enough progress in financial reforms and undergone sufficient austerity to successfully complete their bailout programs. Most of their banks have been recapitalized and saved. Cyprus is also recovering well. As of 2016, Greece continues to struggle and limp along with additional aid payments from its Troika of lenders the EU, ECB, and IMF.

European Stability Mechanism (ESM)

The European Stability Mechanism is a significant part of the financial stability and safeguard mechanisms in the Euro Zone area. It replaced the EFSF European Financial Stability Facility in 2013. This original EFSF was never intended to be permanent. Instead it was designed as a temporary solution to financial problems within the EU.

The European Stability Mechanism that took over for it was better established to deliver financial help to those Eurozone member countries that found themselves either threatened by or actually experiencing financial difficulties.

These two financial facilities ran concurrently from October of 2012 through June of 2013. Beginning in July of 2013 the EFSF could no longer begin new programs for financial support or help. The program still exists to manage and collect repayments of debts that are outstanding.

Once all of the existing loans that the EFSF program made have been repaid and all funding instruments and guarantors have received full payment for their contributions, then the EFSF will cease to exist entirely. This makes the replacing ESM the only and ongoing internal means for delivering aid in response to new calls for financial assistance from Eurozone member nations.

The European Stability Mechanism proves to be the principal means of resolving crises for nations which participate in the Euro. It obtains its money by issuing debt obligations. This permits it to fund financial aid and loans to the member countries of the Euro area. The European Council actually created the ESM in December of 2010. Participating Euro member states came together and signed a treaty between the governments on February 2 of 2012. October 8 of 2012 was the day they inaugurated the new ESM.

This ESM has great flexibility in funding its distressed member states. As various conditions are met, it is able to deliver loans as part of a program for macroeconomic adjustment. The mechanism is also able to buy member countries' debt in either the secondary or primary markets.

It can help to recapitalize banks of member states by loaning the governments money for this purpose. It can also deliver credit lines as a means of providing financial help as a precaution. In worst case and last resort conditions, the facility is allowed to recapitalize banks and other financial institutions directly. This is limited to times when resolution funds and bail ins are not enough to make the bank financially viable again.

The resources of the ESM are considerable. It has a capital base that has been subscribed in the amount of €704.8 billion. Of this amount, €80.5 billion has been paid in to the facility. The remaining €624.3 billion is classified as callable capital when it is needed. The fund is able to loan out a maximum total of €500 billion.

The ESM is based in Luxembourg. It is governed by public international law as an intergovernmental organization. It has only government shareholders making up its ownership. These are the 19 member countries that make up the Euro area. In 2016, 153 staff members worked under the direction of Klaus Regling the managing director.

European countries which are in trouble have other outside recourses for help besides the ESM. The principal other provider of assistance is the International Monetary Fund. The EU has supported having its own ESM, along with the predecessors the EFSF and the European Financial Stabilization Mechanism because it feared the consequences of some of its member states' problems with debt. Not all of the EZ countries suffered from debt issues. One EZ country failing could have contagious effects and widespread repercussions on the other national economies' health.

Eurozone Crisis

The Eurozone Crisis proved to be the gravest threat facing the world back in 2011, per a warning issued by the OECD. The situation became even more perilous as it worsened in 2012. The crisis erupted seemingly from nowhere back in 2009. This was the point when the world finally woke up to the headlines that Greece could completely default on its massive debt load.

Over the next tumultuous three years, the crisis grew and magnified to the point that it presented the serious possibilities for national sovereign debt defaults from neighboring European nations Spain, Italy, Ireland, and Portugal. The European Union under the leadership of Germany and France struggled to contain the crisis by supporting the ailing peripheral economies. They did this through bailouts they began issuing from the European Central Bank and the International Monetary Fund. Despite these strenuous efforts to bottle the crisis back up, many critics (even within the EU) began to question the validity of the euro common currency itself.

This tragic Eurozone Crisis arose from a number of complicated causes. It began because the rules set out by the Maastricht Treaty which ultimately governed the percentages of debt to GDP levels in member states were simply ignored. Penalties for violators simply did not exist in any enforceable fashion. Even economic leaders and supposed role models Germany and France overspent their own imposed limits. This stripped them of the ability to criticize the other nations while their own financial houses were in proverbial disarray. The sanctions for breaking the rules lacked teeth, save for the ultimate penalty to expel offenders from the eurozone itself. That would have only weakened the block and the single currency had it been rigorously enforced.

Nations of the Eurozone at first were benefiting from the historically low interest rates which led to higher investment capital all made conceivable thanks to the strength of the euro common currency. The vast majority of these capital flow went from Germany and France down to the southern peripheral nations like Greece, Portugal, and Spain. While this boosted liquidity and increased prices and wages in the receiving countries, it also made southern nations' exports far less competitive abroad.

Being on the euro currency and under the ECB limitations, these nations had no ability to raise their interest rates or devalue their currencies in order to cool inflation. As public spending rose, tax revenues declined, making it increasingly difficult in the Eurozone Crisis and recession that ensued for the national governments to cover their safety net benefits such as unemployment payments.

A third cause of the Eurozone Crisis came from the austerity Germany mandated to those who received initial bailouts. This caused slower economic growth in the nations like Greece that desperately required higher growth. Austerity did manage to increase the Greek exports, but all this came at the expense of slashed public expenditures, a far weaker economy and lowered output, and massively cut pensions for retirees. As a result of bowing to the requirements of its bailout creditors, Greece received forgiveness for half of its simply unsustainable debt load. The measures also served to raise unemployment, decrease the capital available for lending, and slash consumer spending dramatically.

Ultimately, a six point plan solution was presented by German leader Chancellor Angela Merkel to stem the Eurozone Crisis. It launched rapidly starting programs to foster more business start ups. It lessened protections against employees being wrongfully fired. It created mini jobs through lower taxes. It targeted the stratospheric youth unemployment with vocational education and apprenticeship program combinations. It developed special tax benefits and funds to help privatize the still state owned enterprises as in Greece. It set up special economic zones as China already utilized. Finally it made significant investments in renewable energy.

This plan had worked in the integration of East and West Germany at the conclusion of the Cold War. Merkel believed that a devotion to austerity would increase the whole Eurozone's competitiveness ultimately. The plan followed along the lines of the approved intergovernmental treaty of December 8th 2011.

This treaty performed three actions. It began to concretely enforce the restrictions on budgets which the Maastricht Treaty had mandated. It also assured the bank lenders of the EU that the EU and ECB would guarantee its members and their sovereign debts. Finally it permitted the EU as a whole to work in a more unified, structured, and cohesive unit.

It followed on the heels of a May 2010 bailout fund which the EU set up with 720 billion Euros ($928 billion US dollars at the time, called the "Big Bazooka") worth of euro bonds, which was intended to stop any other type of Wall Street styled collapse from occurring. This bailout ultimately rebuilt faith in the shaken euro and created a potentially dangerous new rival for the American Treasury bonds.

Experian

Experian is one of the three main credit reporting bureaus in the United States. As such it maintains a credit report, history, and FICO score on all adult Americans. The company does so much more than this most commonly understood function.

The company is also an international leader for global business and consumer credit reporting as well as marketing services. Experian is headquartered in Dublin, Ireland and is based on the London Stock Exchange where it is a member of Britain's FTSE 100 stock index. The company has customers in over 80 countries of the world and maintains offices and employees in 37 countries. Besides its Dublin base, Experian has operations headquarters found in Nottingham in the United Kingdom, California in the United States, and Sao Paulo in Brazil.

Experian serves as the corporate leader in global information services. The company received the 2015 honor of "World's Most Innovative Companies" from Forbes magazine for being among the leaders in driving improvements and change.

They deliver analytical tools and data to their clients found all over the world. The company helps businesses to prevent fraud, to manage their credit risk, to automate functions of decision making, and to specifically target marketing offers.

Experian also assists individuals with information and security needs. They aid individuals in checking out their credit reports and credit scores through copies that they can purchase and download directly over the Internet. They help people to safeguard themselves against the very real dangers of identity theft with credit report monitoring services. The company also provides a great source of information for education that is both hands on and interactive. This education helps both marketing personnel and credit professionals along with individual consumers.

Experian prides itself on its analytic and data services. They are in the business of assisting businesses and individuals with managing, protecting, and optimally using their data. They offer a number of different services to help people to do this effectively.

Their Experian Credit Tracker product gives consumers their FICO score, Experian credit report, and a credit monitoring service that comes with fraud alerts. They also staff a dedicated support team for fraud resolution when individuals become victims of identity theft. Help with identity theft or credit fraud is an area that is critical to consumers when they become victims.

Consumers can also choose from their higher level Experian Protect My ID service. This gives individuals an Experian credit report, 3 bureau credit monitoring services and alerts, daily checking of ID via Internet scanning, and access to their dedicated support for fraud resolution.

Experian provides a higher level view of individuals' credit reports and scores also. Their 3 Bureau Credit Report and FICO Scores service delivers copies of the person's credit report and FICO score for Experian, TransUnion, and Equifax. They also sell just their own credit report and FICO score for a lower price.

Experian offers even more services to its big business customers. Among their business product offerings are customer acquisition, customer management, fraud management, risk management, debt recovery, consulting services, regulatory compliance, and thought leadership. In customer acquisition, the company offers direct mail tools and big data analytics.

For risk management they verify applicants' identities and backgrounds. Experian can manage data breaches and prevent money laundering as part of their fraud management offerings. Debt recovery services include locating debtors and managing collection efforts. Among their consulting services are strategy, product, and fraud consulting areas.

Small business customers also have a variety of services offered to them by Experian. These include help with business and consumer credit, marketing and managing the business, and collecting debt.

Fair Credit Billing Act

Congress passed the Fair Credit Billing act back in 1975. They enacted this national law in order to safeguard consumers from unfair or prejudiced billing actions. It created mechanisms for dealing with billing errors that affect credit accounts which are open ended. This includes credit cards and charge card accounts.

There are many different and all too common types of billing errors that the Fair Credit Billing Act specifies and protects against in its statute. Charges which are an incorrect amount are one. It also covers charges showing up on a bill that the consumer did not process. These are often known as unauthorized charges. Consumers can never be responsible for more than $50 of these. The act also covers the costs of any goods that did not come as they were supposed to when the consumer bought them, as well as for those goods that the consumer never received.

Consumers are similarly protected by the Fair Credit Billing Act from errors in calculation. They can not be held responsible for billing statements which the companies send out to the wrong address. Changes of address are required to be submitted by the account holder in writing and received by the creditor more than 19 days before the billing period ends. Consumers are similarly protected against any charges which they request proof of or clarification for on a statement. They may also not be held liable for a creditor improperly showing payments or charges to their credit accounts.

Customers are able to avail themselves of the protections spelled out in the Fair Credit Billing Act. To do so, they have to begin the process by writing the creditor at their business address specified for billing inquiries. They must include their name and address, account numbers, and any information on the billing dispute in question. The letter must be received by the creditor within 60 days or less of the original bill mailing date.

Such a letter should be dispatched by certified mail with return receipt so that the consumer has conclusive proof of when the creditor received it. All relevant copies of receipts and supporting documents need to be included with the letter. The creditor concerned is required by law to acknowledge that they have received the letter of complaint in 30 days or less after they receive it. The creditor then has up to 90 days (as in two billing cycles) to research and resolve the dispute per the terms of the Fair Credit Billing Act.

The Fair Credit Billing Act also governs what happens when a bill is placed in dispute by a consumer. The person is allowed to not make payments on any charges pertaining to the disputed amount in question. Such a period of withholding only applies throughout the time frame in which the investigation is ongoing. All remaining portions of the bill and relevant interest amounts have to be paid as per the governing credit agreement and terms. The creditor may not engage in any legal action or collection activity against the borrower so long as the investigation phase is ongoing. The account of the borrower is not permitted to be closed or restricted in this phase.

The creditor is also forbidden to make threats against the borrowers' credit ratings when charges are under investigation and in dispute. The dispute itself can be reported to the credit ratings agencies. Creditors are not allowed to discriminate by withholding credit approval from any consumer who uses his or her rights to dispute a credit charge. This means in practice that consumers may not be refused credit because they have filed disputes against charges on a bill.

Fannie Mae

Fannie Mae is the acronym for the FNMA Federal National Mortgage Association. This entity is a GSE Government Sponsored Enterprise along with brother organization Freddie Mac. It became a publicly traded company in 1968. This home lending giant proves to be the largest mortgage financing provider anywhere in the United States. As such, it funds significantly more mortgages than any competing company or entity. It ensures that homebuyers, homeowners, and renters around the U.S. all can obtain financing options which they can afford.

As the GSE became established in 1938, it has provided funding for the housing market of the country for over 75 years. Franklin D. Roosevelt's New Deal established the company in the midst of the Great Depression. This is why the mission of the company is to aid individuals in purchasing, renting, or refinancing a home whether economic times in the country are good or bad.

The company's explicit purpose is to boost the size of the secondary mortgage market. They do this when they securitize mortgages and package them into MBS mortgage backed securities. This process returns the mortgage loaned money to lenders who are then able to reinvest this money into additional lending. It also acts to grow the numbers of lending institutions who are issuing mortgages. This ensures that there are more than just savings and loan associations making local loans for housing.

The model worked well until between 2003 and 2004. At this point the subprime mortgages crisis started. It began when the mortgage market turned away from the GSEs like Freddie Mac and Fannie Mae and began to migrate rapidly to unregulated MBS Mortgage Backed Securities that major investment banks put together. This shift to private MBSs caused the GSEs to lose their control over and ability to monitor mortgages in the country.

Increased competition between the investment banks and the GSEs reduced the power and market share of the government mortgage backers further and boosted the mortgage lenders at their expense. This radical change in the way mortgages were overseen and made caused the underwriting standards for mortgages to dangerously decline. It turned out to be one of the major reasons for the ensuing mortgage and financial crises.

The situation became so severe at Fannie Mae by 2008 that the FHFA Federal Housing Finance Agency had to get directly involved. FHFA Director James Lockhart on September 7, 2008 placed both this organization and Freddie Mac under FHFA conservatorship. This proved to be among the most dramatic and far reaching government involvements in free enterprise financial markets for literally decades.

Among Lockhart's first actions, he fired both companies' boards of directors and CEOs. He then made the companies issue a new class of common stock warrants and senior preferred stock to Treasury for 79.9% of both GSEs. Those who had been holding either preferred or common stock in either entity before the conservatorship began saw the value of their shares massively decrease. All prior shares' dividends became suspended to try to hold up the mortgage backed securities' and company debt values. FHFA pledged that it had no intentions of liquidating the GSEs.

Since 2009, Fannie Mae has made great strides in its business of helping make housing work better for individuals and families. They have injected trillions of dollars into the mortgage markets in lending liquidity. This has gone a long way to helping the housing markets and overall economy to recover.

The company has also gone back to high quality eligibility and underwriting standards. In the first quarter of 2016, they have extended $115 billion in mortgage credit that has allowed for 210,000 homes to be purchased and 256,000 mortgages to be refinanced. They also financed the construction of 161,000 multifamily rental units.

Federal Debt

The federal debt is also known as the national debt. This represents the entire dollar value of the money which the U.S. federal government has borrowed from its various creditors over the years. Creditors to the government are made up of all governments, businesses, individuals, and other national and international entities which own the debt instruments of the U.S. government.

This national debt has resulted from numerous government deficit budgets where they spent more than they earned in revenues. It is important to realize that this federal debt never includes any of the money owed by municipal or state governments, companies, or individuals. Instead it is the total of all federal government outstanding obligations. This figure contains not just the money the federal government originally borrowed. It is also made up by the interest amounts that it has to pay back with the borrowed funds.

Governments fall into debt when they are not able to bring in sufficient revenues to pay for their expenses on a variety of government programs. This includes military spending and domestic programs such as retirement benefits, Medicare, welfare, and constructing bridges and roads. Revenues are derived from a number of sources. These are made up of personal income and corporate taxes as well as government fees on things like passports, cigarettes and alcohol, and national park admissions fees.

For 2016, the national debt had risen to an enormous amount of greater than $19 trillion. As a percentage of GDP this is over 105%. It has rapidly increased from the years 2006 to 2016, as in 2006 the debt came in at less than half as much at $8.4 trillion. This represented only 66% of the national GDP at the time. Because of this dramatic and ongoing increase, the debate is always heated regarding what should be done with the national debt. Many individuals and observers like the Congressional Budget Office feel that the debt needs to be paid down. Others argue that the debt proves to be a needed catalyst to keep up economic growth.

The debt has come from successive increases in the federal government's annual budget deficit. These annual deficits represent the amount of additional money the government spends over what they take in for receipts. All of these deficits combined together plus interest paid equal the national debt.

When investors see the debt grow higher and anticipate that there will be greater levels of inflation, they become concerned about the value of their debt holdings. Some economists have conjectured that the government only intends to inflate away the value of the debt over time. This is why debt holders can ask for higher interest rates when they make future loans to governments they suspect of inflating away their debts.

Federal surpluses can be used to pay down the federal debt. This has happened on rare occasions. Since World War II, the federal government has only managed to run less than 10 such surpluses. President Harry Truman was the first to turn the government finances around after President Franklin Roosevelt's years of deficits. President Truman had surpluses in 1947, 1948, and 1951.

President Dwight Eisenhower also managed to run smaller surpluses in 1957 and 1958. There was not another government surplus for more than forty years until 1998 when President Bill Clinton signed a deal with Congress that achieved an $87.9 billion surplus. This surplus grew to $290 billion by 2000.

The last surplus came under President George W. Bush who had a $154 billion carryover surplus in 2001. On these rare occasions, the Federal government was able to pay down the federal debt temporarily. These surpluses were followed by half a trillion to trillion dollar deficits per year for most of the next decade.

Federal Deposit Insurance Corporation (FDIC)

The U.S. government started The Federal Deposit Insurance Corporation back in 1933. They created it because of the literally thousands of failed banks that went down in the 1920s and 1930s. The FDIC began insuring bank accounts at the beginning of 1934. Since then, no depositors have lost any insured bank account money despite a consistent number of banks failing every year.

The first role of the FDIC is to insure and to increase the public's confidence in the American banking system. They do this in several ways. The FDIC insures minimally $250,000 in bank and thrift accounts. They watch for and take action on any risks to the deposit insurance funds. They also stop the spread of any bank failures when one of the banks does fail.

The Federal Deposit Insurance Corporation only insures deposits. This means that it does not cover mutual funds, stocks, or any other investments that some banks offer to their customers. They offer a standard $250,000 amount for each depositor's account. This single limit amount does not apply to other types of account ownerships and accounts at other banks. To help individuals understand if the insurance provided is enough to cover their various kinds of account, the FDIC provides its Electronic Deposit Insurance Estimator.

Another important role of the FDIC lies in its supervisory position. The outfit oversees over 4,500 different savings and commercial banks to make sure that they are operationally safe and sound. This represents more than half of the banks. Those banks that are set up as state banks may choose to become a member of either the Federal Reserve System or the FDIC. Any banks that are not overseen by the Federal Reserve System are watched over by the FDIC.

Another job of the FDIC is to check on the various banks to make sure they abide by the government's consumer protection laws. These laws include The Fair Credit Reporting Act, the Fair Credit Billing Act, the Fair Debt Collection Practices Act, and the Truth in Lending Act.

Lastly, the FDIC checks banks to make sure the different institutions are abiding by their responsibilities under the Community Reinvestment Act. This law ensures that banks help the communities where they were started to achieve their needs for credit.

Despite all of these roles, the only one that members of the public really encounter on a personal basis is the FDIC protecting insured depositors. When a bank or thrift goes down, the FDIC immediately reacts to the situation. They come in fast with the group that chartered the bank to close it down. The charter group could be the Office of the Comptroller of the Currency or the state regulator.

The next step is for the FDIC to wind up the failed bank. In their preferred method, they sell both the loans and the deposits of the bank to another banking institution. Customers rarely feel the transition in the majority of the cases. This is the FDIC's goal, to make sure that people do not lose access to their accounts and money.

The FDIC carries out its several mandates through six regional branches. It has more than 7,000 staff members that help it to carry out these goals. The organization is based in its headquarters in the capital Washington, D.C. Besides these locations, they also have various field offices throughout the nation.

The leadership of the FDIC is supplied by the Federal Government. The President appoints the board which the Senate confirms. There are five members of their Board of Directors. No more than three of them may belong to one political party to ensure bipartisanship in the decisions.

Federal Housing Finance Agency (FHFA)

The Federal Housing Finance Agency is a government regulating agency. They are independent and responsible for overseeing several agencies within the secondary mortgage market. These include Freddie Mac, Fannie Mae, and the Federal Home Loan Banks. They work to keep these critical government sponsored organizations, along with the entire American housing financial system, in good health.

As such, the FHFA labors constantly to build up and safeguard the secondary mortgage markets in the United States. They do this through their leadership in and delivering excellent research, dependable data, strong supervision, and pertinent policies. The three government sponsored entities of Freddie Mac, Fannie Mae, and the Federal Home Loan Bank system together deliver over $5.5 trillion in financial institutions and mortgage markets funding throughout the United States.

The FHFA helps to keep this all possible by providing their independent regulation and careful oversight of these vital mortgage markets. Besides this, they are also the conservator of both Freddie Mac and Fannie Mae since the financial crisis and Great Recession that began in 2007-2008 wreaked havoc on the two giant government sponsored agencies along with the housing market they guaranteed.

The Federal Housing Finance Agency is concerned with creating a better market of secondary mortgages for the country's future. To this effect, they are working on a sequence of strategies and initiatives to boost the housing financial system in the future. Among these new ideas is the construction of a new and improved database called the Common Securitization Platform. This will have dual roles. It will take the presently outdated infrastructures and modernize them. It will also allow for the possibilities of other players in the market choosing to utilize this same infrastructure.

The FHFA considers itself to be in a partnership. They strive alongside the entities they regulate to keep home ownership alive and affordable through a variety of programs. These include the HARP Home Affordable Refinance Program and the HAMP Home Affordable Modification Program. The two programs deliver significant and tangible aid to both communities and their homeowners. So far such programs have assisted literally millions of home owning Americans to keep or stay in their houses.

The FHFA does not have a long history. It is a new organization that grew out of the housing market collapse and Great Recession. President Obama signed the Housing and Economic Recovery Act of 2008 to create the Federal Housing Finance Agency back on July 30, 2008.

The ongoing mission of the FHFA is to make certain that the government sponsored enterprises for housing function in a manner that is both economically viable and safe. This is so that they can continue to provide a dependable source of both funds and liquidity for investment in communities and the financing of home purchases. As part of this, they envision a housing financial system that is stable, dependable, and liquid for both the present and the future.

The FHFA values four virtues. They prize excellence in all areas of their work. The organization appreciates respect for their team members, resources, and the information they collect. They value integrity and commit themselves to the greatest possible professional and moral standards. The group also encourages diversity in all of their business dealings and employment arrangements, as well as in the entities which they regulate and for whom they are the conservator.

FHFA is also an important member group of the Financial Stability Oversight Council. Chief among their tasks is to identify financial stability risks in the U.S., to respond to rising threats to the American financial system, and to encourage discipline in the market. They serve on this council with fellow members that include The Federal Reserve governors, CFTC, FDIC, Comptroller of the Currency, SEC, and Treasury Department.

Fiat Dollars

Fiat dollars refer to dollars that do not possess any sort of intrinsic value. They are not backed up by gold or any other tangible asset, only by the full faith and trust in the United States government. Since the United States abandoned the venerable and stable gold standard back in 1971, the U.S. currency has been one of only fiat dollars.

Fiat actually refers to the Latin for "let it be done." Dollars that are fiat dollars are valued based on the decree of the government. They are not redeemable for anything else.

Until 1971, the dollar proved to be convertible into a certain set quantity of gold. This had been the case along with all other major currencies around the world for nearly two hundred years. Gold backed dollars and other currency proved to be extremely stable and constantly valued for huge spans of time stretching from forty to sixty years before some turbulence like the Civil War would impact their value for a few years. This resulted in part from governments only being able to print as many dollars and other currency as they had gold.

Since the U.S. currency became one of fiat dollars, its stability has vanished, along with its former constant value. One ounce of gold only represented $38.90 valued U.S. dollars at the end of 1970. Today the same ounce of gold equates to $1,350. Another way of putting this is that one 1970 gold backed dollar is equal to nearly $35 fiat dollars in 2010. You might also say that the Fiat dollar has declined by more than ninety-seven percent in the time span of almost forty years since it began its life as a Fiat dollar.

This says several important things about Fiat dollars. They are at the mercy of the international markets, since they are not backed up by any tangible value. They are also able to be printed or electronically multiplied in infinite quantities, since they are not restricted by a given fixed amount of gold. It also means that they are unstable in their values and can collapse fairly easily and quickly, since their real worth is only one of perceived value as determined by the confidence of buyers and sellers.

Fiat dollars are not the only currency that has been decoupled from real valued backing like gold. Euros, Japanese Yen, British Pounds, and practically all major currencies of the world are similarly only based on the faith and trust of their respective governments. The only currency among the major developed economies that might be considered to be non fiat is the Swiss Franc.

The Swiss constitution requires that the government holds a full quarter of the number of Swiss Francs in existence in gold in their vaults. This would give them a twenty-five percent gold backing to their currency. The truth is that since the Swiss value their gold reserves at $250 per ounce, and gold is trading consistently well over $1,200 per ounce to even $1,350 per ounce, at over five times the Swiss value of their gold, this means that they actually have their currency covered by in excess of one hundred percent of actual valued gold holdings, since five times their twenty-five percent gold reserve amounts to one hundred and twenty-five percent.

Fiat Money

Fiat Money proves to be money that has no real intrinsic, or actual, value. It instead derives its worth from governments accepting it as legal tender. The concept of fiat money on a large scale is a relatively new one. Throughout practically all of history, the majority of currencies around the world derived their value from silver or gold. Fiat money is instead entirely based on trust and faith in the issuing monetary authority.

The problem with fiat money lies in the ability of the governments to inflate its value away. They can do this by over printing it. Since fiat currencies are not restricted by a requirement of hard reserve assets, they can be created in any quantity that the issuing government desires. As the supply continues to rise while the demand remains constant, its purchasing power will fall. When the supply is drastically increased, then hyperinflation will result. Fiat money that falls by hundreds of percent in value is deemed to be a victim of hyperinflation.

The other disadvantage is that only peoples' trust in it ultimately gives it practical value. It suffers from inflation and finally hyperinflation, then the confidence in it becomes shaken. Fiat money that lacks the confidence of its citizens will finally collapse in value and then no longer be of any trading use for daily transactions. When it fails, people either return to barter systems, or the government establishes a currency based on hard assets once again.

The history of money has proven on a number of occasions that governments debase currency to the point of fiat money when it suits them. They do this because it allows them to print as much as they need to pay for things. While this creates inflation for their citizens, it gives the money issuing government the ability to repay their debts with cheaper fiat money. Finally, as a society has had enough of the devalued money and currency instability, they force the government to return to asset backed money. This has happened before, and some monetary experts say that you are starting to see this happen again nowadays.

FICO Score

FICO Score refers to the overwhelmingly most popular and heavily utilized credit score in the United States. The company which created, owns, and manages it to this day is Fair Isaac Corporation. Financial institutions that loan out money employ this FICO score for an individual to assess any credit risk and decide whether or not they will offer the person credit. Sometimes they also consider specific information on the credit report of the borrower, but this is increasingly uncommon.

The reason for this is that the FICO score contemplates a well-rounded set of risk parameters for the would-be borrowers. These five areas it considers and draws upon to issue a credit score for credit worthiness include the individual's payment history, present amount of debts, types of credit utilized, amount of credit history, and new credit inquiries and issued accounts.

Ninety percent of financial institutions in the United States that offer loans rely on the FICO score for assessing the creditworthiness of an individual. These scores vary from as low as 300 to as high as 850. Generally speaking, scores over 650 represent desirable credit history. Individuals who boast less than 620 conversely typically find it hard to get decent financing offers approved at reasonable interest rates. Financial institutions claim that they also consider various other details besides FICO scores. These include history of time at a job, applicant's income, and the kind of credit they are seeking.

It is interesting and illuminating to understand how the three main credit bureaus calculate this FICO Score. Fair Isaac Corporation has its proprietary model in which they weigh all categories differently for every individual. This makes it more difficult to say with certainty what percentages in each of the five categories they consider.

Yet generally speaking, payment history represents 35 percent of the total. Amount owed on accounts comprises 30 percent generally. Amount of years of credit history equals approximately 15 percent. Credit mix equates to around 10 percent. New credit inquiries and accounts represent about 10 percent.

Payment history is the simple answer to the question, "does the individual borrower pay the accounts in a timely fashion?" Thanks to the exhaustive nature of credit history, the bureaus clearly demonstrate the payments which have been made for every single line of credit. The reports make special note if any of the payments came in 30, 60, 90, 120, or still more days later than due.

Amounts owed on accounts pertains to the dollar amounts individuals owe on their various accounts as a percentage of the total available credit. This does not mean that possessing a great amount of debt ruins a credit score. What the Fair Isaac Company is considering is the ratio of amount owed to amount available. A clear example shows that when Ringo owed $100,000 yet was not near his limits on any of the accounts, he had a higher credit score than George who only owed $25,000 yet had nearly maxed out his credit card accounts.

Credit history length is a complex category. FICO considers the age of the oldest account as well as the age of the most recent one. They then compile the average account age and come up with a value for this category. Those with shorter credit histories can still get a good credit score.

Credit mix pertains to the variety in types of credit accounts. Higher category credit scores go to those people who have a strong and varied mix of credit cards, retail accounts, and installment loans like mortgages, vehicle loans, and signature loans.

Finally, the Fair Isaac Company does not like recently opened accounts in much of any quantity. When borrowers take out a range of new credit lines and accounts in only a brief amount of time, this tells them that the person is becoming a credit risk and thus decreases the total FICO score.

Fiduciary

A fiduciary is an organization or individual which owes its trust and good faith to another person or group. It means that one party takes on the most serious legal responsibility to the other party. Fiduciaries are ethically and legally required to carry out their activities in the best interest of the other person or organization.

This could involve another's well being, but it usually revolves around finances. People who manage another individual's assets or finances are good examples of fiduciaries. This means that a fiduciary could be a board member, banker, accountant, money manager, estate executor, or corporate officer.

The responsibilities and duties of a fiduciary turn out to be not only ethical but also legal. After a group or individual willingly takes on such duties for another, they must carry out the tasks with the very best interests of that party at heart. This means fiduciaries have to manage any assets for the benefit of those individuals instead of to benefit themselves or realize personal gain. This level of responsibility is called a prudent person standard of care that came out of court ruling in 1830. This prudent person rule means that the individual functioning in the fiduciary's role must always carry out the duties with the beneficiaries' needs foremost.

Conflicts of interest are not allowed to arise between the principal and fiduciary. Per an English High Court ruling on the case of Keech versus Sandford in 1726, fiduciaries are not allowed to profit from holding such a position of trust. Because of this, the only exceptions are when the beneficiary grants specific consent when the relationship starts. When the principal gives such approval, fiduciaries are allowed to enjoy any benefits received, whether they are monetary in nature or opportunities.

Where business relationships are concerned, there are many different kinds of fiduciary duties. The most typical of these occur between trustees and their beneficiaries. There are also a number of other kinds of relationships where this can occur. Some of these are between executors and legatees, company board of directors and shareholders, stock promoters and stock subscribers, guardians and wards, investment corporations and investors, and attorneys and clients.

As the trustee and beneficiary relationship is the most common for fiduciaries, it is important to understand. Trustees handle arrangements for estates and also implement trusts. The beneficiary is the one whom they are serving. The fiduciary in this case is the person who will be the estate trustee or the trust. The beneficiary is also the principal.

In this type of arrangement, the trustee commands legal possession of the assets and/or property. The trustee is fully empowered to manage assets in the trust's name. Because the beneficiary has equitable title of the property or asset, the trustee has to engage in best interest decisions. Such a relationship as trustee and beneficiary is critical in effective and all inclusive estate planning. This is why the trustee should be chosen with great care and thought.

Blind trusts are those where the trustee who has authority over the investment does not allow the beneficiary to be aware of the way the assets are being invested. The trustee still has the legal duty to use the prudent person conduct standard, especially because the beneficiary is unaware of what is happening. Politicians and other public figures create such blind trusts so that they can stay away from scandals involving conflicts of interest.

Financial Crisis

A financial crisis refers to a period where the value of assets and/or financial institutions declines quickly. Such a crisis is commonly connected with runs on the banks or at the least fear and panic. In these difficult and dangerous economic periods, investors will fire sell any assets they can to pull back their cash out of investment and savings accounts. They do this hoping to repatriate their funds home before they decline or vanish altogether at the financial institution.

Such a financial crisis happens because of assets and banks becoming overly valued. They are typically made far worse because of the inexplicable behavior of mass groups of investors. Often times, a rapid-fire domino effect of selling leads to still lower prices of the associated assets in the crisis and even more bank account withdrawals. If the crisis does not become resolved relatively quickly, it can lead an economy and nation into a deep and painful recession or even a lasting and devastating depression.

The sad part of finance is that it is not only prone to numerous incidents like these, but it is also shaped by financial crisis. There have been many such significant financial crises over the past three hundred years. These included the 1720 South Sea Bubble crisis, the Panic of 1792, the Latin American Crisis of 1825, the Cotton Crisis of 1837, the Railroad Crisis of 1857, the Long Depression of 1873, the Knickerbockers Crisis of 1907, Black Monday and the Wall Street Crash of 1929, the 1973-1974 Arab Oil Crisis, 1987 Black Monday, the Asian Crisis of 1997, and the Dotcom Crash of 2001.

The most recent financial crisis which rocked the international world was the Global Financial Crisis of 2008. Economists have determined that this proved to be the most devastating economic disaster for the world since the 1929 Great Depression which lasted nearly a decade. It led to what has become known as the Great Recession. Strangely enough, while the other financial crises which preceded it could be pinpointed to a main reason or singular event, the Global Financial Crisis could not be.

Instead this economic disaster resulted from a chain of events. Each of these had their own trigger. The crisis was so severe that it nearly caused a complete failure of the American and global banking systems. Economists have made the case that the crisis' roots dated back to the decade of the 1970s. The Community Development Act proved to be responsible for developing the market for the one-day toxic subprime mortgages. It was this act that mandated banks had to relax their credit standards for those minorities who were lower income earners.

It turned out to be these quasi-government agency guaranteed subprime mortgage debts that expanded dangerously through the early years of the 2000s. Both the primary government sponsored entities Fannie Mae and Freddie Mac were guaranteeing the toxic mortgages. As these loans were booming, the Federal Reserve (American Central Bank) was drastically slashing interest rates after the dotcom crash of 2001 to stave off a national recession from the stock market collapse. In the end, these dual scenarios of cheap money fueled by dramatically lower interest rates and loosened credit requirements brought on by the Community Development Act worked together to create a housing bubble. The ensuing speculation and positive feedback only encouraged home prices to rise still further.

At the same time, the wily investment banks were seeking easy money gains after the 2001 recession and dotcom bust. They invented the fanciful CDOs collateralized debt obligations from mortgages they bought up on the secondary market. By bundling both prime and subprime mortgages together into single instrument investments, they deceived unknowing investors into purchasing highly risky CDO products.

As the CDO market really took off, the housing bubble started bursting. Along with falling home prices, the subprime borrowers started defaulting on their loans en masse. They either could not or would not make payments any longer on those loans that then turned out to be higher than the value of the homes. This only exacerbated the home price decline situation.

Investors next realized that the CDOs they had bought in droves were declining to near worthless. This resulted from the toxic mortgage debt that underlay them. Investors attempted to offload the paper, but they found the market had disappeared. This then led to a perilous wave of subprime lending institution failures. It caused a dry up in liquidity and a subsequent contagion which filtered through to the highest echelons of the banking world and system.

Thanks to their huge exposure to the subprime mortgages and CDO debt obligations, the two enormous investment banks Bear Stearns and Lehman Brothers collapsed without warning. Over 450 other banks then subsequently failed throughout the following five years. Had it not been for a government-administered and taxpayer-funded bank bailout, a few of the mega banks would have failed as well alongside those that did, including such national venerable institutions as Washington Mutual, Wachovia, and Merrill Lynch.

Financial Stability Oversight Council

The Financial Stability Oversight Council is an organization that was created by the Dodd-Frank Act following the financial crisis of 2008. It possesses a clear legal mandate that provides an accountability to look for risks and respond to perceived upcoming threats to the United States' financial stability.

This is the first time that a single organization has held such important responsibility. The group is actually headed by the Secretary of the Treasury. It combines the various experience and knowledge of state regulators, an insurance expert who is both independent and Presidentially appointed, and federal financial regulators.

The Financial Stability Oversight Council was granted first time powers by Congress to restrain and head off dangerous risks within the financial system. This Council can select a financial firm that is not a bank and mark it for intense supervision so that the firm can not threaten to blow up the financial system and its stability. As an aid in determining what qualifies potential risk to the country's financial stability, this FSOC is allowed to obtain information and analysis from and supply information to the recently established OFR Office of Financial Research that is headquartered in the Treasury building.

Before the financial crisis erupted, the financial regulation in the United States focused exclusively on specific markets and institutions. This permitted gaps in supervision to expand amidst inconsistencies in the regulation. Standards weakened as a result. There was no one regulator responsible for watching over and dealing with the various risks to American financial stability. The threats often revolved around various financial firms which functioned at once in numerous interrelated markets. Because of this, critical portions of the financial system remained unregulated. The Dodd-Frank Act dealt with these failures by creating the Financial Stability Oversight Council.

The Financial Stability Oversight Council has many roles. It facilitates and coordinates regulation. They are tasked with sharing information and coordinating action with the agencies involved to deal with examining, making rules, developing policy, reporting, and enforcing their actions.

They are also to encourage gathering and sharing information among their various member organizations. If they are unable to gather enough information, they are to turn to the OFR to obtain information from individual companies they need to evaluate. Gathering and evaluating such information is supposed to eliminate blind spots in the financial system. By doing this they are fostering a more stable and less dangerous overall financial system in the United States.

The Financial Stability Oversight Council is also to select nonbank financial entities that need to be consolidated. Dodd-Frank identified companies that did not receive appropriate supervision and then led to the outbreak of the financial crisis back in 2008. The act provides the Financial Stability Oversight Council the authority which it needs to force supervision on such companies at entirely its own discretion.

The council also has the power to make recommendations for harsher standards for those firms they deem to be the biggest and most interconnected operations which provide increased risks to the system. This includes both banks and non bank financial organizations. As the Council learns about activities and practices that are threatening financial stability in the country, they are able to recommend tougher standards to the appropriate financial regulators.

The extensive powers of this Financial Stability Oversight Council are most clearly shown in their ability to choose to break up companies at will which they perceive to represent a clear and present danger to the nation's financial stability. They can decide if action should be followed to break up these kinds of firms which they deem to be a grave threat to the United States and its financial stability.

Flash Crash

The Flash Crash has also been called the 2010 Flash Crash and the Crash of 2:45. It occurred on May 6 in 2010. This stock market collapse occurred in the United States and caused a trillion dollars of equity to be temporarily wiped out. It began officially at 2:32 EST. The crash happened over only the next 36 minutes.

During this crash, major stock indices including the Dow Jones Industrial Average, the S&P 500, and the NASDAQ composite fell apart and then rebounded with unparalleled speed and volatility. At one moment, the DJIA set its largest point drop within a single day to that time. It fell 998.5 points representing over 9% of its value.

Most of this drop happened in only minutes. The index then went on to recover a substantial portion of the drop a little later. Up to this point, this represented the second biggest point swing in a single day at 1010 points.

Trading volume exploded briefly as volatility increased. The prices of stock indices, individual stocks, futures on the indices, options, and ETF exchange traded funds were all over the board. In 2014, the CFTC Commodities Futures Trading Commission released a report that called this just over thirty minute crash among the most chaotic points in all of the history of global financial markets.

The government responded by putting a number of new regulations into play after the 2010 Flash Crash. Despite this fact, they were insufficient to stop another such rapid crash on August 24, 2015. During this second episode, bids on literally dozens of stocks and ETFs plunged to as little as a single penny per share as ETFs decoupled from their underlying value, per the Wall Street Journal article of December 6, 2015. As a result of this second incident, regulators placed ETFs under additional scrutiny. This also led to the analysts at Morningstar stating that legislation from the Depression era was governing the digital age technology of ETFs.

It took the Department of Justice almost five years to charge an individual with criminal misconduct that contributed massively to the original flash crash. They charged the trader Navinder Singh Sarao with 22 counts of market manipulation and fraud. Apparently he had utilized spoofing algorithms to trick the exchanges.

Immediately before the crash unfolded, Sarao had put in orders for thousands of the stock index futures contracts known as E-mini S&P 500 contracts. These orders constituted $200 million in bets that the markets would then decline. Before the orders were cancelled by his algorithm, it modified or replaced them 19,000 times. Thanks to this individual action, the government and regulators banned front running, layering, and the spoofing of orders.

In the investigation that the CFTC conducted, they came to the conclusion that Sarao bore substantial responsibility for the imbalances of the orders in derivatives markets. These impacted the stock markets and made the crash so much more severe. The small time trader Sarao was operating from his parent's house in the suburban part of west London when he carried out these actions. He had started manipulating the markets back in 2009 when he purchased and modified trading software that would permit him to quickly and automatically place and cancel his orders.

A later CFTC report in May 2014 determined that the high frequency traders who were assigned much of the blame for the flash crash did not cause it themselves. They did contribute to the severity of it as their orders were taken before those of other participants in the market.

Forced Liquidation

Forced liquidation involves a business or other organization selling its securities or assets in order to produce liquidity because of a deteriorating financial position and scenario. It is also referred to as forced selling. This activity is commonly pursued involuntarily, as a response to a series of economic or financially devastating events, business regulations, or court imposed legal orders.

Where stock securities and investments are concerned, this type of forced liquidation can happen if an investor possesses a margin trading account. Should the investor be negative with the account balance and refuse or be unable to raise the account value back over the mandatory margin requirements once a margin call has been issued, then the broker has the rights to begin forced selling of the account securities and positions. Typically, the brokerage will provide one or more warnings that an under-minimum margin situation has occurred before pursuing this drastic option. If the holder of the account refuses to respond to the repeated calls for margin leveling, then the broker can simply force sell off all positions.

It is helpful to consider a few real world examples in order to better understand this forced selling in a brokerage margin trading account. This could be the case with stocks, bonds, commodities, or futures holdings. Assume that brokerage Jean Paul Brokers enforces a minimum margin level requirement of $1,000 for all of its account holders. Gwen's personal margin trading account had a stock portfolio originally valued at $1,500. Meanwhile, Jean Paul Brokers adjusted their margin requirements up to $2,000. They begin to issue margin calls to Gwen. She is instructed to either sell some stocks or deposit additional funds to raise her account value up to the new margin amount of $2,000. If Gwen refuses or ignores the order for the margin call, Jean Paul Brokers has the legal authority to force sell off at least $500 of her account position stocks.

In another scenario with the same account, Gwen has her account net value at $1,500 while the margin requirement remains at the original $1,000. Her stocks begin to plunge in value and are now only worth $800 all together. Jean Paul Brokerage will now send her a margin call demanding that she raise the account value by depositing an additional

$200 cash to reach $1,000 in the account. Should Gwen not react by raising the now- delinquent account to this amount so that it is in good standing, then Jean Paul Brokerage will force liquidate her stock positions and shares so that it is able to decrease the amount of leveraged risk to which is it ultimately exposed as the broker responsible for the positions.

There is also an opposite of forced liquidation in such margin accounts. This is called forced buy-in. It happens in the event that the short sold shares of a margin account of a short selling trader are recalled by the broker or holder from whose account they were originally borrowed. In the unusual event when this triggers, the brokerage will buy back the shares to return them to the original owner and thus force close out the short position in the account. In such a case, the brokerage is not required to notify the account holder before performing such an account action. They must alert the account holder once they have done this.

With hedge funds and mutual funds, portfolio managers sometimes run into unanticipated financial crises. In this case, they may be required to sell off some of their holdings in order to cut their losses and free up cash. A real world example of this is Valeant Pharmaceuticals International. In May of 2016, the drug maker experienced a 90 percent stock price crash from its prior 2015 high. A number of hedge funds had poured in literally hundreds of millions of dollars into the pharmaceutical firm stock. They force liquidated their long holdings of the stock in order to salvage what remained of the investment and to safeguard their funds and clients from any further deterioration in the underlying share price.

Foreclosure

Foreclosures represent houses or commercial properties that have been seized by a bank or other mortgage lender. These properties are then sold to recoup mortgage loan losses after an owner and borrower has not made the payments as promised in the mortgage agreement.

Foreclosure is also the legal procedure in which the lender gets a court order for the termination of the mortgagor's right of redemption. This is the case since most lenders have security interests in the house from the borrower. The borrower will secure the mortgage using the house as the collateral.

Borrowers fall into home foreclosure for several reasons, most of which could not be predicted in advance. Owner might have been let go from their job or forced to take a job transfer to another state. They might have suffered from medical problems that prevented them from working. They might have gone through a divorce and split up assets. They could have been overwhelmed by too many bills. Whatever the reason, they are no longer able to make their promised monthly mortgage payments.

Foreclosures represent potential opportunities for investors. They may be purchased directly with a seller in advance of a bank completing foreclosure proceedings. Many investors who concentrate on foreclosures prefer to deal with the owners directly. They have to be aware of many laws pertaining to foreclosures, which are different in every state. For example, while in some states home owners can stay in their properties for a full year after defaulting on payments, while in others, they have fewer than four months in advance of the trustee sale.

Practically all states also allow a redemption period for the delinquent homeowner. This simply means that a seller possesses an irrevocable ability to catch up on back payments and interest in order to retain ownership of the house. The owner will likely be required to pay any foreclosure costs experienced by the bank up to that point.

Another means of purchasing a foreclosure home is to buy it at the Trustee's Sale. When this means is pursued, it is better to bid on a house that allows you to look it over in advance of putting up an offer. This is helpful so that you can determine how many repairs will be needed to make it salable and even possibly habitable. It is also worth knowing if the occupants are still living in the house and will have to be forcefully evicted. The process of going through an eviction can be both expensive and time consuming.

Many Trustee Sales will have certain rules in common that have to be followed for a foreclosure house to be purchased. They may demand sealed bids. They could require you to demonstrate your proof of financial qualifications. They might similarly insist on you putting up a significant earnest money deposit. Many of them will state that the property is being purchased in its present condition, or as is.

Fractional Banking System

The fractional banking system is also known as the fractional reserve banking system. This system is the way that virtually all modern day banks around the world operate. In a fractional reserve banking system, banks actually only maintain a small amount of their deposited funds in reserve forms of cash and other easily liquid assets.

The rest of the deposits they loan out, even though all of their deposits are allowed to be withdrawn at the customers' demand. Fractional banking happens any time that banks loan out money that they bring in from deposits.

Fractional banking systems are ones where banks constantly expand the money supply beyond the levels at which they exist. Because of this, total money supplies are commonly a multiple bigger than simply the currency created by the nation's central bank. The multiple is also known as the money multiplier. Its amount is determined by a reserve requirement that the financial overseers set.

This fractional reserve system is managed ultimately by central banks and these reserve requirements that they enforce. On the one hand, it sets a limit on the quantity of money that is created by the commercial banks. The other purpose of it is to make certain that banks keep enough readily available cash in order to keep up with typical withdrawal demands of customers. Even though this is the case, there can be problems. Should many depositors at once attempt to take out their money, then a run on the bank might occur. If this happens on a large national or regional scale, the possibility of a banking systemic crisis emerges.

Central banks attempt to reduce these problems. They keep a close eye on commercial banks through regulations and oversight. Besides that, they promise to help out banks that fall into difficulties by acting as their ultimate lender of last resort. Finally, central banks instill confidence in the fractional reserve banking system by guaranteeing the deposits of the customers of the commercial banks.

A significant amount of criticism has been leveled against this fractional reserve banking system. Mainstream critics have complained that because money is only created as individuals borrow from the banking system, the system itself forces people to take on debt in order for money to actually be created. They say that this debases the currency. The biggest problem that they have with the commercial banking system growing the money supply is that it is literally creating money from nothing.

Other critics associate fractional banking with fiat currencies, or money that is only valuable because the governments say that they are. They decry these as negative aspects of current money systems. They dislike that fractional banking systems and fiat money together do not place any limits on how much a money supply can ultimately grow. This can lead to bubbles in both capital markets and assets, such as real estate, stock markets, and commodities. All of these can be victims of speculation, which is made easier by the creation of money through debt in the fractional reserve system.

Freddie Mac

Freddie Mac is a semi-private company that Congress chartered in 1970. They created the entity to offer stability, liquidity, and affordable prices for the country and its housing markets. They have grown to be responsible for the home purchases of one out of four buyers.

Besides this the company is also among the biggest financing sources for multifamily housing in the nation. From 2009 to 2016, the company has dispersed mortgage market funding that amounts to over $2.5 trillion. This has enabled in excess of 13 million American families to refinance, purchase, or rent a home in that time frame.

In 1970 Congress was seeking to stabilize the mortgage markets of the country. They wanted to grow and improve opportunities for rental housing that was affordable and for home buying. Because of this, Freddie Mac's mission has always been to bring stability, liquidity, and affordability to the national housing market in the United States. They do this in a variety of ways. The company helps the secondary mortgage market. They buy both mortgage securities and mortgage loans outright as investments. They then package and sell these as guaranteed mortgage securities known as PCs. In this secondary market, there are entities which buy and sell mortgages as complete loans or as mortgage securities. Freddie Mac never makes loans to home owners directly themselves.

Because of the collapse of the mortgage backed securities markets in 2007 and 2008 and its impact on their finances, the company is now being run under conservatorship. The FHFA Federal Housing Finance Agency oversees their business to make sure loans are carefully scrutinized and securitized. They want to avoid the mistakes of the financial crisis becoming repeated here.

Freddie Mac operates in three main business areas to ensure that a continuous supply of mortgage funding goes through to the housing markets in the country. They make rental housing and home buying more affordable through their single family credit guarantee business, their multifamily business, and their investment business. They utilize all three of these to promote financing for affordable housing.

The single family line is essentially a recycling operation. They work with securitizing mortgages so that the entity is able to provide funding to millions of different home loans annually. This securitization proves to be the means where they buy up different loans lenders have made and then package these up into various mortgage securities. They then sell these on the worldwide capital markets. The money from the sale of these securities they next funnel back to the lenders. In this way home loan operations have sufficient mortgage money for lending.

The company is also interested in supporting renters as well. This is the role of their multifamily business. In this line, the outfit cooperates with a group of lenders to help finance the construction of various apartment buildings throughout the United States. The lenders make the loans and Freddie Mac buys them to package and resell. This way the lenders receive back the proceeds so they can issue more loans. This is a critical line as multifamily loans prove to be a few million dollars each and require unique underwriting from one property to the next.

Their investment business actually purchases some of their own mortgage backed securities which they and other financial entities like Fannie Mae guarantee. This portfolio further invests into individual loans which they guarantee but choose not to securitize. By bidding on some of their own securities, the investment business and portfolio serves the markets. It gives these mortgage backed securities greater liquidity and offers more funding for mortgages. They do this by issuing their own debt which creates net income for the company after they pay their interest to the bond holders.

Global Debt

Global debt is an issue that has become especially troublesome since the financial crisis of 2007-2009. Eight years following this crash and Great Recession, the planet is experience a debt problem that has never before been seen in the whole history of the world.

Total debt outside of the financial sector has increased by more than double in real dollars since the century began through 2016. By 2015, it had climbed to over $152 trillion. This figure that includes the debt of governments, households, and non financial firms continues to grow.

Global debt levels as of October 2016 reached a record setting 225% of the entire gross domestic product for the globe, per the IMF's Fiscal Monitor semi annual publication. Roughly two thirds of the total non-financial firm debt is owed by the private sector of businesses and consumers. The balance nearly a third of the total is considered to be government public debt. While other measures have this percentage higher, the IMF claims that government debt is up to 85 percent of GDP versus the 70 percent seen in 2015.

This enormous amount of global debt has made the job of worldwide policy makers much more challenging. Central banks have found that their efforts to stimulate economies are diminishing. It is up to government fiscal policy to increase growth to try to keep up with rising global debt. So far, few countries have seen much success in these efforts.

The surge in global debt borrowing hails back to the private debt boom that occurred before the financial crisis in 2008. Corporations and consumer households within the world's advanced economies began to retrench after the crisis. Despite this, debt deleveraging did not proceed evenly and in other cases debts continued to rise. Bad debts of banks especially proved problematic. Many of these have wound up on the balance sheets of governments instead.

The low interest rate environment that followed the financial crisis also encouraged a rising tide of corporate debt in the emerging nation markets. Private debt levels were already dangerously high in advanced countries.

Now they are also problematic in such important emerging economies as Brazil and China. Both of these are rightly thought of as systemically critical in the world's financial system.

The problem with deciding how dangerous global debt has become is there is no consensus on what percentage of debt versus GDP is critical. It is well known that financial crises are related to an overabundance of private debt in developing and developed economies. Beyond this, research has demonstrated that higher levels of debt come with lower rates of growth, even though a financial crisis may be side stepped. The IMF has been warning especially about the need for deleveraging to happen in both the euro zone area and China.

There are two more problems associated with rising debt levels. As debt increase outpaces economic output growth, more government debt equals a greater level of state involvement in the overall economy. It also guarantees a higher tax rate and number of taxes for the future.

Besides this, debt has to be rolled over regularly. The repetition of having to auction debt creates a scenario where governments face a vote of confidence on a routine basis. Should a government fail to inspire enthusiasm for its debt auction as has happened with a number of euro zone governments in past years, then the erring nation plunges head long into serious crisis.

Good Debt

Good debt is debt that benefits a person or business to carry. Such good debts demonstrate both the creditworthiness and the responsibility of a borrower. They also create a good base to build on in the future. There are many examples of good debt, which stands in contrast to bad debt.

Good debts are typically those debts that are taken on to acquire an item or investment that only grows in value with time. Examples of this include things like real estate loans, schooling loans, home mortgages, business debt, and passive income investments. Each of these items could provide a significant and real advantage with time. Real estate could increase in value and be resold for profits.

Higher education commonly leads to greater amounts of earnings. Loans on homes are commonly wonderful for building credit and provide properties that serve as excellent collateral. Loans for businesses may result in profits earned from trade and sales. It is important to note that cars and other items are not included in these lists. This is simply because they lose value the moment that they are purchased and driven away.

Bad debts in contrast are those that result in higher interest rates and considerable deprecation of the items purchased with time. Goods that are for short time frame use and bought on credit are commonly considered to be bad debts. Since the item's life span will only decline with time, and the interest rates are typically high, no benefit is derived from purchasing these things with debt. A great number of such purchases rapidly decline in value, even after one use.

A significant benefit to good debts lies in the increase in cash flow that they commonly create. Properly structured good debts lead to tax advantages, to the ability to invest in still more assets that can produce cash, and to higher credit scores as well. Good debts that are paid on time furthermore build up a good financial base for the future. Good debts create cash flow, which stands in contrast to bad debts that do not.

Investments that produce passive income are among the best good debts. For example, purchasing an apartment building using debt will result in both income revenue and substantial tax deductions. This proves to be good debt, since although you are borrowing money, you are receiving passive income and gaining the ability to depreciate assets that can actually appreciate with time. On top of this, you are allowed to live there while you accrue all of these other benefits.

When considering a good debt, you should make certain that the income that the investment will provide is high enough to make the investment and the accompanying debt worth while. A number of experts offer advice on this. They suggest that not tying up in excess of twenty percent of your overall value in debt is a better practice. Higher debt levels than this can sound off warning bells with banks and other lenders.

Government Bonds

Government bonds are debt instruments that governments issue to pay for government expenditures. Within the United States, federal government issues include savings bonds, treasury notes, treasury bonds, and TIPS Treasury inflation protected securities. Investors should carefully consider the risks that different countries' governments possess before they invest in their bonds. Among these international government risks are political risk, country risk, interest rate risk, and inflation risk. Governments generally have less credit risk, though not always.

Savings bonds are a type of United States government bonds that the Treasury department sells. They are available in an electronic form. The Treasury offers them directly from their website, or individuals can buy them from the majority of financial institutions and banks. When savings bonds reach maturity, the investors get back the bond's face value along with interest which accrued. These savings bonds may not be redeemed the first year of issue. Any investors who redeem them in their first five years of issue lose three months interest for cashing out too early.

The Treasury of the United States also issues intermediate time frame bonds known as Treasury notes or T-Notes. These notes provide interest payments semiannually at a coupon rate which is fixed. These notes typically are denominated in $1,000 face values. Those with three or two year maturity dates come in $5,000 denominations. Before 1984, T-Notes were callable and gave the Treasury the right to buy them back given specific conditions.

The U.S. government's longest term bonds are Treasury Bonds, or T-Bonds. These have maturity dates ranging from ten to 30 years time. They also provide interest payments on a semiannual basis and come in $1,000 denominated values. These T-bonds are important because they pay for federal budget shortfalls, are a form of monetary policy, and ensure the country is able to regulate its money supply. As all bond issuers, the Treasury department looks at return and risk requirements on the market when it goes to raise capital so that it can be as efficient as possible. This helps to explain the different kinds of Treasury securities and government bonds they offer.

U.S. government bonds have generally been considered to be without risk, which is why they trade so easily in extremely large and liquid markets. The downside to this is that they offer considerably lower returns than do other bonds. TIPS do provide protection against inflation so that any inflation increases will not exceed the interest rate of the bond. The prices of government bonds are based on current interest rates. This means that the fixed rate bonds will decline in value as the interest rates rise, since there is lost opportunity to obtain newer bonds at higher interest rates. Similarly, if interest rates fall, the bond's values will rise.

The federal government is able to control the money supply in part by its issue of the government bonds. If they wish to increase the money supply, they can simply buy back their own bonds. These funds then find their way to a bank and expand the money supply as banks keep small reserves and loan the rest out (in the money multiplier effect). The government is also able to lower the money supply by selling additional bonds which takes money out of circulation. If the government were to retire the funds received from the sale of these bonds, it would reduce the available money supply. More often than not, the U.S. government spends the money.

Government Debt

Government debt refers to the total amount of government issued IOUs which have not been paid back at any given point. Governments issue such debt any time they chose to borrow money from the public or from overseas nations and companies.

As a government borrows this money, it provides government securities that give all of the important information on this investment debt. The face of the certificates states the interest rate which the government will pay on the original principal, the amount which they are borrowing, and the payment schedule for both principal pay back and interest payments. These outstanding securities are equal to the total debt amount which the government has not paid back. It is also the government debt.

Governments actually issue a variety of debt types. Economists classify such debt in different categories. The first would be by the form of governmental agency that issued such debt in the first place. Within the U.S., the principal governmental agencies which issue debt are state, federal, and local jurisdictions. Local debt is also further subdivided into sub-classes including city-, county-, or parish-issued government debt. All of these are considered a type of government bonds.

Yet another way to classify such government debt is according to the dates of maturity. This is why bond investors and U.S. Treasury officials with the Federal Reserve discuss thirty year and ten year bonds. These are the amounts of time between when the government originally issued the bond and the due date of the principal. With federal government debt, there are three easy to understand and remember types of maturities.

Treasury Bills are the first of these. They come with maturities amounting to a single year or under. This could be three month T-bills or year long T-bills. Treasury notes are the second designation. They have maturities that range from a single year to ten years long. Treasury bonds are the over ten year long maturity dates. With local or state level government debt, the terminology used is just bonds. This is true regardless of when they mature.

There are also bonds that carry infinite repayments. Analysts call these perpetuity bonds. With these bonds, the principal never becomes repaid. Interest payments will then be made forever. This would practically be until the government defaults, the country collapses financially, or the government buys back the bonds. Such bonds were at one time issued by the government of Great Britain. They called these consols.

A final means for classifying government debt bonds comes down to the revenue source which underlies the bonds' repayment. Those government debts that the entity plans to repay by utilizing revenues they garner from taxing their constituents they call general obligation bonds. Revenue bonds are those bonds that they pay back by employing particular user fees, sometimes from the project itself which the bonds will finance. This could be tolls on a new highway or a bridge. Only local and state government debt is classified this way.

The United States government debt has radically and exponentially increased over the past 15 to 20 years. Consider that in 2004 early in the year, the outstanding federal government debt amounted to around $7.1 trillion. In early 2017, that amount topped $20 trillion for the first time ever. Roughly half of this enormous debt amount the government owes to its pension funds - the Social Security Trust and Medicare Trust Funds.

Some economists like to say that the internal debt does not carry any public welfare or economic impacts, but they are incorrect with this assertion. Since the Social Security Fund will start to need its loaned out money paid back in 2020, it will require the government to issue either new debt to non-governmental buyers or to raise taxes dramatically to pay back the pension funds for the social security recipients' monthly benefits to continue.

This problem will only worsen over time through 2032 or 2033, when the funds will have exhausted all of their money the government owes them back. At this point, the federal government will either have to abandon the Social Security and Medicare programs entirely, dramatically reduce the benefits to where they are sustainable, hugely increase the age when retirees can draw on them, or vastly increase government revenues from somewhere.

Great Depression

The Great Depression represented the most serious economic contraction that affected the world in the twentieth century. It occurred the decade before the Second World War broke out, in the 1930's. The Great Depression began and ended in differing years in the various countries and economies of the world. In general it started around 1929 and held countries in its grip through the end of the 1930's and the early years of the 1940's.

The Great Depression turned out to be the deepest, hardest, longest, and most geographically encompassing depression that the world had seen. Nowadays, the Great Depression is still held up as the model for how badly the economy of the world can collapse. In the eighty years since the great depression began, economists have not named another economic contraction in the world or the United States as a depression.

The Great Depression began in the United States. It commenced with the stock market crash that began on September 4, 1929. The far steeper stock market decline of October 29, 1929 became known as Black Tuesday and eclipsed the worldwide newspaper headlines. This rapidly spread from the U.S. to nearly all countries around the globe.

Practically all nations of the world, whether rich or poor, felt the tragic and crushing impacts of the Great Depression. International trade plummeted by as much as one half to two thirds of its previous level. Along with this, profits, personal incomes, tax revenues, and prices plunged. In the United States, unemployment soared to twenty-five percent, but in other countries, this level reached even thirty-three percent.

Cities all over the globe suffered especially, particularly those that relied on heavy industry as their economic mainstay. In a great number of nations, construction came practically to a stop. Even farming suffered terribly with the prices of produce crashing by around sixty percent. The areas that depended on industries in the primary sector took the worst hit, including logging, mining, and cash cropping. Job losses in these industries turned out to be among the worst.

A few nations' economies began recovering in the middle of the 1930's. For most countries around the world, the terrible consequences of the Great Depression remained until the outbreak of the Second World War. The military output required by the conflict rapidly increased production and employment everywhere.

Numerous events and problems caused the Great Depression's original economic collapse of 1929. Structural weaknesses were present, only waiting for particular events to turn the crash into a worldwide depression. It is particularly interesting how the contraction ran from one country to the next like a wildfire in a forest. Regarding the structural weaknesses of the 1929 economic contraction, historians are quick to point out that enormous and widespread bank failures only became worse as the stock market crashed. Others hold up specific monetary policy like the Federal Reserve in the United States contracting America's money supply, and the British Empire choosing to go back to the pre-World War I parity of the Gold Standard with one pound equal to $4.86.

Great Recession

The Great Recession proved to be the worst American and world wide economic downturn since the 1930's era Great Depression. It began within the U.S. in December of 2007 and is said to have ended in June of 2009 officially. There is ongoing debate with some economists as to whether the full effects of the Great Recession have really ceased, or this is merely a lull in between bouts of a greater depression.

The Great Recession started in the U.S. but later spread to most industrialized countries around the globe. This world wide recession led to a severe drop in trade and a significant drop in economic activity. The financial crisis of 2007-2010 actually kicked off the Great Recession.

The financial crisis and resulting Great Recession ultimately stemmed from irresponsible lending policies practiced by banks on a widespread level and encouraged by the U.S. and British governments. Along with this, the increasingly common practice of securitizing real estate and mortgages led to the financial collapse. Mortgage backed securities from the United States were promoted and sold around the globe. They turned out to be far more speculative and risky than anyone had predicted or disclosed.

Besides this, a worldwide boom in credit encouraged a speculative asset bubble in stocks and real estate. As prices continued to rise, the risky lending only grew more prevalent. The crisis actually flared up as a result of severe losses on sub prime loans that started in 2007. These demonstrated that other loans were also at risk amid too high real estate prices. As the loan losses continued to rise, Lehman Brothers suddenly collapsed on September 15th of 2008.

An enormous panic ensued in the inter-banking loan markets. With stock and real estate prices sharply declining, historical and major commercial and investment banking institutions throughout both the U.S. and Europe showed how much they had over extended themselves with major leverage as their losses quickly mounted. The governments of their home countries had to step in with enormous amounts of public tax dollars in order to save many of them from imminent bankruptcy.

This resulting Great Recession has led to a substantial decline in international trade, dropping commodity prices, and high and mounting unemployment around the world. Although the National Bureau of Economic Research declared the Great Recession officially over at the end of 2009, other economic experts are not convinced. Nobel prize winning economist Paul Krugman has said that this Great Recession heralds the start of a second Great Depression. Others who are less pessimistic have claimed that true recovery in the United States will not emerge until the end of 2011.

A number of events have been blamed for causing the financial crisis and Great Recession. The environment that preceded the crisis included an unnatural rise in asset prices along with an accompanying boom in worldwide economic demand. These are believed to have resulted from the multi-year period of too easily available credit, insufficient regulation, and poor oversight from the regulatory bodies who all too often simply looked the other way when times were good.

Home Equity Line of Credit (HELOC)

A home equity line of credit is also known by its acronym HELOC. It represents a viable alternative to the more commonly used home equity loan. Whereas home equity loans provide lump sum amounts, Home Equity Lines of Credit provide cash as and when the borrower needs it. The downside to a HELOC is that a bank can decide to reduce the amount of available credit or cancel the line altogether without warning. This can happen before a borrower has utilized the funds.

In a home equity line of credit, borrowers use the equity within the home to be their collateral with the bank. The lending institution decides on the maximum amount that the borrower can obtain. The home owner then determines how much of this they want to borrow for the amount of time the bank permits. This might be until the monthly payments reduce the line to a zero balance, or it could be for a certain number of months. This makes these HELOCs much like a credit card in the ability to draw on the resources only when and as they need them.

The main difference between a home equity line of credit and a home loan is that the former is a revolving loan instrument. Borrowers are able to use the money then pay it off. They can then draw on it once again. Home equity loans pay a single lump sum up front amount one time. HELOCs also feature variable interest rates that will change over time, while home equity loans come with interest rates that are fixed. The payment amounts on the home equity loans are also fixed every month, while the payment on the HELOC depends on how much of the line is used.

In order to be able to obtain a home equity line of credit, the home owner must have significant equity in the house itself. Banks will insist that owners keep at least 10% to 20% equity within the property all the time. This must be the case after the line is approved as well. The HELOC approval process will also require verifiable proof of income, consistent documented employment, and a high credit score that is generally more than 680.

It is important for prospective borrowers to determine what they will use the home equity line of credit money for before they draw on it. Home renovations lend themselves better to home equity loans. This is because the one time large amount would enable the borrower to finish the renovations and then repay the loan. A HELOC is a better fit for a revolving bill such as the children's college tuition. Borrowers can use them to cover the tuition, then pay them off hopefully before the next tuition payment become due. At this point they can re-utilize the HELOC for the next semester tuition.

The home equity line of credit can also be a good choice for individuals who wish to consolidate the balances on their credit cards which feature high interest rates. The rates for the HELOC are typically much lower. This strategy requires some discipline. Once the credit cards have been cleared, there is the danger that the home owner might be tempted to run them back up again while they are still making payments on the line of credit. This would put borrowers in a worse situation than before they chose to consolidate.

Home equity lines of credit can get a home owner into the bad habit of constantly borrowing and paying them back as with a credit card. This can be a problem if the borrowers take on more debt with the HELOC than they can afford to pay in monthly payments. Missing these payments would put their home at jeopardy of being seized by the bank.

Home Equity Loan

A home equity loan is a means for home owners to borrow money using the value of their house. Borrowers find these loans appealing because they can usually borrow significant sums of money. Besides this, they are much simpler to get approved for than with many competing kinds of loans. A home owner's house secures these home equity loans. The borrowers may utilize these funds for any purpose that they wish. They do not have to be spent on expenses related to the house that secures the loan.

Such a home equity loan is actually a kind of second mortgage on a house. The first mortgage allows the buyer to purchase the home. When sufficient equity is established in the house, owners can attach other loans to the property to borrow against it.

There are a number of benefits to obtaining a home equity loan. They appeal to both lenders and borrowers. Borrowers get better APRs or interest rates from them than with other loan types. Because they are secured by the value of the home, they can be easier to get approved for even with bad credit. The IRS allows home owners to deduct interest expenses from these home equity loans from their taxes. Finally, borrowers are able to obtain substantial loan amounts using these loan vehicles.

The lenders like these loans because they consider them to be safer loans. The house acts as collateral in the process. This means that banks are able to seize the house to liquidate it and regain unpaid balances if the owner fails to make the payments. Because of this, banks know that borrowers will make the payments of these loans a high priority so they do not lose their house.

Banks protect themselves in any case by not lending too much against the value of the property. In general, lenders will not allow borrowers to obtain a greater amount than 85% of the value of the house. This includes both the amount that remains on the first mortgage as well as the second mortgage home equity loan. This percentage is known as the loan to value ratio. It can vary somewhat from one bank to the next.

The way home equity loans work is relatively straightforward. Borrowers receive a one time cash payment. They then make fixed payments each month to pay back the loan over a pre-set amount of time. The interest rate will be set by the bank at the beginning of the loan. With every payment, the loan balance declines after part of the interest costs are covered. This makes these amortizing loans.

Sometimes borrowers do not require all of the money at one time. An alternative to the home equity loan in this case is the HELOC home equity line of credit. This delivers a set amount of money which home owners can draw on only when and if they require it. The borrowers only have to pay interest on money which they physically draw and borrow. It is possible for the interest rate to change on these HELOC loans. Banks may also cancel such a line of credit before the borrower has utilized all or part of the funds.

Home equity loans can be used for many different needs. It is wise to improve the value of the house with the money through renovating, remodeling, or increasing the appeal of the property. Other common uses borrowers employ them for are to help pay for a second home, to afford college tuition and expenses for family members, or to consolidate bills with high interest rates.

Hyperinflation

In the field of economics, hyperinflation proves to be inflation, or rising prices over time, that is extremely high and even beyond controlling. This state of the economy exists as the overall levels of pricing in a certain country are rising sharply and quickly at the same time as the actual values of these economic goods remain roughly the same price as measured in other more stable currencies. In other words, the nation's own currency is diminishing in value rapidly, commonly at rate that grows in pace.

The IASB, or International Accounting Standards Board, gives a precise definition of hyperinflation. They state that when the rate of inflation during three cumulative years nears one hundred percent total, or at least twenty-six percent each year compounded annually for three consecutive years, then hyperinflation has been reached. Other economists such as Cagan have declared hyperinflation to be when inflation is greater than fifty percent each month. Hyperinflation can witness the overall price levels go up by five to ten percent and higher even in single days for extended periods of time. This stands in sharp contrast to regular inflation which is commonly only reported over a quarterly or annual basis.

As greater and greater amounts of inflation are created in each printing of money instance, a truly vicious cycle takes effect. Such hyperinflation is clearly evident as the money supply grows at an uninterrupted rate. It is typically seen alongside the population's unwillingness to keep the hyper-inflationary currency for any longer than they have to in order to use it for any hard good that will prevent them from losing more actual purchasing power. Hyperinflation is typically a part of wars and their after effects, social or political upheavals, and currency meltdowns such as seen in Zimbabwe.

Hyperinflation is a phenomenon that is unique to fiat currencies that are not backed up by anything but a government's faith and trust. As the money supply is not limited by normal restraints like gold in a vault, it is instead run by a paper money standard. The supply of it is completely dependent on the discretion of the government.

Hyperinflation commonly leads to intense and long lasting economic depressions. This is not always the case though. In Brazil which suffered in the grips of hyperinflation for thirty years in the 1964 to 1994 period, the government managed to avoid economic collapse by valuing all non-monetary goods, services, and investments for the whole economy in an involved index. The government supplied this daily updated index that they measured with the daily Brazilian currency against the United States dollar.

In contrast to Brazil, Zimbabwe did not bother to set up such an index measured against the dollar. They did offer the day by day changes in the U.S. dollar as a comparison for everyone in the country to see. This voluntary comparison only served to worsen the problem and finally destroyed the real value of non monetary items that did not get updated as expressed against the Zimbabwe dollar. All monetary items in the country finally lost every bit of value during the hyper-inflationary meltdown.

Inflation

Inflation proves to be prices rising over time. It is specifically measured as the increase in a given basket of goods and services' prices. These goods and services are taken to represent the entire economy. Inflation is also the going up in cost of the average prices of goods and services as measured by the CPI, or consumer price index. The opposite of inflation is known as deflation. Deflation turns out to be the falling of an average level of prices. The point that separates the two from each other, both deflation and inflation, is price stability, or no change in the costs of goods and services.

Inflation has almost everything to do with the amount of money available. It is inextricably tied to the money supply. This gives rise to the popularly remarked observation that inflation is actually an excessive number of dollars chasing too small a quantity of goods. Comprehending the way that this works is easier when considering an example.

Pretend for a moment that the world possessed only two commodities: oranges that are gathered up from orange trees and paper money created by government. In seasons where rain is limited and the oranges are few as a result, the cost of oranges should go up. This is because the same number of printed dollars would be competing for a smaller number of oranges.

On the other hand, if a bumper crop of oranges are seen, then the cost of oranges should drop, since the sellers of oranges have no choice but to cut prices to sell off their large inventory of oranges. These two examples illustrate inflation in the former and deflation in the latter. The main difference between the real world and this example is that inflation measures changes in the price movement on average of many or all goods and services, and not simply one.

The quantity of money in an economy similarly impacts the amount of inflation present at any given time. Should the government in the example above choose to print enormous amounts of money, then there will be many dollars for a relatively constant number of oranges, as in the lack of rain scenario. So inflation is created by the number of dollars going up against the quantities of oranges that exist, or overall goods and services existing. Deflation, as the opposite of inflation, would be the numbers of dollars dropping compared to the quantity of oranges available.

Because of this, levels of inflation result from four different factors that often work together in combination. The demand for money could drop. The supply of money could expand. The available supply of various other goods might decline. Finally, the demand for other goods increases.

Even though these four factors do work in correlation, economists say that inflation is mostly a currency driven event. This means that in the vast majority of cases, it results from governments tampering with the money supply. Generally, they do this by over printing their own currency to have money to pay for spending, resulting in higher inflation.

Inflationary Bias

Inflationary Bias refers to the opposite of deflationary bias. Both of these are government monetary and/or fiscal policy prejudices. Governments are forced to take one of two positions with reference to their monetary policy and interventions in an economy. Inflationary bias turns out to be the one which the vast majority of central banks and sovereign nation policy makers pursue for several important reasons.

Such an Inflationary Bias results from discretionary policies of national governments. If they are utilized properly with regards to the labor market, these biases cause a higher than ideal inflation level without leading to any transitions in income increases. At the same time, this bias results from the goals of those nations which are saddled with public debt levels. They would pursue these policies with a goal of fostering inflation over the medium to longer term.

There are economic theories that persuasively argue governments have a natural affinity for and tendency towards Inflationary Bias policies. The Barro-Gordon model demonstrates that the government's ability to manipulate the economy will cause it to skew towards a bias that is inflationary by nature. According to such a model, countries will try to maintain the country's national unemployment rates at lower than the naturally occurring levels. This causes a wage and price inflation that is higher than their normally occurring level. In the end, this will lead to an aggregate inflationary level that proves to be greater than the normal level of inflation.

The economic theories that are more traditional also suggest that this Inflationary Bias will be present any time that fiscal and monetary policies become enacted at the discretion of the policy makers and central bankers instead of being rules based. Still other economists argue that this bias will even be present if the policy makers are not bent on reducing unemployment to lower than normal levels and even if the policies operate off of rules instead.

As there are so many perils from such Inflationary Biases, economists have suggested a variety of measures to stop it from occurring. Some of them have argued for appointing only conservatively ideological central bankers. According to these arguments, the countries ought to set out aimed for inflationary targets and goals. When these rates of inflation are surpassed by real economic data releases, there could be a punishment of some type given out to the central bankers.

In truth and point of fact, the majority of important countries now do state their optimal inflation rate targets in their policy setting meetings, press conferences, and notes from closed door meetings alike. For most Western nation policy makers and central banks like the United States Federal Reserve, Great Britain's Bank of England, the Euro Zone's European Central Bank, and the Japanese Central Bank, this level amounts to a desired two percent inflation target over the medium to long term time frame.

For those nations that opt to go with the opposite of an inflationary bias, the only other choice is the deflationary bias. The problem with deflationary biases is that they only work for countries, businesses, and consumers which are not saddled down with enormous debt levels. This is because a deflationary bias will cause debts to progressively cost more in real terms over time even as they reward savers and creditors. Governments are especially afraid of this policy bias as they are mostly running budgetary deficits year in and year out. Only a handful of countries run government budget surpluses in point of fact.

Insolvency

Insolvency refers to the point where an individual, business, or even governmental organization is not able to cover its various financial obligations any longer. This means that it is unable to settle debts with its creditors and lenders as they are due. Many times, before such an indebted individual, company, or government becomes embroiled in any type of insolvency or bankruptcy procedures, they will try to enter into informal negotiations with creditors. This could involve setting up other payment schedules and arrangements.

Insolvency can happen for a variety of reasons. Among these is a decrease in cash flow and profitability forecasts, poor management of cash resources, or a rapid expansion in costs and expenses. Where businesses are concerned, this type of insolvency is classified according to one of two separate categories. The first of these is Cash Flow insolvency. This happens as a corporation or company simply can not pay the business debts as they become due. The second form is Balance Sheet insolvency. This type results from a company reaching the point where it possesses a negative net asset position. It simply means that the corporation's aggregate debts are greater than its total assets.

It is entirely possible for firms to be solvent by balance sheet figures but at the same time be insolvent by cash flow. The opposite scenario could also occur. If a company is bankrupt according to its balance sheet while still solvent by cash flow, it simply means its incoming revenues permit it to cover its current financial obligations. There are numerous companies which possess longer term debt obligations that continuously operate in this balance sheet-bankrupt status.

Technically, insolvency and bankruptcy are not exactly the same thing. The former is a condition of being in financial trouble or at least difficulties. Bankruptcy is instead a court order. It describes the ways in which a debtor which is no longer solvent will continue to meet its obligations or instead have its assets sold off to settle with the creditors.

This means that it is entirely possible for a company, individual, or government entity to be no longer solvent but not yet be officially bankrupt.

This could result from a temporary or sometimes fixable problem. The reverse is never the case. An entity can not be bankrupt yet still be solvent. Such a lack of solvency often translates into an eventual bankrupt state when the debtors are not able to improve their financial conditions.

Corporations and firms that have become insolvent are able to improve their financial state. They might slash costs, borrow money, sell their assets, renegotiate the terms of their debts, or seek out a bigger corporation to acquire them. The buyer could settle their debts as part of the assumption of their services, products, technology, and proprietary trademarks.

Several unfortunate events can lead to a company becoming insolvent. If they do not have enough management in human resources or accounting departments, this could contribute to the problem. A lack of qualified accounting staff could cause a company's budget to be either ignored or misappropriated.

There might also be sharply increasing vendor prices which the company is powerless to stop. Higher prices for their goods and services mean that companies will have to raise their prices in an effort to pass these along to the consumer. The problem arises when customers then shop another company or product to get a better price. Lost clientele nearly always translates into a drop in cash flow. This means that they no longer have the cash coming in to cover the bills due to the company creditors.

There could also be lawsuits brought by employees or customers that break a company's finances. The firm could be forced to pay enormous bills for both defense and in settlement damages which make it impossible for them to continue ongoing operations. As operations cease and revenue naturally drops, the ability to pay bills disappears quickly.

A final reason centers on the lack of evolution in a company product line. It might be customers simply change their needs and therefore purchasing habits. This could lead them to rival firms which offer a broader product range or line. The company which could not or did not adapt its products will find its revenues and profits decreasing to the point where they are unable to cover their expenses with their remaining income.

Interest Rate

Interest rates are the levels at which interest is charged a borrower for using money that they obtain in the form of a loan from a bank or other lender. These are also the rates that individuals and businesses are paid for depositing their funds with a bank. Interest rates are central to the running of capitalist economies. They are commonly written out as percentage rates for a given time frame, most commonly per year.

As an example, a small business might require capital to purchase new assets for the company. To acquire these, they borrow money form a bank. In exchange for making them this loan, the bank is paid interest at a pre set and agreed upon rate of interest for lending it to the company and putting off their own use of the monies. They receive this interest in monthly payments along with repayments of the principal.

Interest rates are also used by government agencies in pursuing monetary policies. Central banks set them to influence their nation's economic performance. They impact many elements of an economy such as unemployment, inflation, and investment levels.

There are several different interest rates to consider. The most commonly expressed one is the nominal interest rate. This nominal interest rate proves to be the amount of interest that is payable in money terms. If a family deposits $1,000 in a bank for a year, and is paid $50 in interest, then their balance by the conclusion of the year will be $1,050. This would translate to a nominal interest rate amounting to five percent per year.

The real interest rate is another type of rate used to determine how much purchasing power is received. It is the interest rate after the level of inflation is subtracted. Determining the real interest rate is a matter of calculating the nominal rate and removing the amount of inflation from it. In the example above, supposed the economy's inflation level is measured at five percent for the year. This would mean that the $1,050 in the account at year end only buys what it did as $1,000 at the beginning of the year. This translates to a real interest rate of zero.

Interest rates change for many reasons. They are altered for political gains of parties in power. By reducing the interest rate, an economy gains a short term boost. The help to the economy will often influence the outcome of elections. Unfortunately, the short term advantage gained is often offset later by inflation. This reason for changing interest rates is eliminated with independent central banks.

Another main reason that interest rates change is because of expectations of inflation. Since the majority of economies demonstrate inflation, fixed amounts of money will purchase fewer goods a year from now than they will today. Lenders expect to be compensated for this. Central banks raise interest rates to fight this inflation as necessary.

Jumbo Loan

Jumbo loans are specific types of loans made by banks for home mortgages. They are special because these loans are for larger sized house loans. In order for a loan to be qualified as a jumbo one, it must be larger than the conforming loan limits.

The government Federal Housing Finance Agency sets these conforming loan limits through regulation. They are the agency that oversees the mortgage buying government sponsored entities Freddie Mac and Fannie Mae. Both of these groups purchase mortgages from the traditional lenders like banks and credit unions.

For the majority of the United States, jumbo loan limits start at $417,000. There are several states and a few hundred counties that have different loan limit amounts. Some of these limits range as high as $625,000 for their loan limits in areas that are the most expensive property markets.

Counting Louisiana parishes, Alaska boroughs, and the District of Columbia like counties, the U.S. has 3,143 counties. This does not consider the Virgin Islands, Guam, or Puerto Rico. An overwhelming majority 2,916 of these counties have the traditional limit amount of $417,000 for jumbo loan minimums.

Another 115 counties have loan limits that are in between the typical $417,000 and $625,000 maximum. This would include higher than usual priced real estate markets but not the most expensive ones like Los Angeles. In Colorado Denver County is one such example with a jumbo loan minimum of $458,850. Another 108 counties contain higher jumbo loan limits that start at $625,500. Included in these are the most expensive housing markets. Among these are such pricey counties as those found in New York City, Los Angeles, and San Francisco.

Several states and their counties are allowed to have higher conforming loan limits than the maximum amounts set out by the government housing authority. This includes Hawaii, Alaska, the Virgin Islands, and Guam. These are all treated specially because of a long time exception to the regulation. In Hawaii for example, four of its five counties have the highest limits for jumbo loan cutoffs. They range from $657,800 to $721,050.

Obtaining a jumbo mortgage involves some extra paperwork and proofs. Underwriting for these jumbo types is much the same as with standard conforming mortgages. There are more requirements for appraisals and down payments than with smaller mortgages. Some jumbo mortgage lenders have a requirement for two appraisals rather than the standard single one.

Down payments are also often more demanding for jumbos than for the traditional mortgages. Usually these lenders will want a higher down payment to ensure the individual can really afford and is committed to the loan. The minimum down payments for these more expensive home purchases will vary with each lender. They might be as high as 30%, or they could be as low as 15% to 20%.

Only applicants with significant finances need apply for these jumbo loans. A great number of their lenders require a minimum high credit score of 700 or better. They also insist on a debt to income ratio that does not exceed 43%. These lenders will want to see minimally from six to twelve months' cash reserves in bank accounts as well.

Jumbo loans are not only made to individuals for their primary residences. Lenders will also issue them for vacation or second homes. Investment properties may also involve jumbo loans. They come with a wide range of terms and interest rates.

Jumbo loans can be issued as adjustable rate loans or fixed rate loans. They often come with higher interest rates than individuals would pay for conforming loans or for high balance conforming home loans. Sometimes in addition to the bigger down payment the underwriting standard will be stricter as well.

Junk Bonds

Junk bonds are almost the same as regular bonds with an important difference. They are lower rated for credit worthiness. This is why in order to understand junk bonds, individuals first must comprehend the basics of traditional bonds.

Like traditional bonds, junk bonds are promises from organizations or companies to pay back the holder the amount of money which they borrow. This amount is known as the principal. Terms of such bonds involve several elements. The maturity date is the time when the borrower will repay the bond holder. There will also be an interest rate that the bond holder receives, or a coupon. Junk bonds are unlike those traditional ones because the credit quality of the issuing organization is lower.

Every kind of bond is rated according to its credit quality. Bonds can all be categorized in one of two types. Investment grade bonds possess medium to low risk. Their credit ratings are commonly in the range of from AAA to BBB. The downside to these bonds is that they do not provide much in the way of interest returns. Their advantage is that they have significantly lower chances of the borrower being unable to make interest payments.

Junk bonds on the other hand offer higher interest yields to their bond holders. Issuers do this because they do not have any other way to finance their needs. With a lower credit rating, they can not borrow capital at a more favorable price. The ratings on such junk bonds are often BB or less from Standard & Poor's or Ba or less by Moody's rating agency. Bond ratings such as these can be considered like a report card for the credit rating of the company in question. Riskier firms receive lower ratings while safe blue-chip companies earn higher ratings.

Junk bonds typically pay an average yield that is from 4% to 6% higher than U.S. Treasury yields. These types of bonds are placed into one of two categories. These are fallen angels and rising stars. Fallen angels bonds used to be considered at an investment grade. They were cut to junk bond level as the company that issued them saw its credit quality decline.

Rising stars are the opposites of fallen angels. This means the rating of the bond has risen. As the underlying issuer's credit quality improves, so does the rating of the bond. Rising stars are often still considered to be junk bonds. They are on track to rise to investment quality.

Junk bonds are risky for more reasons than the chances of not receiving one or more interest payments. There is the possibility of not receiving the original principal back. This type of investing also needs a great amount of skills in analyzing data like special credit. Because of these risk factors and specialized skills that are needed, institutional investors massively dominate the market.

A better way for individuals to become involved with junk bonds is through high yield bond funds. Professionals research and manage the holdings of these funds. The risks associated with a single bond defaulting are greatly reduced. They do this by diversifying into a variety of companies and types of bonds. High yield bond funds often require investors to stay invested for minimally a year or two.

When the yield of junk bonds declines below the typical 4% to 6% spread above Treasuries, investors should be careful. The risk does not become less in these cases. It is that the returns no longer justify the dangers in the junk bonds. Investors also should carefully consider the junk bond default rates. These can be tracked for free on Moody's website.

Lease

Leases are contracts made between an owner, or lessor, and a user, or lesee, covering the utilization of an asset. Leases can pertain to business or real estate. There are a variety of different types of leases that vary with the property in question being leased.

Tangible property and assets are leased under rental agreements. Intangible property leases are much like a license, only they have differing provisions. The utilization of a computer program or a cell phone service's radio frequency are two example of such an intangible lease.

A gross lease is another type of lease. In a gross lease, a tenant actually gives a certain defined dollar amount in rent. The landlord is then responsible for any and all property expenses that are routinely necessary in owning the asset. This includes everything from washing machines to lawnmowers.

You also encounter leases that are cancelable. Cancelable leases can be ended at the discretion of the end user or lessor. Other leases are non cancelable and may not be ended ahead of schedule. In daily conversation, a lease denotes a lease that can not be broken, while a rental agreement often can be canceled.

A lease contract typically lays out particular provisions concerning both rights and obligations of the lessor and the lessee. Otherwise, a local law code's provisions will apply. When the holder of the lease, also known as the tenant, pays the arranged fee to the owner of the property, the tenant gains exclusive use and possession of the property that is leased to the point that the owner and any other individuals may not utilize it without the tenant's specific invitation. By far the most typical type of hard property lease proves to be the residential types of rental agreements made between landlords and their tenants. This type of relationship that the two parties establish is also known as a tenancy. The tenant's right to possess the property is many times referred to as the leasehold interest. These leases may exist for pre arranged amounts of time, known as a lease term. In many cases though, they can be terminated in advance, although this does depend on the particular lease's terms and conditions.

Licenses are similar to leases, but not the same thing. The main difference between the two lies in the nature of the ongoing payments and termination. When keeping the property is only accomplished by making regular payments, and can not be terminated unless the money is not paid or some form of misconduct is discovered, then the agreement is a lease. One time uses of or entrances to property are licenses. The defining difference between the two proves to be that leases require routine payments in their term and come with a particular date of ending.

Lease-to-Own Purchase

A Lease-to-Own Purchase is a combination of a lease on a house with a purchase option on the home. This option is valid for a specific amount of time, typically for 3 years or less. The price for the purchase is agreed on in advance and is a part of the contract. These types of arrangements became far more common after the housing crisis and Great Recession. Many individuals who wanted to buy a house could no longer qualify for the stricter loan requirements. This also impacted sellers who could not obtain a selling price with which they were satisfied by any other means.

With a Lease-to-Own Purchase, the contract is typically designed and provided by the seller. The benefits of the arrangement can be set up to provide advantages to both buyer and seller parties. They might also be arranged so that the majority or even all of the benefits accrue to one side. This means that buyers should beware before entering such an agreement. It is wise for them to share the contract with a real estate attorney before they sign.

In a traditional Lease-to-Own Purchase contract, borrowers first pay an option fee that goes against the cost of buying the house. This generally amounts to from 1% to 5% of the home price. The renter will also pay a fair market value rent alongside a rent premium that also goes towards the price of buying the house. Everything is negotiable in these contracts, including option period, option fee, rent premium, rent, and the price of the house. Should the purchase option not be exercised by the renter, then he or she forfeits the rent premium and the option fee to the seller.

Buyers will naturally want a longer option period. This gives them a greater amount of time in which to repair their credit and save up money for a down payment. The downside to a longer option period in a Lease-to-Own Purchase comes into play if they can not exercise the option to buy. In this case, the renters forfeit both the option fee and the monthly rent premium which they have paid continuously. Sellers will want a shorter time period on the option. If they make it too short, they will be unable to sell the house to the renter.

It is possible for a Lease-to-Own Purchase to work out to be a win-win situation for both parties. The rent premium and option fee to the buyers represent equity they are paying into the house which they expect to buy. Such payments are compensation towards a guarantee for the seller that the house will sell. The seller will get to keep the additional payments as income if the buyer is unable to obtain the mortgage needed to purchase the property.

Some Lease-to-Own Purchase contracts will provide the renter with the ability to sell their option to another party. Such an option gives buyers additional confidence in the deal in the event that they are unable to personally exercise their buying option. This is a concession from sellers who would rather keep the house along with the fees they have collected. Some lease contracts will also have clauses that can cancel the buyer's option. These are often set as penalties for late rent payments.

One advantage to leasing the house before buying it lies in buyer awareness. The renters have time to consider any significant problems with the house, neighbors, or the neighborhood before they commit. If these are substantial issues, the buyers are able to cut their losses and not go through with the buying option.

Ledger

A Ledger is also often called a general ledger. It refers to a firm's set of (numbered) accounts that it maintains for its corporate accounting records. With such a record, the firm has a full history of all its financial transactions it has entered into throughout the entire existence of the firm. In this master set of company books, the firm keeps all of the necessary information it must have to compile its financial statements. The data will always cover such useful facts and figures as liabilities, assets, cash flow and positions, revenues, expenses, profits, and owners' equity.

Accountants work with these general ledgers as part of their book keeping system for drawing up the company financial statements. All transactions must be included in the master document. Accountants will first pursue creating a trial balance. This represents a report of all account balances and the corresponding accounts. It is this adjusted trial balance which will be employed to create all relevant corporate financial statements.

These general ledgers are employed continuously by those firms which utilize the method of book keeping known as the double entry system. In such a methodology of accounting, every financial transaction will impact minimally two different ledgers and accounts. It also signifies that every entry will have an equal and opposite credit and debit transaction. Such double entries will be arrayed in two separate columns. Generally the debit postings will be to the left while the credit entries will be posted to the right column. It is imperative that all credit and debit entries balance out all the time.

It helps to look at a concrete example to better understand this challenging concept. When a customer pays a $300 invoice, the cash account will rise. The accountant will book a $300 credit to cash. At the same time, he or she will then log a $300 debit on the other column for the accounts receivable. In this way, both the credits and debits will equal out.

There are four key financial statements which accountants can produce from these general ledgers. The balance sheet is one of them. Under balance sheets there are sub divisions including accounts receivable and cash accounts reports. The formula for any balance sheet proves to be assets minus liabilities equals equity. The one cash account in the example above gains by $300 while the accounts receivable category becomes reduced by the amount of $300. Thanks to this simultaneous increasing and decreasing of the balance sheet equation left side, the equation will stay in perfect balance.

A second critical financial report which is impacted by the general ledgers proves to be the income statement. It also has a formula, which amounts to revenue minus expenses equals net income (also called profit). It is crucial that this formula similarly remains balanced for the financial statements to be correct. A single given transaction might also affect both the income statement and the balance sheet. Consider another example. Firms might bill their clients $750. They would note a $750 debit on to the accounts receivable category. At the same time, they would put up a $750 credit on to the revenue (or cash) categories. Both the credits and debits grow by $750 this way. The two totals remain in balance.

This double entry accounting contrasts with single entry accounting methods. In either methodology of book keeping, the common element will be the accountant or book keeper working with a general ledger of some type.

Lender

Lenders are individuals or more commonly institutions that loan out money. The person who receives this money is a borrower. A number of different kinds of lending organizations exist. These include commercial, mutual organizations, educational, hard money, and lenders of last resort.

Commercial lenders are the most common of the traditional lenders. Commercial types are usually banks. Another kind of commercial lender would be a private financial organization. Commercial lenders provide offers on their loans to their borrowers at a set rate of loan terms. Such terms include time frame of the loan and the interest rate. Their goal is to make as much money as possible relative to the chances of the borrower not repaying the loan.

Mutual organizations are another type of lender. They are composed of members of the mutual who cooperate together to loan money to the membership. The members pool their money into the organization. From there it is loaned out to the members who need to borrow money. They do this with favorable terms and at advantageous rates.

Mutual organizations are not driven to make profits. This allows them to offer lower interest rates on the loans they make and higher interest rates on the deposits they take. Among these mutual groups are community based credit unions. Friendly Societies are another example of them.

Educational lenders provide loans to individuals who are looking to further their education at an institution of higher learning like a college or university. They offer borrowers subsidized or unsubsidized loans. When the loans are subsidized, the Federal Government guarantees the loans and ensures that the lender provides a low and often fixed interest rate.

Hard money lenders make special types of loans that are short term. These are loans principally secured by real estate collateral. The downside to this kind of a lender is that they often provide higher interest rates than a traditional commercial bank. The tradeoff is that they will often take on a larger variety of deals.

Typically these hard money lenders give terms that are more flexible to their borrowers. Some states have stricter laws on interest rates that may be charged than does the Federal government. This forces hard money lenders to operate under different rules and with lower interest rates when they are in conflict with usury laws in give states.

Many times these loans that lenders make to individuals become brokered loans. In such cases, third parties consider the borrower's case then send the loan request out to a variety of lenders. This is often done over the Internet. They pick these different lenders because of their chance of approving the borrower in question. Sometimes the terms can be improved by one or more of these competing lenders in order to win over the borrower's business.

Lenders of last resort are an interesting final category. They are often governmental organizations whose goal is to save national economies and important banks from failure. These types of organizations loan money out to too big to fail banks which are close to collapse. They do this to safeguard the bank's depositors and to prevent panic from pushing the nation's economy into a downward spiral.

Lenders of last resort can also be private organizations that make loans to individuals. These groups loan out money to borrowers who present great risks of default or who have extremely low credit scores. Interest rates with these lenders are substantially higher than with traditional lenders. They charge these rates in order to make up for the losses they suffer from their borrower's greater default rates. Such lenders that charge even higher rates are sometimes known as loan sharks.

Lender of Last Resort

Lender of Last Resort refers to an official central financial institution which provides emergency loans to commercial and savings banks as well as other financial institutions which are suffering from extreme financial hardship or are believed to be nearing collapse. Generally such a lender turns out to be a national central bank. Within the U.S., it is the Federal Reserve which functions as the last case lender to those institutions which find themselves without any other way to borrow funds quickly. Their inability to gain access to funds and credit could lead to a devastating consequence for the greater economy in general. This is why the central banks will provide credit extensions on an expedited basis to those financial institutions which are undergoing extreme financial stress and so in consequence cannot get funds from anywhere else.

The principal job of such a Lender of Last Resort is to maintain the financial system stability and the banking system integrity through safeguarding the deposited funds of individuals and businesses. This is critical to foster confidence in the financial system and to prevent wholesale panic from taking hold of depositors who might otherwise cause runs on the banks by attempting to draw out all of their funds at once. Such an action would create an illiquidity event for the bank and force them to close their doors.

It has been over a century and a half since central banks made it their missions to head off great depressions through being the effective Lenders of Last Resort when financial crises erupted. The action does deliver the liquidity funds with a penalty interest rate. As open market operations take over the funding facility, the interest rate drops for safe assets as collateral. The process also includes direct support to the market.

Commercial banks do not enjoy borrowing from the Lender of Last Resort at any time. It would be a sure fire warning that the bank was undergoing financial stress or even experiencing a crisis of liquidity and a crisis of confidence would next follow. This is the reason that critics of this type of arrangement feel that it tempts banks into taking on a higher level of risk than they should in a form of moral hazard. This could happen because they believe that consequences for engaging in risky financial behavior will not be so severe.

The alternatives to a trustworthy central banking institution not functioning as a Lender of Last Resort can be serious. Bank runs are what result in times of financial crisis when the customers of banks begin to show concern over the solvency of their home financial institution. These customers can be seized with sudden panic and descend en masse on the bank demanding to withdraw all of their funds when confidence in the individual bank or the banking system as a whole erupts.

Banks only maintain s tiny percentage of their deposited funds on hand in their vaults. This is how a bank run can result in the liquidity of a bank rapidly disappearing. Literally these panicked customer actions can set into motion a self-fulfilling prophecy which leads to the bank failing as a result of insolvency.

This actually occurred in 1929 and throughout the 1930s. Bank runs led to catastrophic and widespread bank failure throughout the United States after the 1929 stock market crashes. This snowballed into the Great Depression which gripped the country and developed world economies for the next roughly fifteen years. The American federal government responded too late with tough new legislation which mandated severe reserve requirements on the banks. It required by law that they keep a specific minimum percentage of their deposits as available cash reserves.

Liabilities

Where a business is concerned, liabilities prove to be amounts of money that are owed by the company at any given point. These liabilities are displayed on the firm's balance sheet. They are commonly listed as items payable, or simply as payables.

There are two types of liabilities. These are longer term liabilities and shorter term liabilities. Long term liabilities turn out to be business obligations that last for greater than the period of a single year. Mortgages payable and loans payable are included in this category.

Short term liabilities represent business obligations that will be paid in less than a year. There are many different kinds of short term liabilities. They include all of the items detailed below.

Payroll taxes payable are one of these. They represent sums automatically collected from the employees and put to the side by the employer. They have to be given to the IRS and any state taxing agencies at the pre determined time.

Sales taxes payable are another short term liability. The business collects them from its customers when sales are made. They hold them until it is time to give them to the proper revenue collecting department within the state.

Mortgages and loans payable are another short term liability. These represent payments made every month on mortgages and loans. They are not large single payments or the total amount of a loan that is eventually owed, but instead represent recurring monthly obligations.

Liabilities for individuals are another type of liabilities altogether. They also represent money that has to be paid out. For people, they are debts owed, as well as monthly cash flow that goes out of the individual's accounts.

Liabilities and assets are the opposites of each other, yet people often get them confused. While assets are things that contribute positive cash flow to a person's finances, liabilities are those that create negative cash flow, or money that leaves an individual's accounts every month. For example, a house that an individual owes money on and makes monthly payments on is a liability, not an asset. The house takes money from the person in the form of monthly mortgage payments each month. For a house to be an asset, it would have to be completely paid off. Even still, if monthly taxes and insurance payments are being made, then technically it would still be a liability. Houses can only be assets really and truly when they are rented out and the rental income that a person receives is greater than all of the expenses associated with the house every month, including any mortgage payments, taxes, insurance, upkeep, and property management fees. When the net result of a property is money coming in, then it is an asset and not a liability.

Lien

A lien is a claim on one individual's property by another person or entity. The party that holds the lien is able to recover the property if a debtor will not follow through with making payments. There are also other circumstances in which liens would allow the lien holder to take the property. Mortgages on houses or buildings prove to be one kind these. Vehicle loans for a business or individual represent other types that are put on the value of the vehicle. When the obligation is paid off, the lien becomes discharged.

Before individuals are able to receive their money after the sale of an asset like a car or house, the lien must be paid off first. With a vehicle, this means that the lender will not send out the title until they receive complete repayment of the principal.

The majority of liens allow for the individuals or businesses to utilize the property as they are paying it. There are scenarios where the lender or creditor physically holds the property while the borrower is making payments. These are a part of bankruptcy procedures as well because they are secured loans with debt repayment rules that have to be addressed in a case.

While there are a number of different types of liens, the most typical one is on a vehicle. Individuals buy a car from the dealer. The bank loans the money and secures the loan. They do this by placing a vehicle lien which allows them to hold on to the automobile's title. The lender files a UCC-1 form to record this. So long as the debtor continues to make payments, the loan will be paid off finally. The bank would then release to the individual the title.

If the individuals stop making their payments, the bank is able to take possession of the vehicle back while still holding the title. If the vehicle owners choose to sell the automobile when they still owe principal, they must clear the bank loan in order to obtain the title. Without the title, a person can not sell the vehicle.

There are a variety of different types of liens in the world. Consensual ones are those which individuals voluntarily accept when they buy something. Non consensual ones are also known as statutory. These come from a court process where an entity places a lien on assets because bills have not been paid. Three of these are fairly common.

A tax lien occurs when individuals do not pay local, state, or federal income taxes. These are put on the offender's property. A judgment lien comes as a result of a case in a small claims court. When a court gives a judgment to one party, the offending party might refuse to pay. In this case the court will place a judgment lien on the offender's property.

A mechanic or contractor lien happens when a contractor performs a job for a home owner. If the owner refuses to pay, the contractor can ask a court to place a lien on the property in question. This would have to be paid off along with other security interests before the property owner is able to sell.

Liquidation

The meaning of liquidation depends on the use of the word. In financial terms, there are three different definitions of it. In economics or finance it refers to a failed company. A company that is insolvent is unable to pay its bills when they are owed. Liquidation is the process of winding up the company. The operations of the company cease at this point. The assets would then be divided up among its creditors and stock holders. This is done based on whose claims have priority.

Insolvent companies that choose to go into liquidation generally do so under U.S. bankruptcy code Chapter 7. This legal statute gives the rules on liquidation of companies. Companies that are still solvent but are in trouble may also file a Chapter 7 bankruptcy. This is less common. There are also bankruptcies for companies that do not force liquidation. One such provision that covers this scenario is Chapter 11. In a Chapter 11 filing the trustee saves the company and restructures its debts.

When the process of liquidation occurs, the company halts all operations. All of its assets are tallied up and then distributed to the various claimants. After this is finished, the trustee finally dissolves the business. The debts actually have not been discharged in this process. They still exist to the point where the statute of limitations on the debts expires. There is no debtor in existence to pay off these debts. Creditors simply write them off in practice.

The assets in this liquidation process are handled in a certain methodical way. The Department of Justice appoints a trustee. This individual supervises the process. Assets are distributed to those who have claims based on their priority. Secured creditors are first in line. This is because their loans are backed up by collateral.

The lenders are allowed to seize this collateral and then to sell it. Many times they receive far less than the actual asset value because there are limited time frames. Sometimes the assets are not enough to cover their debt. These creditors are compensated from any other liquid assets in this case.

Unsecured creditors come next in the process. In this category are holders of bonds, the IRS, and employees. Bond holders are a form of unsecured creditors. The company may owe the IRS taxes. Employees may be waiting on payroll or other money they are due. The last category to receive compensation is shareholders. If any assets are left they receive them. Preferred stock investors receive priority before the common stock holders. Usually there is nothing left for either class by the time the creditors are paid.

Another definition of liquidation surrounds huge sales. Sometimes a company needs to close out a great deal of inventory. They would do this by liquidating their inventory at deep discounts. Any company can do this. They do not have to file for bankruptcy in order to sell off inventory.

A third definition of liquidation involves closing out an investment. This generally occurs when an investors sells their holdings in exchange for cash. An individual might also liquidate out of a one position and into an opposite one. If he or she held long shares in a stock, they could instead take on the identical number of short shares.

Brokers can force liquidate trader positions in certain cases. Traders who have acted or traded recklessly with risk can have this happen. If traders' account values drop below the minimum margin requirements they can suffer from forced liquidation as well.

Liquidation Value

Liquidation Value represents the full value of a corporation's complete range of physical assets if and when it declares bankruptcy or actually goes out of business. This value is compiled when every asset on the company books and balance sheet becomes tallied up. This value then includes real estate, equipment, factories, fixtures, and inventory. Those assets that are intangible would never be a part of the firm's final liquidating value.

This is one of four key types of value assigned to a corporation or company's various assets. These include book value, market value, salvage value, and liquidation value. With every category of value, this delivers an alternative view point for both analysts and accountants alike to classify the total value of all assets. For individuals and investors who engage in workouts and bankruptcies, this Liquidating Value is absolutely essential to know.

Book value and market value generally vie for the crown of largest assets' category valuation. In cases where any group of assets' market value has deteriorated because of decreasing market demand instead of the business using it up, this proves to be true. With book value, the asset value equates to the one declared upon the corporate balance sheet. Since the company balance sheet declares these assets for their historical price and cost, this means that the book value could equate to more or less than the relevant market prices which apply on a given day. When the all around economy is growing and prices in general are rising, then this book value is traditionally less than the relevant market value.

With liquidation value, the sum represents the anticipated price for the asset after it has been sold, generally for a loss as compared the original price. Salvage value refers to the one assigned to the assets once they reach the conclusion of their natural and useful life. This then would represent the scrap value of assets. Liquidation value typically proves to be less than the book and market values yet still higher than basic salvage value. Liquidating assets are still valuable, they just sell for less than they otherwise should and would because of the proverbial fire sale in a shortened time frame. It causes them to be sold for losses versus their listed book value.

There are reasons why such liquidation values never include any intangible asset prices. Such intangible assets comprise the goodwill, intellectual property, and brand recognition of the company or corporation. When firms are sold off instead of being liquidated, the firm's value will include both intangible assets' value and liquidation value. This is why traditional value investors will consider and contemplate the variances between the ongoing concern value and the market cap value. They are able to decide this way whether or not the stock of the corporation represents a good value.

It is always useful to consider an example in order to clarify the concept of liquidation value. A given corporation the Snappy Pop Company has $550,000 in liabilities. They also possess book valued assets of $1 million on their company balance sheet. The auction value of these assets might be $750,000, which represents three-quarters of their fair value. At the same time, the salvage value is $75,000. To determine the liquidation value, analysts simply subtract out any liabilities (in this case $550,000) off of the auction value (in this case $750,000). This gives a value of $750,000 minus $550,000 for a grand total of $200,000 liquidating value.

Loan Modification

A loan modification proves to be a set of changes on the original terms and conditions of a mortgage loan agreement. These must be agreed to by both the borrower and the lender. The housing crisis of 2007 caused many American homeowners to be on the verge of foreclosure. The numbers of imminent and in process foreclosures increased dramatically.

Loan modifications were amended to be a means for home owners to stay out of foreclosure and keep their houses. The process is not simple or quick, and it can be time consuming. Consumers also have to watch out for scams that prey on the vulnerable owners of homes.

Before the financial crisis erupted, a loan modification turned out to be a means for borrowers to ask for better interest rates on their mortgages without having to undergo an entire refinancing ordeal. Every mortgage company did not offer them. The ones that featured these would provide them for a cost to borrowers on the condition that their mortgage had not been resold to another firm. Now they are far more commonplace since lenders needed unorthodox solutions to help homeowners who were struggling to keep up with their payments and avoid foreclosure.

For the process of a loan modification to begin, the borrower must first request such a change to the loan terms. These changes once only affected the interest rate and made them lower. The more recent packages offered since the Great Recession are even able to change adjustable rate mortgages into standard fixed rate types. It is possible that a lender could suggest such a change to its borrowers as a possibility. Usually the borrowers initiate the process by determining they can not keep up with their loan payments and asking for help and a modification.

The next step is for the lender to consider the borrower's request. They are not required to agree to these petitions. A great number of lenders have very strict guidelines on which borrowers they will approve for modifications and which they will not. This is the case even when the homeowner has foreclosure looming. It is partly because such modification programs were not created to save home owners from rising adjustable interest rates or payments they could not handle. They were made to create a cheaper way of refinancing down to better interest rates. Each lender makes its own rules for which modifications they will accept and which they will reject.

Finally the lender will decide whether to approve or reject the modification request. They will then notify the borrower in writing. Many borrowers are rejected because they have been late with their mortgage payments frequently or too recently. Other lenders might not be in possession of the original loan any more. Whatever the reason is, the lender will state this in the letter.

If the request for modification gains approval, the request goes through to the department that handles loan servicing. There the loan will be modified to the new terms and conditions. Usually this will only reduce the interest rate and not change the loan's amortization. It may require several payment periods before these changes take effect. This is why borrowers should always keep making the payments in the amount and time for which they are scheduled.

Mortgage Backed Obligations (MBO)

Mortgage Backed Obligations are also called mortgage backed securities, or MBS. These are real estate-based financial instruments. They represent an ownership stake in a pool of mortgages. They can also be called a financial security or obligation for which mortgages underlie the instrument.

Such a security offers one of three different means for the investor getting paid. It might be that the loan becomes paid back utilizing principal and interest payments that come in on the pool of mortgages which back the instrument. This would make them pass through securities. A second option is that the security issuer could provide payments to the investing party independently of the incoming cash flow off of the borrowers. This would then be a non-pass through security. The third type of security is sometimes referred to as a modified-pass through security. These securities provide the security owners with a guaranteed interest payment each month. This happens whether or not the underlying incoming principal and interest payments prove to be sufficient to cover them or not.

Pass-through securities are not like non-pass through securities in key ways. The pass through ones do not stay on the issuer of the securities' or originators' balance sheets. Non-pass through securities do stay on the relevant balance sheet. With these non pass through variants, the securities are most frequently bonds. These became mortgage backed bonds. Investors in the non-pass through types often receive extra collateral as a letter of credit, guarantees, or more equity capital. This type of credit enhancement is delivered by the insurer of the mortgage backed obligation. The holder of the MBO will be able to count on the security which underlies the instruments in the event that the repayments the pools of mortgages make are not enough to cover the payments (or fail altogether) for the bond holder investors.

These offerings of Mortgage Backed Obligations, Mortgage Backed Bonds, or Mortgage Backed Securities are all ultimately backed up by mortgage pools. Analysts and investors usually call these securitized mortgage offerings. When such types of investments are instead backed up by different kinds of assets and collateral then they have another name. An example of this is the Asset Backed Securities or Asset Backed Bonds.

They are backed up with such collateral as car loans, credit card receivables, or even mobile home loans. Sometimes they are referred to as Asset Backed Commercial Paper when the loans that underlie them are short term loan pools.

With these Mortgage Backed Obligations, they are often grouped together by both risk level and maturity dates. Issuers, investors, and analysts refer to this grouping as tranches, which are the risk profile-organized groups of mortgages. These complicated financial instrument tranches come with various interest rates, mortgage principle balances, dates of maturity, and possibilities of defaulting on their repayments. They are also highly sensitive to any changes in the market interest rates. Other economic scenarios can dramatically impact them as well. This is particularly true of refinance rates, rates of foreclosure, and the home selling rates.

It helps to look at a real world example to understand the complexity of Mortgage Backed Obligations and Collateralized Mortgage Obligations like these. If John buys an MBO or CMO that is comprised of literally thousands of different mortgages, then he has real potential for profit. This comes down to whether or not the various mortgage holders pay back their mortgages. If just a couple of the mortgage-paying homeowners do not pay their mortgages while the rest cover their payments as expected, then John will recover not only his principal but also interest. On the other hand, if hundreds or even thousands of mortgage holders default on their payments and then fall into foreclosure, the MBO will sustain heavy losses and will be unable to pay out the promised returns of interest and even the original principal to John.

Mortgage Backed Securities (MBS)

Mortgage backed securities turn out to be a special kind of asset which have underlying collections of mortgages or individual mortgages that back them. To be qualified as an MBS, the security also has to be qualified as rated in one of two top tier ratings. Credit ratings agencies determine these ratings levels.

These securities generally pay out set payments from time to time which are much like coupon payments. Another requirement of MBS is that the mortgages underlying them have to come from an authorized and regulated bank or financial institution.

Sometimes mortgage backed securities are called by other names. These include mortgage pass through or mortgage related securities. Interested investors buy or sell them via brokers. The investments have fairly steep minimums. These are generally $10,000. There is some variation in minimum amounts depending on which entity issues them.

Issuers are either a GSE Government Sponsored Enterprise, an agency company of the federal government, or an independent financial company. Some people believe that government sponsored enterprise MBS come with less risk. The truth is that default and credit risks are always prevalent. The government has no obligation to bail out the GSEs when they are in danger of default.

Investors who put their money into these mortgage backed securities lend their money to a business or home buyer. Using an MBS, regional banks which are smaller may confidently lend money to their clients without being concerned whether the customers can cover the loan itself. Thanks to the mortgage backed securities, banks are only serving as middlemen between investment markets and actual home buyers.

These MBS securities are a way for shareholders to obtain principal and interest payments out of mortgage pools. The payments themselves can be distinguished as different securities classes. This all depends on how risky the various underlying mortgages are rated within the MBS.

The two most frequent kinds of mortgage backed securities turn out to be collateralized mortgage obligations (CMOs) and pass throughs. Collateralized mortgage obligations are comprised of many different pools of securities. These are referred to as tranches, or pieces. Tranches receive credit ratings. It is these credit ratings which decide what rates the investors will receive. The securities within a senior secured tranche will generally feature lesser interest rates than others which comprise the non secured tranche. This is because there is little actual risk involved with senior secured tranches.

Pass throughs on the other hand are set up like a trust. These trust structures collect and then pass on the mortgage payments to the investors. The maturities with these kinds of pass throughs commonly are 30, 15, or five years. Both fixed rate mortgages and adjustable rate ones can be pooled together to make a pass through MBS.

The pass throughs average life spans may end up being less than the maturity which they state. This all depends on the amount of principal payments which the underlying mortgage holders in the pool make. If they pay larger payments than required on their monthly mortgages, then these pass through mortgages could mature faster.

Mortgage Insurance

Mortgage Insurance refers to a policy that helps would-be homeowners to buy a house with a smaller amount of down payment than traditional bank mortgages require upfront. It is these large typically 20 percent down payments that keep many people from the American dream of home ownership. Such insurance is also known by its popular acronym MI.

Thanks to private mortgage insurance, individuals are able to buy a house and put down a smaller amount than 20 percent. Most lenders and investors alike will insist on such mortgage insurance on any down payment that amounts to under 20 percent. Such MI gives lenders the peace of mind and financial backing that if a loan falls into foreclosure, they will receive financial compensation. This kind of guarantee helps many (if not most) lenders to work with less than the standard 20 percent down payment in home loan scenarios.

The real world application of such MI happens like this. A home buyer wants to purchase a $200,000 house. He is only able to put down 10 percent, amounting to $20,000, for his down payment. The lender will then get the privately issued mortgage insurance on the remaining $180,000 which is the mortgage amount. This will reduce the lender's total exposure from $180,000 down to $150,000. This is because the MI will cover the top 25 percent to 30 percent of the mortgage amount. In this example, the MI has protected 25 percent, or $30,000 beyond the $20,000 down payment, from any end-losses the lender would take in the event of foreclosure on the house. Meanwhile the monthly premiums will become a part of the monthly mortgage payment amount, added on to the monthly amount due for the mortgage repayment.

There can be no doubt of the clear advantages this offers lenders. Yet home buyers also gain from MI in several important ways. The first of these is that they are able to purchase a house far sooner than they would be able to otherwise if they had to save an entire 20 percent standard down payment up themselves. It also boosts their ultimate buying power since they are no longer required to put down a full 20 percent. It is partially refundable according to a pro-rated schedule of premiums when it is cancelled through selling the house before the mortgage has been paid off.

PMI helps to secure quicker approvals for home buyers. Finally, home buyers gain greater cash flow alternatives and flexibility on money that they do not have to put down at closing and tie up with the purchase of the house.

Most MI policies are allowed by the lender to be cancelled out after the loan balance declines to less than 75 percent to 80 percent of the total value of the house. The associated premiums also can be paid according to flexible means with many policies. Some will allow buyers to pay for part or even the entire premium in an initial lump sum during closing so that the monthly premiums will be lower. In either case, the policy can be cancelled when it is no longer needed or the buyer sells the house and pays off the mortgage in the process.

Some lenders will offer to pay the MI premium on the behalf of the home buyer. This is rarely done for free however. The tradeoff to the home buyer is that the lender will boost either the interest rate throughout the life of the mortgage loan or the fees they assess at closing time. This is why it is so critical to understand what the costs are when a lender offers to cover the premium on private mortgage insurance.

Mortgage Modification Package

Mortgage Modification Package refers to an agreement that reduces the homeowners' mortgage payments and possibly overall mortgage debt when they are suffering from significant financial struggles. The idea is to help the borrowers become capable of making their loan payments. This way they can keep their home and not forfeit it in costly foreclosure proceedings.

This does not mean that it is easy to get approved on a Mortgage Modification Package. The mortgage company ultimately will determine if they will allow for such a modification. These changes to the mortgage agreements really are to the advantage of the lender and are often in their best interest. Through helping borrowers to make their payments in a timely fashion, the financial institutions get to keep performing loans and sidestep the tremendous costs, time, and hassle of foreclosing on the property.

The name Mortgage Modification Package describes precisely what occurs in these arrangements. Current mortgage terms become modified so that the interest rate, payments, and overall final balance of the loan are manageable for the borrowers' in question. Amounts which are past due can be paid down either utilizing installments or otherwise can be deferred to the end point of the mortgage. The repayment timeframe of the loan can be extended as well. This lowers the principle payments which are due each month. There are cases where the financial institution will even consent to writing down the remaining loan principle to a manageable amount the borrower can truly afford.

Sometimes these modifications will be temporary. This is often the case where interest rates alone are lowered. They may provide a several year break in the rate that will finally rise back to its original amount. Other times, the lender will permit the borrowers additional time to catch up the late payments without incurring additional fines and fees.

In other scenarios, these modifications can be permanent. This is more common when the financial institutions opt to push out the loan repayment schedule or agree to write down some of the principle which borrowers owe on the mortgage. Without a doubt, such permanent changes to a mortgage are not as easy to receive as are the more temporary in nature ones.

It is not necessarily the financial institution which issued the mortgage loan in the first place which has to approve such a Mortgage Modification Package. Rather the loan servicer is the entity responsible for changing the terms of the loan. This is often another company from the one which extended the mortgage loan upfront.

Loan modifications should never be confused with refinancing, even though they have some similar end results. Both routes will make the payments more affordable in most cases. Yet in order to successfully achieve refinancing, the borrowers will require solid credit and dependable finances. In fact the majority of applicants for loan modifications do not enjoy these significant advantages.

Refinancing is instead actually closing out the existing loan and re-making a new mortgage with which to replace it. The new terms will be more beneficial. Even as borrowers had to qualify for the first mortgage, they must re-qualify for the new one. For some borrowers who are late on or are missing payments altogether (because finances are no longer sufficient to cover the obligations of the mortgage), this will practically rule out qualifying for a traditional refinancing offer.

Mortgage Modification Packages alternatively were purposefully established for those individuals who find themselves in financial straights. They will change the existing mortgage terms in order to help the borrower catch up on late payments and possibly to help make the mortgage terms overall more manageable. This arrangement can be either permanent or temporary.

Negative Interest Rates

Negative interest rates are those that fall below 0%. In the past, negative interest proved to be only a theoretical discussion that economists played around with for the sake of argument. In 2010 Sweden's central bank put these rates into practice as a means of stemming the flow of outside money into the country. Denmark followed suite in 2012. Since then, minor to major central banks have moved into the mostly uncharted waters of these negative rates.

The reason that central banks would be interested in such negative interest rates is that they help the economy. Central banks cutting the rates into negative territory creates a similar effect as simply lowering interest rates. Lower rates help consumers to spend and businesses to invest more.

They also boost prices in the stock markets and other risk assets. They reduce the level of the nation's currency. This helps exports to be more competitive against other country's goods. Finally lower rates cause people to expect higher inflation rates in the future. This encourages consumers to spend their money now as opposed to later when it will be worth less.

The world has many decades of knowledge of what happens when central banks influence economies by reducing rates from 3% to 2% because of downturns in the economy. In theory this shifting to negative interest rates is similar with the difference of a starting point at or below zero.

Such NIRP negative interest rate policies are called unconventional monetary tools. The idea is to move benchmark interest rates into negative territory. Doing so means breaking the centuries' long barrier of 0%.

Deflation is what caused desperate central banks to pursue these negative interest rates and policies. In times where deflation pervades an economy, the businesses and consumers tend to hold their money rather than invest and spend it. Eventually this creates a reduction in total demand that in turn causes prices to fall even more. Output and production slow down and unemployment increases as a result.

Stagnation like this is typically avoided when central banks pursue a loose monetary policy. The problem arises when the deflation becomes so powerful that dropping interest rates to zero is no longer enough to encourage lending and borrowing.

The result of negative interest rates is profound. Central banks charge their commercial banks money (negative interest) in order to keep their deposits at the bank. Commercial banks then pass along these costs to their larger account holders as they are able. The financial institutions have not much stooped to official negative rates on their depositors. Instead they charge fees for keeping money in these current accounts. This amounts to negative rates under the guise of a different name.

Central banks hope that the commercial banks will loan out money instead of paying to hold it. Instead many banks have been paying the fees themselves, and this has impacted bank profits. Banks fear passing along fees to small deposit account holders who may withdraw their money instead.

As of 2016, the negative interest rate policy has been adopted by the European Central Bank, the Swiss National Bank, and the Bank of Japan besides the Scandinavian Central Banks. Early evidence suggests that the Euro zone did manage to reduce interbank loans with the negative interest rates. Companies have not so far much benefited from the negative interest rates. This is because the risk is perceived to be higher with corporations who borrow than with governments. One notable exception is with Nestle the Swiss food conglomerate that has issued negative interest rate corporate bonds.

Overdraft

An Overdraft refers to the extension of credit where a bank or other lending institution allows for debits to be paid after an account has hit zero dollars. Thanks to these overdrafts, individuals are able to keep drawing down the account value below zero, although there is no money left in it or an insufficient amount to resolve the withdrawal. Another layman's definition of this term is when the bank permits its clients to borrow a given sum of money.

When individuals possess an account with overdraft facilities, the bank will courtesy cover any checks that will put it into overdraft instead of returning them unpaid (bouncing them back to the check depositor). Naturally the outstanding overdrawn balance will have interest charged on it, as with any loan. Typically such interest rates prove to be far lower than those offered by credit cards though. Sometimes there may be other fees for utilizing the overdraft protection. This would decrease the overdraft protection amount available. Some of these could be per withdrawal or per check insufficient funds assessed fees.

Such overdrafts on money market savings accounts, regular savings accounts, and checking accounts happen when the customers do not keep sufficient funds within this account to cover the incidents such as check and ATM withdrawal transactions. In order for it to equal an overdraft, the bank will have to be willing to process and cover the transaction regardless of the shortfall of funds.

Many banks will pay overdrafts on four kinds of banking transactions. These include recurring transactions of debt cards, checks and related transactions that rely on the account number, online banking transfers and payments, and auto bill payments.

Banks might decide to utilize their own corporate funds in order to pay a client overdraft. They might also have customers link the overdraft on to one of their credit cards. When banks deploy their own money in order to pay an overdraft, then this does not usually impact a client's credit score. As credit cards are utilized to cover overdrafts, this could increase the client debt to the amount where the credit score became negatively impacted.

This does not directly result from checking account overdrafts however.

The problem comes when the overdrafts do not become repaid in a prearranged time frame. The bank might opt to hand over the account into the hands of a collection agency. Such a collection activity might negatively impact the credit score if it becomes reportable to any or all of the three primary credit agency bureaus of TransUnion, Experian, or Equifax. This comes down to how the collection agency reports its accounts to the agencies. It will determine whether the overdraft protection on a checking account shows up as a problem or not.

Such Overdraft protection will deliver a useful tool to help manage the checking account on a day to day basis. For example, a person might easily forget that they drew out money for a Starbucks or Costa Coffee run. The overdraft protection will make sure that the ATM is not turned down or that the ATM Debit card purchase does not get rejected at the merchant point of sale. Banks will commonly assess an overdraft fee and use this to make money from the convenience they are delivering. This is why such protection should not be too commonly used and over-utilized. Instead it is to be reserved for emergency needs and situations.

Every overdraft protection dollar amount is not equal. Each bank and type of bank account will vary the level of protection they deliver. This could also vary on a case by case basis. When such protection is overused, the bank or other financial institution may simply elect to remove the courtesy off of the bank account. Getting it reactivated after such a penalizing move is never easy.

Personal Assets

Personal assets are items of value that belong to an individual. There are many examples of such tangible personal assets. Among these are houses, real estate, cars, and jewelry. Personal assets can also be any other thing with cash value.

When individuals go to a bank or other institution to apply for loans, such personal assets and their values are often considered. These assets are also the bedrock of the formula for net worth for consumers. The value of people's personal assets can be higher than they expect and surprise them as so many different items can be included under this label.

There are many personal assets that are material and easy to measure. These include such financial assets as savings accounts, checking accounts, and retirement accounts. Assets that have a value that can not be easily accessed are also included in the personal assets category. This includes life insurance policies and annuities that have cash values. Other items of value which would be included in a list of personal assets cover such items as antiques, art collections, electronics, personally owned businesses, and other valuable items.

Personal assets can do more than simply help people get loans and count towards net worth. They are also sometimes able to create income for their owners. Bank accounts and savings accounts accrue interest. Holders of real estate are able to lease or rent it out. This brings in rent or lease fees. Individuals who have personal assets should educate themselves in the best practices for managing them so that they are able to increase their total wealth by generating the highest income possible from them.

It is important to keep a careful track of rent or other income obtained from personal assets as the money will be taxable. Income that is not properly reported to the government on the correct tax forms can incur penalties from the Internal Revenue Service.

It is also important to know the value of an individual's personal assets. There are two different methods of learning this. In the first method, individuals examine the item's market value. This is the value for which the asset would sell if a person were to put it straight on the market. Another way to determine the value of these assets is to have a personal asset appraised.

Appraised values can be substantially greater than market values. This is because an appraisal value relies on the possible future price of the item in question. This difference matter significantly, particularly when having an item insured. Individuals generally have to obtain appraised value insurance coverage. This means that they will likely have to pay for a greater amount of insurance.

When properly managed, personal assets can greatly contribute to an individual's personal financial situation. It is also true that these assets can prove to be a liability if they are not well taken care of or managed. Part of managing assets well involves asset allocation.

Financial experts warn against placing all or the majority of personal assets into a single asset type or location. This type of practice causes people to take on additional risk than is prudent. Instead, it is better to spread around an individual's wealth into a variety of different assets so that if one suffers or decreases in value, some of the other assets may offset this by outperforming or increasing in value.

Taking care of personal assets is also an important part of maintaining their value. Individuals can break expensive electronics if they are not careful. Not engaging in proper maintenance for works of art can also lead to their value declining over time.

Power of Attorney

A power of attorney is an agreement in writing that grants another individual the authority to make some choices if the grantor is not available. This person who receives the power does not have to be an attorney. Attorneys are typically only involved in drafting up or potentially witnessing such an agreement. The phrase comes from an individual receiving status as an agent or attorney in fact.

When people implement such a power of attorney they do not lose the ability to make their own decisions. Instead they are allowing another individual to act for them in matters specified within the written text. This can be very helpful if people are out of the country or in the hospital as an example. Someone else with this authority would be able to cash checks at the bank or pay bills on their behalf. It is simply a matter of sharing power with another person. The agent is only carrying out the grantor's wishes, not actually making choices for them, so long as they are coherent and mentally capable.

People who will be out of town for an extended period of time might find these arrangements particularly useful. With a power of attorney, the agent could carry out major decisions such as selling cars or other personal assets. The Internet has eliminated the need for some of these functions as computers and mobile devices make it possible for people to buy and sell stocks and handle many financial transactions from anywhere they have an online connection. There are still cases where a transaction will require an in person agent to handle them.

There is also a special kind of power of attorney that is used by individuals who lose their ability to handle decisions for their personal financial affairs. This is known as a durable power of attorney. In this case, the word durable refers to the ability of the agent to make the choices on the grantor's behalf when he or she can not mentally do them. This type of arrangement grants the agent the legal authority and responsibility to make the best possible physical and financial decisions for the grantor.

It means that the agent is able to spend the individual's money as appropriate, cash checks, deposit checks, and even withdraw money from the personal bank accounts. The agent further gains the authority to sign contracts, sell personal property, take legal actions, and file and follow up on insurance claims.

When people decide to enter a durable power of attorney arrangement, a notary public or lawyer should witness the document before they sign and execute it. If such individuals need to have a durable agreement established and are not mentally able to do it, courts can do this for them as they deem necessary.

Agents who become appointed to this position are expected to keep correct and segregated records on each transaction they perform. The records must also be easily available at all times. When the individual dies, his or her power of attorney becomes null and void. The will is responsible for the dispensation of the deceased person's estate.

Powers of attorney can be rescinded. If individuals feel unhappy in the ways that their agent is managing their personal affairs, they can simply revoke the authority back at any point. It is always wise for people to choose an individual to be agent whom they know and implicitly trust.

Prime Rate

The Prime Rate is the most typically utilized shorter term interest rate for the United State banking system. All kinds of lending institutions in the United States employ this U.S. benchmark interest rate as a basis or index rate to price their medium term to short term loans and products. This includes credit unions, thrifts, savings and loans, and commercial banks.

This makes the Prime Rate consistent around the country as banks strive to be competitive and profitable in their lending rates which they provide to both consumers and businesses. A universal rate like this simplifies the task for businesses and consumers as they shop around comparable loan products that competing banks offer. Every state in the country does not maintain its own benchmark rate. This makes a California Prime or New York Prime identical to the U.S. Prime.

Commercial and other banks charge this benchmark rate to their best customers. These are those clients who have the best credit ratings and loan history with the bank. Most of the time banks' best clients are made up of large companies.

The prime interest rate is also known as the prime lending rate. Banks typically base it on the Federal Reserve's federal funds rate. This is actually the rate that banks loan money to each other for overnight purposes. Retail customers also need to be aware of the prime lending rate. It directly impacts the lending rates that they can access for personal and small business loans as well as for home mortgages.

The federal government and Federal Reserve Bank do not set the prime lending rates. The individual banks set it. They then utilize this base rate or reference rate to set the prices for a great number of loans such as credit card loans and small business loans.

The Federal Reserve Board releases a statistics called "Selected Interest Rates." This is their survey of the prime interest rate as the majority of the twenty-five biggest banks set it. It is this publication which reveals the Prime Rate periodically. This is why the Federal Reserve does not directly set this important benchmark rate. The banks more or less base it on the target level of the federal funds rate that the Federal Open Market Committee sets and changes at their monthly meetings.

Different banks adjust their prime lending rate at the same time. The point where they change it is generally when the Federal Open Market Committee adjusts their own important Fed Funds Rate. Many publications refer to this periodically changing reference rate as the Wall Street Prime Rate.

A great number of consumer loans as well as commercial loans and credit card rates find their basis in the prime lending rate. Among these are car loans, home equity loans, personal and home lines of credit, and various kinds of personal loans.

The rates above the prime lending rate that banks charge their less then prime (or subprime) customers depend on the credit worthiness of the borrower in question. The banks attempt to correctly ascertain the risk of default for the borrower. For the best credit customers who have lower chances of defaulting, banks can afford to assess them a lower interest rate than others. Customers with higher chances of defaulting on their loans pay larger interest rates because of the risk associated with their loans not being repaid.

As of June 15, 2016, the Federal Open Market Committee voted to maintain its target fed funds rate in a range of from .25% to .5%. As a result of this, the U.S. prime lending rate stayed at 3.5%. Once per month the Federal Reserve committee meets to determine if they will change the fed funds rate.

Principal

Principal has several different meanings. It most commonly pertains to the initial amount of money that a person either invests or borrows with a loan. A secondary meaning has to do with a bond and its face value. Sometimes the word pertains to the owners of a company or the main participants in any type of transaction.

Where borrowing is concerned, this term relates to the upfront amount of any loan. It also is utilized to describe original amounts which the individuals still owe on the loan in question. Looking at a clear example always helps to clarify the concept. When people obtain a $100,000 mortgage, this Principal is the same $100,000. As the individuals pay down $60,000 of this amount, the remainder of $40,000 that is left to pay off is similarly referred to as Principal.

It is the original Principal that decides how much interest borrowers will pay. If borrowers take out a loan with an initial amount equaling $20,000 that comes with a yearly interest rate at seven percent, then they would be required to pay $1,400 in annual interest for each year that the loan remains open. As borrowers pay the monthly payments to the loan servicer, the interest charges for the month will first be paid off. What remains goes toward the initial amount which the individuals borrowed. Paying down this original amount borrowed remains the only means of lowering the interest amount that accrues on a monthly basis.

Another form of mortgage that operates differently has the name of zero principal mortgages. Bankers think of these as interest-only loans. They represent a unique form of financing where the routine monthly payments of the borrower only apply to the loan's interest. This means that the initial loan amount never gets paid down unless the borrower makes extra payments. It also translates to no equity building up in the property which backs the mortgage loan.

Because of this, financial advisors will typically not recommend these types of mortgages to home buyers as they are rarely in the true interest of the purchaser. Despite this fairly obvious assessment, there are a few unusual cases when they could work out for certain people. When a home buyer is starting out on a career path that pays very little initially but will later on earn substantially more in the not too distant future, it could be worthwhile to lock in the home price now while it is lower. Once the income increases apace, the borrowers always have the ability to refinance into a more traditional mortgage which would cover payments on the initial amounts borrowed as well.

Another scenario where these loans make sense relates to unusual and fantastic opportunities for a particular real estate investment deal. When huge returns on investment dollars can be anticipated, it is practical to go with these mortgage's far lower payments that are interest-only. Meanwhile the borrower can plow the additional monthly payment money savings into the exceptional investment opportunity.

Principal also finds use describing the first initial outlay on an investment. This does not take into consideration any interest that builds up or earnings on the investment. Savers might deposit $20,000 at a bank in a savings account with interest. After a number of years, the balance will grow to $21,500. The principal remains the original $20,000 the savers gave the bank. The additional $1,500 will be called interest or earnings on top of this initial outlay.

It is interesting to note that inflation will not change the nominal value of a loan or financial instrument's principal. Yet the effects of inflation do very much reduce the real value of the initial amount.

Recession

A recession is literally defined as the declining of the nation's GDP, or Gross Domestic Product, by a smaller amount than ten percent. This drop in GDP has to occur over greater than a single consecutive quarter in a given year. Gross domestic product stands for the total of all goods and services that a country produces, or the actual total of all business, private, and government spending on the categories of investment, labor, services, and goods.

The terms recession and depression are typically confused and sometimes used interchangeably. They are quite different from each other. Recessions are typically less severe than are depressions. Recessions are generally corrected in significantly less time and with less economic pain for individuals. Depressions furthermore involve drops in GDP of greater than ten percent.

There is no universal consensus on what makes a recession within an economy. Most economists agree on a few different factors that are commonly involved in causing such recessions. Prices might decrease substantially, or alternatively they could go up substantially. The decrease in prices shows that people are spending smaller amounts of money, and this will cause the Gross Domestic Product to go down. Conversely, higher prices can diminish the amounts of public and private spending, similarly causing the Gross Domestic Product to decrease.

As much as governments, individuals, and businesses hate recessions, many economists feel that they are normal for economies to go through, particularly mild ones. They claim that such economic pull backs are a built in part of society and economics. Prices go up and down, and spending and the amount of consumption similarly decreases and increases over time as well. Still, natural decreases in spending are not sufficient to provoke a recession into occurring. Some other factor changes suddenly and leads to sharp spikes or drops in real prices.

For example, the early 2000's recession came about as a result of the dot com industry suddenly and precipitously decreasing in activity. One day, the demand that they had anticipated turned out to be far less than expected. This created enormous failures of companies and significant layoffs that led to production decreases and finally spending cuts. This dot com drop created a shock effect on the gross domestic product, leading to a significant fall in production and output as spending dropped.

The recession had ended by 2003, yet the consequences of it turned out to be dramatic and can still be felt. High paying jobs suddenly disappeared, only to be outsourced to foreign countries. These jobs will likely never return to the United States. Still, as the Gross Domestic Product began growing again, the recession was deemed to have ended. This does not change the fact that numerous individuals still feel the impact of it in their own personal lives.

Similarly, the Great Recession that you saw stem from the financial collapse of 2007-2010 came about as a sudden seizure in the banking industry and credit markets. It has led to the highest levels of real unemployment since the Great Depression, reaching nearly twenty percent when measured by the formula that had been used until President Bill Clinton changed it. Even though this recession has been called over, the unemployment levels have not declined meaningfully. This means that for several more years at least, a great amount of economic pain and hardship will continue to be felt by those countless millions who have lost their jobs in the recession.

Repayment Penalty

A repayment penalty is commonly associated with paying back a loan before the end of its term. If you are contemplating paying off your loan balance in advance of its due date, then you should be aware that a number of loans come with these repayment penalties for liquidating the balance early. Different types of loans utilize different names for these same fees. Repayment penalties can also be called redemption charges, early redemption fees, prepayment penalties, or financial penalties.

The fees associated with repayment penalties vary depending on the loan in question. These repayment penalties are commonly stated as a percentage of the balance that is outstanding when prepayment is offered. Alternatively, they might be figured up as a certain number of months of interest charges. In general, when they are figured up using months of interest, they are comprised of one to two months' interest in fees. The sooner in the loan's life that you choose to repay the loan, the greater amount of charge you can expect to pay. This is because the anticipated interest portion of the loan comprises a great part of the repayment earlier in the loan's time frame. Early repayment penalties might increase the total cost of your loan significantly.

If you wish to avoid a repayment penalty in paying off your loan in advance of the term's end, then you will have to be aware of the loans that come with these fees and the ones that do not. Even if you change a currently existing loan into a loan for debt consolidation, you will have to cover the early repayment penalty if one is in the terms. The only way to avoid early repayment penalties is by selecting loans that specifically do not have ones attached to them. It is ironic that some of the least expensive loans out there do not include repayment penalties for early pay off actions.

Another factor of repayment penalties involves a gradual disappearance of the provision over time. With many mortgages, these repayment penalties gradually go down over the years of the mortgage. After the fifth year, the majority of repayment penalties no longer even apply. In many cases, repayments of as much as twenty percent of the original balance are permitted in a given year without you having to be penalized.

Besides this, there are different kinds of penalties for repayments. Penalties that only apply to your refinancing of the mortgage are called soft penalties. Penalties that include the sale of the house and a refinancing are known as hard penalties.

Repossessed

Repossessed means that an article of personal (or occasionally business) property for which an individual (or business) did not pay for has been reclaimed by the financier or original owner of the asset. There are two cases in which it is commonly utilized. The first is when the real owner of said asset re-acquires the asset in question from the party that borrowed it, leased, or rented it. This could be done whether the asset has been leased, rented, or loaned out without compensation or with it.

In the second case, a lienholder can take possession of the asset from the owner to whom it is registered. This happens in cases where the item was pledged to be collateral on a loan. Some analysts describe the act of repossession as an action which is really self-help for the actual owner in a difficult situation. The party has the rights of ownership to the given real estate or asset, and they simply get it back from the party which formerly had the rights of possession. They do this without having to rely on court proceedings.

Once a property is successfully repossessed, the actual owner is allowed to sell it either via a third party realtor or agent or utilizing a financial institution. In various jurisdictions, there are different rights of repossession that are government-authorized. The authorities also determine how they can execute such repossession in practice.

There are other cases when the lenders are unable to track down their collateral. They also might not be able to obtain it peaceably, or the legal jurisdiction simply may not permit such repossession to occur in the first place. In these cases, the alternative to repossessing something is for the holder of the asset to return the goods before a court ordered judgment mandates it. This is called replevin.

In the United States, laws can allow for repossession of items. Liens refer to the collateral's security interest. Lienholders are the creditors or lenders. Lienholders will have a non-delegatable obligation that states they cannot disturb the peace when they repossess the item. If they do, the repossessed item will be reversed back to the holder of the asset. The entity which ordered the repossession would then be liable for any and all damages. Foreclosure is the name analysts and lenders give when a real estate property is repossessed.

State laws govern the actual act of repossession within the U.S. Creditors who possess security interests in assets are allowed to reclaim possession of such assets when the debtor of the item defaults on his contract which originally established the security interest in the first place. All fifty states and D.C. enacted into law the Uniform Commercial Code Article 9 that allows for repossession of goods when the debtor defaults and such a repossession can occur without breaching the peace. Defaulting means that the one who owes the debt failed to carry out the obligations of the contract. It generally occurs when debtors refuse to or are unable to make their necessary payments in a timely manner or if they do not keep the agreed upon insurance levels current on the item in question.

In particular, a number of American states decided to enact other laws which pertain to repossessing leased or bought motor vehicles. These laws were established to protect consumers from predatory practices of lienholders. Auto lenders have to give opportunities to redeem or reinstate the lease or purchase contracts once their car has been repossessed. Such a reinstatement means that the consumer successfully caught up on all of their overdue amounts along with the repossession expenses of the creditor. Redemption means that the consumer pays off the whole balance remaining on the contract. They would then acquire full and undiluted ownership of the vehicle without any further contractual obligations.

Residual

Residual refers to residual income. Residual income can have several different meanings depending on the context that you use. For an individual, residual income proves to be the money that remains at the end of a month after all financial responsibilities for the month are covered.

These include living costs, taxes, and housing costs. Where business is concerned, residual incomes are the operating income that is additional as compared to the typical minimum amount of operating assets that are controlled. Residual income furthermore refers to passive income that is earned. In this form of the term, it relates to all income that is created as a result of activities that are indirect. These might include royalties, rental income, investment portfolio returns, website revenues, or passively managed businesses, all of which qualify as residual income.

The word residual is a variation on the word residue. Residue means anything that stays behind because of some other substance or cause. So, residual income proves to be additional money made because of another activity like penning a novel and collecting royalties for the sale of every book.

Rental incomes are residual as they remain from the action of buying a house and then renting it to a tenant who pays you a monthly rental fee. Work is involved in this activity, although a property management company can do it on your behalf. The rewards for this rental project can be significant, as you enjoy the continuous rental stream as well as any increases in the value of the real estate property underlying it. Rental income can be utilized to pay for potentially an entire mortgage.

Income from investment portfolios is similarly considered to be residual income. Both dividends and interest are acquired as an additional, passive benefit of possessing stocks, bonds, mutual funds, and other instruments. This residual income is not guaranteed from these investments, but it is common for investors.

A form of residual income that is growing in popularity these days is website, or Internet based, revenues. Internet revenues are commonly those that you make from having advertising on a given website. The dollar value of the advertising is mostly based on the number of visitors to the page. A significant amount of start up work is required to create the website and get it highly ranked on the major search engines. After this, you can see continuous monthly profits that you earn as a result of the advertising, which builds up a residual income. This amount of money could be as little as a few dollars a month to possibly thousands of dollars per month.

A last form of residual income can result from a business. If your company becomes large enough, you may be able to hire a manager to run it. The income that supports you while the manager runs the business is then considered residual income.

Reverse Mortgages

Reverse mortgages are special types of loans. They are limited to homeowners who are at least 62 years old. These mortgages permit the owners to take a portion of their home equity and convert it to cash. The seniors may use these mortgage proceeds in any way that they like.

The government came up with these unique products because they were looking for a way to help out retired individuals who did not have enough income. The idea was that they might unlock the wealth they had built up in their houses to provide for health care, outside home care, or ordinary monthly costs of living.

These loans are referred to as reverse mortgages because the home owners do not send a lender monthly payments. These are the opposite of traditional mortgages. Lenders provide the borrower with payments instead. The home owners have several advantages. They do not have to repay the loan until they either no longer live in the home or sell it. They also do not make any regular monthly payments against the balance of the loan. The borrowers are required to keep up with their homeowners insurance, property taxes, and any association or homeowner fees.

The most common type of reverse mortgages are known as HECM Home Equity Conversion Mortgages. The U.S. HUD Housing and Urban Development designed and oversees these. These are not loans from the government. Rather they are mortgage loans that lenders provide with insurance from the FHA Federal Housing Administration. In these particular types, borrowers accrue a 1.25% insurance fee as part of the balance on the loan. This increases the loan balance annually.

This insurance is useful for two protections. In case the lender can not make the monthly payment, it provides for it. Should the house resale value be insufficient to pay back the final loan balance at the end, it makes the lender whole. The government and its insurance fund would then clear any balance that remained.

These HECMs comprise the majority of such reverse mortgages in the United States. Included in their regulations is that the senior borrowers must undergo third party counseling to help them with all of the documents and agreements.

The other type of reverse mortgage is a Proprietary Reverse Mortgage. The mortgage lenders that provide these also insure them privately. This means that they do not have to follow the regulations as with the HECMs. The majority of firms that offer these mortgages choose to honor the identical consumer protections featured in the HECM program. This means that mandatory counseling is usually a part of their programs.

These types are also known as jumbo reverse mortgages. Seniors with larger value houses go with these kinds since there is a $625,500 maximum loan limit on the government's HECMs. Two companies in the country presently offer these types of PRMs. These are the Orange, California based American Advisors Group and the Tulsa, Oklahoma based America Reverse Mortgage.

Regardless of the type of reverse mortgage, the lenders have to put potential borrowers through a financial assessment before making the loan. This is so that they can be certain the seniors will be able to pay the future homeowners insurance and taxes and afford to live in the house for the loan's life. To do this, lenders consider all of the income streams of the borrower. This includes their Social Security, investments, and any pensions. The home owners are also required to give the lender their tax returns and bank statements so that expenses and income may be properly documented.

Revolving Credit

Revolving Credit refers to lines of credit that customers draw on and then make payments on to their creditors. In order to have such a facility, the debtor must pay a commitment fee. This enables them to utilize the funds on an as-needed basis. Such a facility is typically deployed for operating expenses. It would therefore vary every month according to the present day cash flow requirements of the customer. Both individuals and corporations alike are able to take out these revolving lines of credit.

An agreement would be established upfront between the bank and the customer. Such a contract would guarantee the maximum potential amount that the bank will loan out to the client. Besides the initial commitment fee, there will naturally be interest costs for the corporate borrowers. These are called carry forward charges when the accounts are set up for consumers.

Banks and other financial institutions will contemplate a number of factors concerning the borrower and its ability to repay such a line before these revolving credit lines become issued. Where individuals are concerned, this means that his or her current income, credit score, and stability of employment will all be evaluated. Where organizations and corporations are concerned, the bank will typically review the income statement, balance sheet, and cash flow statement before making its final decision on approval and maximum line amount.

For those business entities and individuals who suffer from commonplace fluctuations in non-anticipated expenses and cash balance fluctuations, this revolving credit can be crucial and even lifesaving. They provide flexibility, versatility, and convenience, though this comes at a cost. The price for this is a more expensive interest rate which banks and lending institutions levy for revolving credit than they do on more traditional installment types of loans. Many times, this revolving credit facility will come alongside interest rates which are variable and can be quickly adjusted as appropriate.

The credit limit proves to be the highest dollar amount which the financial institutions will allow the borrower to draw. While there are many different examples of revolving credit facilities in the market place today, the most frequently cited ones are the personal lines of credit and the home equity lines of credit. These are also called HELOCs.

It is important to understand the differences between revolving credit and installment loans. Installment loans typically involve a pre-determined and –set number of payments which will be made on a monthly or quarterly basis over a fixed amount of time. By contrast, revolving funds only involve interest payments along with fees which are applicable per the contract established between the actual bank and the client.

When an individual or corporation receives this revolving credit line, it means that a customer has been pre-approved for receiving a loan. It is more convenient to use than taking out loans again and again, as one does not need to have his credit reevaluated or a new loan application taken every time they draw upon the revolving facility funds. This is why revolving facilities were created for smaller loans that are shorter term in nature. With more massive sized loans, the banks will want a better laid out structure that comes complete with installment payments.

There are differences between business credit cards and revolving lines of credit. No physical credit card is necessary with revolving credit lines. Also revolving lines do not require a preset purchase or amount. This credit can be transferred into the company or personal account for whatever reason they wish. This makes the revolving facilities more like cash advances with funds immediately available upfront and without questions asked regarding the purchase. The interest rates on revolving facilities are also commonly substantially less than are those associated with even business forms of credit cards.

Run on the Bank

A run on the bank is the vernacular expression for a bank run. Runs on the banks actually happen as a result of many bank customers deciding to take out their deposits at one time. They do this out of fear that the bank is either broke or on its way to becoming insolvent. When runs on the banks get started, they have a tendency to create their own terrible momentum that leads to a self fulfilling prophecy. The more customers who take out their money, the greater the odds of bank default become, which leads to still more customer deposit withdrawals. If this happens long enough, it will likely upset a bank's finances to the point that the bank encounters bankruptcy as a result.

Runs on the bank can often lead to bank panics. These financial crises result from a large number of banks experiencing bank runs all at once. If the bank panics are not dealt with swiftly and convincingly, then a systemic banking crisis can develop. In such a banking crisis that is system wide, it is not uncommon to witness practically all, or even all, of a country's banking capital disappear.

Once this occurs, numerous bankruptcies follow, many times ending up in a deep and painful economic recession or even depression. Bank runs created a great amount of the economic damage that you saw done in the Great Depression. Associated costs of fixing the mess related to a systemic banking crisis are enormous. Over the last forty years, these expenses around the world have averaged fully thirteen percent of the respective countries' Gross Domestic Products in fiscal costs, leading to losses of economic output that averaged twenty percent of Gross Domestic Product.

Runs on the bank are able to be prevented with a few different strategies. Withdrawals can be suspended. More effectively, deposit insurance systems can be put in place, like the one that the Federal Deposit Insurance Corporation operates in the United States. The Central Bank may also help out banks by performing the function of the lender of last resort in times of banking crises. Such strategies are commonly effective, but not always. Even when countries possess deposit insurance, the bank depositors could still be fearful that they will not have instant access to their bank held deposits while the bank is reorganized by the FDIC.

The reason that runs on the bank are able to happen in the first place is because of the fractional reserve banking system. Modern day banks only keep a small percentage of their demand deposits in cash on hand, typically ten percent in developed nations. The rest of these deposits are tied up in loans that have longer terms than demand deposits. This leads to a mismatch of assets and liabilities. Though some banks keep better reserves than others do, no modern bank keeps sufficient reserves in its vaults to handle the majority of their deposits being withdrawn at a single time.

S Corporation

S Corporation refers to the Subchapter S Corporation type of company filing which measures up to certain requirements set by the IRS Internal Revenue Service. This status provides a corporation which possesses a hundred or fewer shareholders all of the advantages of incorporation while also keeping the benefits of only being tax treated like a partnership.

One of the many benefits to this type of incorporation is that it is able to pass all of the company income straight through to the shareholders, thus avoiding the problems of double taxation which are a real issue with shareholders of public companies. There are some particular requirements that must be met to enjoy these advantages. The firm must be domiciled as a domestic corporation. It cannot possess over a hundred shareholders, and it may only count a single class of stock.

Such S Corporations can pass all of their credits, deductions, losses, and any income straight through to the various shareholders. They may then report this loss or income directly via their own personal tax returns. It allows them to pay out their taxes at generally considerably lower individual income tax rates. There are some built in gains on which the S Corporation will pay the taxes at the corporate level, but these are few and far between.

These S Corporations have to be domestically headquartered firms whose shareholders are estates, certain kinds of trusts, and individuals. A corporation, partnership, or non-resident alien can never qualify for this category of shareholder. There are also some financial institutions, domestic international sales firms, and insurance outfits that are not allowed to incorporate as an S Corporation.

There are some significant advantages to establishing an S Corporation. It builds up real creditability with employees, possible customers, investors, and suppliers as it proves the owner is seriously committed to the firm. Employees may also be shareholders in the company, which allows them to enjoy company salaries while also receiving any corporate dividends and distributions which are tax-free as compared to the investment in the company. This is certainly beneficial for morale.

Paying out distributions in the form of dividends or salaries allows the owners to lower the self-employment tax liability at the same time as it creates wage and expense deductions for the firm. Since this S Corporation will not pay any federal taxes at company level, such losses can be utilized to offset other forms of income for the tax returns of the shareholders. It is always helpful to save money on the onerous American corporate income taxes, particularly for new firms. It is another benefit to these companies that the various interests within the corporation can be easily transferred without creating tax liability events and consequences. Complicated accounting rules do not create restrictions nor does the company have to adjust the basis of property either.

Yet there are also a few downsides to establishing a company as an S Corporation. The IRS closely examines any and all distribution payments made to shareholders in the forms of either dividends or salaries to make sure that they are really employees working in the firm. If wages become characterized as dividends, then the company will lose its compensation paid deduction. Should dividends be characterized as wages, then the company will pay a greater amount of employment taxes. It is also easy for mistakes to be made in the areas of notification, consent, election, filing requirements, or stock ownership requirements that lead to the S Corporation being untimely terminated. There is considerable money and time investment in such a corporate structuring as well.

The owner will have to begin by filling in and filing articles of incorporation to the Secretary of State, get a registered agent on board for the company, and pay any relevant fees and costs involved. Owners often have to pay yearly reporting fees and franchise taxes along with ongoing types of fees. These may be inexpensive, but they can still be deducted under the cost of doing business category. Even if the investors possess non-voting shares of stock in this form of corporate structuring, they will still get distribution and dividend rights.

Sovereign Debt

Sovereign Debt refers to the amount of money which the government of a given nation owes its various domestic and foreign creditors. It is a synonym to country debt, national debt, or government debt since the word sovereign simply equates to an independent national government. Another way of thinking of this term is that it is the amount of money which the nation owes its outside creditors. This is a good reason why it is commonly interchanged freely with the phrase public debt. Sovereign debt is similarly the total accumulation of the yearly deficits run by a government. For this reason, it reveals the additional amount of money which governments spend over what they realize in revenues cumulatively.

It is mostly through issuing bonds that governments are able to finance their deficit spending. A good example of this is the United States' Treasury notes and bills. These instruments come with terms ranging from as little as three months to as far out as 30 years. Governments will pay the holders of the notes interest in order to give them a return for loaning the government the money.

As the likelihood of the bond being paid back increases, the interest rate which accompanies it decreases. This leads to a lower cost for carrying sovereign debt for nations which are perceived as trustworthy and financially viable longer term. Besides this financing avenue, governments are able to take out loans from private businesses, commercial banks, and other nations as well as from international individual financiers.

It is not so simple to compare the various sovereign debts of differing nations. Each debt ratings agency has its own emphasis in figuring up debts for sovereigns. As an example, Standard & Poor's' as an investors and business measuring debt ratings agency only considers those debts which the country owes its commercial lenders. It will not consider the money the country owes other countries, the World Bank, or the International Monetary Fund. It also will only include the national debt, and not the amount that provinces, states, cities, and counties in the nation owe.

With the European Union, it measures debt more broadly. It restricts the total amount of debt that its member states are allowed to maintain while being members of the EU. This would include local and provincial governments' debts and any amounts of future social security types of obligations that have been promised to citizens.

The United States itself considers debt still differently. Money which it owes other departments of its own government, called intra-governmental debt, it does not count. It also never includes any debts that the states, counties, and cities have incurred. As the overwhelming amounts of city and state governments are not permitted to run up deficits, it is generally a non-issue.

It is true that expanding the national debt increases growth. The simple explanation is that when governments increase their spending on health care, social security, or for new warships, they are rapidly flushing money through the economy as a whole. This increases economic growth (even if only temporarily) since businesses will then expand in order to keep up with the government spending-driven, rising demand.

This generally leads to new jobs. A multiplier effect becomes created as this increases growth and demand still more, leading to a virtuous cycle. This is why deficit spending is always considered to be a potent stimulant economically since the demand appears instantly while the cost for the debt is delayed into the future.

So long as the amount of sovereign debt is at a reasonable level the lenders to the nation are not worried. The higher growth means that they can be more easily paid back with their owed interest. The leaders in government want to spend constantly for the very simple reason that expanding economies equate to happy voters who will vote them back into office next election. Motivations for cutting spending simply do not exist in democracies.

Sovereign Wealth Funds

Sovereign Wealth Funds are investment pools made up of foreign capital and currency reserves which the government of the country in question owns. The biggest such pools of investment belong to the few countries with a large trade surplus in their economies. This means that Norway, Singapore, the oil producing and exporting nations, and China are the principle sovereign wealth fund nations of the world. They bring in such foreign currencies as U.S. dollars in token of their substantial and valuable exports. Their respective governments then invest these currency reserves in order to obtain the maximum return they possibly can for the benefit of their nations as a whole.

The idea behind these Sovereign Wealth Funds is that the pools of money which the nation owns in foreign reserves can be invested wisely in yield-producing assets so that the economy of the country and its citizens as a group gain advantage. It is the excess central bank reserves in a net exporting nation which make these funds possible, as they accumulate from either trade surpluses or budgetary surpluses. Exports of valuable natural resources create such revenues which can be used for this kind of a fund.

The total wealth which these Sovereign Wealth Funds contain has increased by more than double since September of 2007. It grew rapidly from $3.265 trillion to fully $7 trillion by 2015. This means that the assets held by such funds have grown to be twice as much as the value for all of the global hedge funds combined. It makes these wealth funds substantial enough to move markets dramatically without ever trying to do so. During the financial crisis, they bought major stakes in troubled lenders Morgan Stanley, Citigroup, and Merrill Lynch. They were guilty of causing an asset bubble in real estate in both London and New York City. Their influence only grows apace as they evolve into increasingly sophisticated investors.

One sovereign wealth fund nation differs from the next in the kinds of permissible investments they are allowed to pursue and include. Some of the nations are worried about liquidity issues. This makes them restrict their investments to only those which are the most liquid types of public debt instruments, such as U.S. Treasuries, British Gilts, and German Bunds.

It was the rising and higher than average oil prices from 2007 to 2014 which actively encouraged the expansion of these enormous sovereign wealth funds. In that same time frame, almost 60 percent of all such assets came from the revenues of oil and gas production, sales, and distribution. Even though the 2008 Financial Crisis destroyed trillions of dollars in global asset wealth, it hardly slowed down the inexorable growth of the national wealth funds. They managed to attain the levels of $4 trillion by December of 2009 and $5 trillion by March of 2012.

There are a number of especially oil and natural gas producing nations which have developed and built up their SWF in order to provide diversification to their national income streams. The United Arab Emirates is one such model example. The overwhelming share of its national income and wealth is derived from oil exports. Because of this, the emirate dedicates part of its foreign currency reserves to a sovereign wealth fund which invests its resources in a range of diversified assets that can provide a hedge against oil-related price shocks. This fund has grown to be massive by any measure. By June of 2015, the UAE Abu Dhabi-controlled fund had increased to around $773 billion. This represented ten percent of all SWF assets at the time. In fact, these Middle Eastern oil exporting-based sovereign wealth funds comprise nearly a third of all wealth found in such national funds.

Despite the size of the UAE fund, it is not the largest on earth. The Norway Government Pension Fund proves to be the biggest in the world, with $873 billion by June of 2015. Its income is derived from the nationally owned North Sea Oil drilling operation. The plummet in oil prices and accompanying decline in the Norwegian Kroner may cause the fund to record a loss of $17 billion by the period which ended in first quarter of 2015. It is so very large that if the money from this national fund were equitably distributed to all Norwegian citizens, each of them would receive over a million Kroner in distributions.

Singapore also possesses two of the largest Sovereign Wealth Funds. Their two funds together contain $458 billion in total. They have amassed this enormous fortune because of the impressive investment and savings rates of the businesses and people in this world leading financial and trading center and city state. The Government of Singapore Investment Corporation, presently known as the GIC Private Limited fund, holds $344 billion as of 2015. Both funds are owned and operated by the government of the city state of Singapore.

China also possesses some of the largest such funds in the world. The China Investment Corporation is their largest at $747 billion. Hong Kong's Monetary Authority owns a $442.4 billion fund as of 2015. This is utilized to support and ensure stability for the public finances of Hong Kong in general and the Hang Seng stock exchange in particular.

Stagflation

Stagflation refers to the simultaneous problems of high unemployment, stagnated economic growth, and persistently high inflation. It is an unlikely scenario, as slowing economies typically reduce demand sufficiently in order to keep higher prices in check. When workers lose their jobs, they purchase less. Businesses are then usually forced to reduce their prices in order to convince remaining customers to buy. It is this typically slower growth in market economies that prevents inflation from running away.

Stagflation policies typically lead to hyperinflation. Central banks that expand the country's money supply as the national supply is restricted do so by printing up additional currency. Monetary policies then create additional credit. This increases demand from consumers. It is the simultaneous supply restrictions that keep companies from producing enough to keep up with the rising demand.

Such a scenario happened in Zimbabwe back in 2004. Their government printed up so much currency that it pushed well beyond stagflation and evolved into ruinous hyperinflation. A stagflation in the United States only transpired in the 1970s. At the time the U.S. government expanded its dollars significantly to try to create additional economic growth. While they did this, President Nixon's wage price controls severely limited business-produced supplies.

The name stagflation actually comes from the 1973 to 1975 era recession. In those six consecutive quarters, the U.S. GDP shrank in size. Inflation literally tripled in 1973 alone, jumping from a relatively tame 3.4% to 9.6%. In the time between February of 1974 and April of 1975, inflation stubbornly remained between 10% and 12%.

Experts today look back at the 1973 Arab-led oil embargo as the crisis that triggered first oil price inflation. At this time, OPEC nations drastically cut their oil exports to the United States, forcing prices to quadruple. The inflation from oil spread to many other parts of the economy dependent on oil and gasoline, such as shipping, rail, and trucking.

The mild recession of 1970 was the precursor to the problems. President

Richard Nixon in his bid to be re-elected introduced as series of four fiscal and monetary economic policies that helped to ensure he won. These unfortunately also created the conditions for stagflation a few years later.

Nixon's first mistake was the start of wage and price controls. U.S. businesses were unable to raise their final prices even as import costs were soaring. They could only respond by reducing costs via worker layoffs. That boosted unemployment and further slowed economic growth by lowering demand. Nixon secondly took the U.S. off the gold standard to stop an international run on American gold reserves. This only crushed the value of the dollar and created still higher import prices and yet more inflation.

In order to fight off the inflation, the Federal Reserve had no choice but to continue raising interest rates. These reached their peak of 20% by 1979. Because the Fed did this in an up and down motion, businesses became confused and chose to keep up higher prices.

Though stagflation has not yet reoccurred in the U.S., Americans became worried it might again in 2011. The Fed had begun employing aggressive expansive monetary policies to save the U.S. economy from the grips of the 2008 financial crisis and Great Recession. This caused many to fear that high inflation would return. The economy only grew at low levels form 1% to 2% at this time.

Economists observed stagflation was a viable risk if inflation rose while the economy continued to struggle. Instead, deflation became the serious concern of the day. Massive increases in global liquidity were used to try to fight off this opposite kind of problem.

Subordinated Debt

Subordinated Debt refers to a security or alternatively a loan which has a lower ranking to other debt securities and loans. This pertains to the claims on a corporation's earnings or assets in the event of repayment default. Analysts also call this a subordinated loan or a junior security alternatively. When the borrower defaults on the loan or security in question, those creditors who extended the loan or investment and who are only holding a subordinated security will not receive any compensation until after all of the senior most debt holders have received payment in full. In principal this means that they will get little if anything at all back in the event of an actual default. Subordinated Debt proves to be the precise opposite of unsubordinated debt.

It helps to explain why such Subordinated Debt is always riskier for creditors or investors than comparable unsubordinated debts prove to be. Those firms which borrow on a subordinated debt basis generally turn out to be huge corporations and other businesses. Their size gives them the air of likelihood to repay a less sure loan or security.

As corporations take on more debt, they will typically issue at least two types of bonds as subordinated and unsubordinated debt. Should the huge corporation later default and then file for bankruptcy, it will be the responsibility of the bankruptcy court to decide on the priority of loan repayments according to seniority of the creditors. They will order the firm to pay off its debts using the proceeds from the sale of the corporate assets according to a certain order of repayment. Lower priority repayment debt turns out to be the unlucky Subordinated Debt. Greater priority debt will be the unsubordinated debt.

As the term implies, the liquidated assets through bankruptcy sale will first pay off the unsubordinated debts. If there is any cash remaining after these creditors are made whole first, then the unsubordinated debt holders will receive a portion of their funds back according to the schedule set out by the bankruptcy court. In the unlikely event that enough cash remains, the Subordinated Debt becomes completely repaid. It is more likely that the subordinated holders will get a payment in part or nothing whatsoever.

This explains why Subordinated Debt is so very risky in practice. Potential lenders or investors always have to be aware of the solvency prospects of the company in question as well as its total assets and other more senior debt obligations when they are considering investing in a given bond issue. Yet risky or not, these less senior bond holders still have seniority over all classes of stock holders in the company, even the preferred stock holders. Subordinated Debt bondholders will receive a greater rate of interest than the unsubordinated ones in order to make up for the possible default risk, which is very real.

Like with any debt obligations, such Subordinated Debt will appear on the principal company balance sheet. First the balance sheet will actually list out the firm's current liabilities. Next comes the senior most debt, the unsubordinated issues, which will appear as longer term liabilities. Lastly, the subordinated issues appear as the longer term liabilities ranked according to their payment priority. As firms issue such subordinated bonds and then bring in the cash from the lender or investor, the cash account goes up, or alternatively the PPE property, plant, and equipment account. The firm's accountants simultaneously record a liability for the exact amount.

Tax Sheltered Annuities 403(b)

Tax sheltered annuities are retirement savings programs and vehicles that the Internal Revenue Service allows for under the 403(b) section of their tax code. They were created for the benefit of employees who work for churches, educational institutions, and specific not for profit agencies.

They offer the advantage of permitting employees who are eligible to participate to contribute nearly all of their annual income towards retirement savings and investments in the plan. As an example of the generous limits with these particular plans, employers who choose to contribute can put in as much as $53,000 as of 2016 for any single tax year.

This supplemental program for retirement savings gives participating individuals a variety of ways in which they can choose to contribute funds. They may invest on an after tax basis, as with a Roth plan. They may also choose to contribute using funds that are pre-taxed. They can also opt to use a combination of the two methods. These plans and their participating contributions are entirely voluntary. Employees generally make the majority of these contributions as there is not always an employer match involved with them.

A variety of employees of eligible organizations may participate in these tax sheltered annuity plans. Employees of public schools, universities, and state colleges are allowed to participate. Many employees of churches are also allowed to become involved. Those who work for the school systems run by Indian tribes and their governments may participate. Not for profit 501(c)(3) churches' and organizations' ministers are included in them, as are ministers who are self employed who serve as part of a tax exempt organization. Chaplains are also usually qualified to participate.

There are several good reasons to become involved with these tax sheltered annuity plans. With automatic payroll deductions, it is a simple and relatively painless means of building up extra savings which individuals will require to increase their after retirement income.

They can get involved in a low cost program that is flexible enough to offer a good selection of investment choices. People can make contributions on a Roth after tax basis, a pre tax basis, or a combination of the two. Finally these plans are portable, meaning the owners can take their retirement vehicles with them when they move to a different job or another not for profit organization.

Thanks to these plans and vehicles, account holders are able to invest tax money that would otherwise go to the IRS. They can move money between the various funds in the plans without suffering from capital gains taxes or additional fees. This gives these TSA pre tax accounts a greater return than a taxable account would enjoy if it earned similar returns. For any individuals who use these account vehicles as Roth after tax accounts, all qualified distributions at retirement will be enjoyed completely tax free.

Money from these accounts can not be taken out without penalties until the individual reaches the government mandated minimum retirement age of 59 ½. They must begin taking distributions by the time they turn 70. An exception to the minimum retirement age is for individuals who stop working for their not for profit company before they reach retirement age. In this case, they are allowed to go ahead and begin receiving distributions without having to pay the extra 10% early withdrawal penalty tax. Only any taxes that were due for monies which had been contributed as pre tax dollars would apply in this particular case.

Term Life Insurance

Term life insurance is a form of life insurance. It offers coverage for a preset and limited amount of time that is called the relevant term. The coverage provided is a fixed rate of payment coverage. Once the term expires, the individual's coverage at the rate of the premiums that were charged before are not assured any more.

The client will be forced to drop their term life insurance coverage or to get a different coverage with varying payments and terms. Should the person who is insured die within the term, the death benefit amounts are paid out to the insured person's beneficiary. This term life insurance proves to be the most affordable means of buying a major dollar value of death benefit coverage based on the premium cost charged.

Term life insurance turns out to be the first type of life insurance created, and it stands in contrast to permanent forms of life insurance like universal life, whole life, and variable universal life. These coverage types promise an individual pre set premiums that can not go up for the person's entire life. People do not usually employ term insurance for strategies involving charitable giving or their needs for estate planning. Instead, they are thinking about a need to replace an income if a person passes away on his or her family unexpectedly.

A great number of the permanent life insurance policies also offer the advantage of increasing in value during the person's contract. This cash value can then be withdrawn when certain conditions are met by the policy holder. Generally, withdrawing these cash amounts closes out the policy. Beneficiaries of permanent life insurance products get the insurance policy face value but not the cash value upon the holder's death. Because of this, financial advisers will suggest that people purchase term life insurance for their insurance needs and then invest the money saved over permanent products in retirement accounts that provide tax deferred contributions and investment gains, like 401k's and IRA's.

Like with the majority of insurance policies, term life insurance pays out claims for the insured, assuming that the contract is current and the premiums are paid as due. Assuming that a claim is not filed, the premium is not given back to the policy holder. This makes term life insurance like home owners' insurance policies that pay claims if a home becomes destroyed or damaged as a result of fire, or like car insurance policies that pay drivers if they have a car accident. Premiums are not refunded when the product is no longer required. Because of this, term life insurance like these other products only provides risk protection.

Total Public Debt

Total public debt refers to all of the national debt which the United States owes to its various creditors and other agencies within the government to whom it owes money. This amount grows in years where there are deficits as the government spends more funds than it receives in taxes.

The aggregate national debt shrinks in surplus years as the federal government receives a greater amount of money that it spends. Every year of the Obama administration has been a deficit year that increased the debt. As of the end of Fiscal 2016, the government's total public debt amounted to $19.7 trillion.

The total public debt includes all money owed to Americans and foreigners as well as other agencies within the government. As such, the gross national debt for the country is made up of two components. The first of these is marketable debt which the public and foreign countries hold. This includes instruments such as Treasury bills, bonds, and notes.

Investors regularly buy and sell this debt on the bond markets. Any investor who is not a part of the federal government is considered to be a part of this class of debt. This means T bills held by consumers, companies, banks and financial institutions, the Federal Reserve, and local, state, and foreign governments are all included in this category of debt. As of July 29, 2016 this portion of the debt amounted to $14 trillion.

The other category of the total public debt is the debt which other government accounts hold. This is also called intra-governmental debt. These debts are also comprised of Treasuries, only these can not be bought and sold. This category of debt is like IOUs kept in federal government administered accounts. The country owes it to beneficiaries of programs, as with the Social Security Trust Fund or the Medicare Trust Fund. These government accounts once had surpluses and invested them over time in Treasury securities. The amount which they are owed includes principal plus interest earnings. On July 29, 2016, this category of the total public debt equaled $5.4 trillion.

Together, the two categories which make up the total public debt equaled

$19.4 trillion on the July 29, 2016 date. This represented fully 106% of the prior twelve month national GDP for the United States. Foreigners held $6.2 trillion worth of the debt at this point equivalent to about 45% of the debt which the public held or 32% of the aggregate public debt. The largest foreign holders proved to be China and Japan. As of May 2016, China owned about $1.25 trillion while Japan held $1.15 trillion worth of U.S. government debt.

Usually, the government's debt goes up as and when the government spends monies on entitlements, interest on the debt, and budgetary programs. It similarly decreases as taxes and other monetary receipts accrue. Both categories change throughout the months of the fiscal year.

The government does not in practice issue Treasury debt itself on a day by day basis as it spends money. Instead, this is issued or redeemed according to the government's money management operations. The total amount of money which Treasury is authorized to borrow is restricted by the debt ceiling of the United States. Congress conveniently lifts this every time the ceiling is hit.

Trust

A Trust proves to be a special type of fiduciary arrangement where one participant the trustor grants the other participant the trustee the rights to possess the property title or assets title for the advantages of the beneficiary, often times a third party. When it is utilized in the world of finance, this similarly refers to a kind of closed end investment fund collectively established as a public limited company.

Settlors ultimately establish such trusts. They elect to shift over all or a portion of their possessions (assets) to the trustees of the trust in this action. It is the trustees who ultimately maintain the assets on behalf of the beneficiaries of said trust. The trusts' rules come down to the particular terms that apply to the given trust in question. Some jurisdictions allow for older members of the beneficiaries' class to ascend to the roles of trustee. Some of these jurisdictions actually allow for the grantor to be both a trustee and lifetime beneficiary together at once.

Two different types of trusts exist, the testamentary trust and the living trust. The testamentary trusts are also known as will trusts. These determine the means in which the assets for the individuals will be allocated after they eventually pass away. The document of such a trust comes into play legally following the death of the testator.

On the other hand, living trusts are known as inter vivos or revocable trusts. These written out documents allow for the assets of an individual to be created in the form of a trust. The individual himself or a beneficiary will then enjoy the advantages of and utilization of the resources throughout their remaining lives. Such assets will eventually be transferred to the legal beneficiaries when the individual dies. The trust creator sets a successor trustee who will carry the responsibility of transferring any remaining assets over to the beneficiary in question.

There are a number of different reasons that individuals employ trusts. One of these is to attain a degree of privacy. Wills and their arrangements are often public domain material in many jurisdictions. Trusts can specify the identical conditions which a will may, without the intrusive nature of being public domain documents available for any and all members of the public to read upon demand. This explains why those people who do not wish to have their wills and terms of their estate disposition revealed publically after they are gone will often choose to utilize trusts for their final bequests instead of the will document.

Besides this, trusts are a useful vehicle for planning the payment of taxes. Trusts have different tax arrangements than do standard planning accounts and competing vehicles. The tax consequences for deploying such trusts are typically less negative and expensive than those of other typical means involved in financial planning. This helps to explain why using trusts has become a standard option in the world of efficient tax planning. This is the case not only for individuals but also for corporations.

Finally, trusts find extensive utilization in estate planning procedures. This allows for the assets of deceased people to be passed on to their spouses. The spouses are then able to equally divide up the remaining assets for the benefit of the children who survive the deceased parent. Those children who do not possess the necessary 18 years of age to be considered legal persons (with possession rights) will be required to have trustees to exercise control over all assets in question until they reach the legal age of adulthood.

Trust Account

A trust account refers to a type of account which a trustee holds on the behalf of the beneficiary. The trustee does not have the ability to utilize the funds in any personal capacity, but merely to safe keep, disburse, and invest them for the advantage of the beneficiary.

An example of this type of arrangement is when an attorney holds funds for the benefit of the client. The attorney will not be able to draw upon the funds until after a certain protocol takes place. As the attorney earns the lawyer fees, the client will have to first review and then actually approve the bill from the attorney before he or she can transfer the client funds from this trust account over to the general account of the attorney for settlement of bills.

There are a number of reasons and situations in which individuals may opt to establish a trust account. In some scenarios, people wish to disperse a pre-determined sum of money to their family or other loved ones over a number of years or throughout the remainder of their natural lives.

As a real world example, consider the following. Parents may wish to establish some trust accounts which will provide money to their dependents and/or children every month if and when they die. In such a scenario, it would normally be banking brokers who would manage such accounts. In fact these broker trustees would draw down the account values by the appropriate amount every month or year as they disbursed the either monthly or yearly funds to the beneficiaries for the individuals who originally formed the trust.

There are other common kinds of trusts as well. One of these is a property tax trust account. Such accounts will be established by entrepreneurs of real estate who own a variety of properties. Rather than have to be concerned about the property tax funds and disbursements to the appropriate taxing authorities themselves, they elect to form a trust account which will pay the taxes. This prevents the entrepreneurs from forfeiting their valuable properties because they forgot to pay the property taxes. There are a number of monetary benefits to having such an account. One of these is that estate taxes will not apply to properties contained in such a trust when the owner dies.

There are two different main types of trust accounts. These are revocable and irrevocable trusts. With revocable trusts, these represent deposit accounts whose owners chose to name one or several beneficiaries. These beneficiaries would then obtain the deposits in the account once the holder of the account died. As the name implies, such revocable trusts may be terminated, revoked, or altered on demand whenever the holder of said account wishes. In this particular case, the owner is the trustor, settlor, or grantor of the revocable trust in question. These types of trusts will be established as either informal or formal. While trustees are powerful and have a broad scope of authority over the assets of the beneficiary, they are not omnipotent, but must be bound by the laws and regulations of the jurisdiction which pertain to trust accounts.

Irrevocable trusts on the other hand are similarly deposit accounts but they are not titled in the name of the owner. Instead these become titled as an irrevocable trust for the name. The owner, trustor, settlor, or grantor also makes deposits of money or other valuable assets to the trust account. The principal difference is that the owners forfeit all ability to alter or cancel the trust once they have established it. These types of trusts also become created once an owner of a revocable type of trust dies. They can be set up through a judicial order as well, or even by a statute as appropriate.

Trust Fund

A trust fund proves to be a specific kind of legal entity. It contains property or cash which it holds to benefit another group, individual, or organization. Numerous different kinds of trusts exist. They are governed by almost as many provisions that determine how they work. Every trust fund involves three critical parties. These are the grantor, the beneficiary, and the trustee.

A grantor is the individual responsible for creating the trust fund. Grantors can do this with a variety of assets. They might give stocks, bonds, cash, mutual funds, real estate, private businesses, art, or other items of value to the fund. They also determine the terms by which the trustee will manage the fund.

Beneficiaries are the individuals who receive the benefit of the fund. The grantor sets it up on their behalf. The assets the grantor places inside of the trust fund are not the property of the beneficiary. The trustee oversees them so that the financial gain benefits this individual according to the rules laid out by the grantor at the time he or she establishes it.

Trustees are the managers of these funds. They could be an institution like a the trust department of a bank, an individual, or a number of trusted advisors. Their job is to make sure that the fund fulfills its duties spelled out by the governing law in the trust documents. Trustees typically receive small management fees. The trustee could manage the assets directly if the trust specifies this. In other cases, trustees have to pick out investment advisors who are qualified to manage money.

Trust funds come to life under the rules of the state legislature where the trust originates. Different states offer advantages to certain types of trusts. This depends on what the grantor wants to do by establishing the fund. This is why attorneys help to draft the trust documents to make sure they are correct and most advantageous. As an example, there are states which allow perpetual trusts that can continue forever. Other states make these illegal because they do now want to enfranchise a class of future generations who receive substantial wealth for which they did not work.

Special clauses may be inserted into these trusts. Among the most heavily used is the spendthrift provision. This keeps the beneficiary from accessing the fund assets to pay debts. It also allows parents to ensure that any irresponsible children they have do not find themselves destitute or homeless despite poor decisions they may make.

Trust funds provide a large number of benefits. They receive special protection from creditors. They ensure that family members follow wills after the grantor passes away. These trusts also help estates to avoid as many estate taxes as possible so that wealth can reach a greater number of generations.

Trusts can be an ideal way to ensure the continuity of a business. Sometimes business owners wish to protect a company and their employees after they die. They might still wish for the profits to benefit their heirs. In this case, the trustee would oversee the management of the business while the heirs reaped the financial rewards but could not break up or ruin the company through mismanagement.

Trusts can also be used with life insurance to transfer significant amounts of money which will benefit the heirs. A small trust could purchase a grantor life insurance. When the grantor dies, the insurance money funds the trust. The trustee will then buy investments and give the rents, interest, and dividends to the beneficiaries.

Trustee

Trustee refers to either a firm or an individual who possesses assets or real estate property on behalf of a third party individual, group, or organization. Trustees are often appointed to perform a great range of functions. These could be for charities, bankruptcies, trust funds, pension plans, or retirement plans.

As the name implies, these individuals or firms are entrusted with taking the optimal decisions which are in the primary interest of the beneficiary. Because of this sacred trust, these are often considered to be fiduciary responsibilities for the beneficiary or beneficiaries of the trust in question. This means that they are legally bound and obligated to perform these duties to the very best of their capabilities.

The granting of the prestigious title and responsibilities of trustee comes in the form of a legal title bestowed by a trust. Trusts themselves prove to be legal arrangements which two willingly consenting parties agree to make. Because of the fiduciary nature of the trustee role in any trust which the individual or organization oversees for the beneficiary or beneficiaries, they must lay aside any and all hopes of individual gain or personal agendas so that they can perform the best actions on behalf of the trust.

In other words, the trustee carries the full responsibility for correctly and optimally managing both the financial assets and real estate types of property which the trust itself possesses. There will always be duties particular to the specific details of the trust which the trustees must perform. The differing types of assets will naturally dictate the activities which the trustees must engage in for the beneficiaries' common good.

It helps to consider a real world example to more fully understand the somewhat complex concept. When trusts are made up of a range of real estate properties, the trustees will be responsible for properly overseeing the maintenance and handling of the particular pieces of property. In other cases, a trust might be comprised of different investments such as stocks, mutual funds, and bond holdings in a stock brokerage firm account. The trustees in this case will have to properly oversee and mange as necessary the account or accounts for the beneficiaries.

Trustees also have certain guidelines to which they must adhere in general. Among these common responsibilities which pertain no matter what the particulars of the trust agreement may actually be, the assets must be at all times kept under the direct control of the trustees so that they are securely accounted for each and every day. Trustees also must fully grasp the often unique terms of their particular trust, the responsibilities they are incurring by taking on the role, and the wishes of the applicable beneficiaries. Assets which may be invested must be considered productive so that they will benefit the beneficiary or beneficiaries in the future.

Besides this, the trustees have to both understand and properly interpret the trust arrangement so that they can effectively administer the assets' distribution to the correct parties and/or beneficiaries. This includes the duties of compiling all appropriate records for the trust. Among these there will be tax returns which they must file and pay and statements that they must produce and deliver to the beneficiaries. As such, the trustees will be expected to maintain regular communication with all beneficiaries so that they remain informed of the value of related accounts and any taxes which will become due.

In the end, all trustees have the distinction of being the ultimate decision makers regarding every trust-related matter. They must make such decisions according to the particular provisions contained within their unique trust arrangement and contract. It also means that if beneficiaries have questions regarding a decision which the trustee is preparing to take, that they must first obtain answers for these beneficiaries before they engage in the given decision.

Trustee Savings Bank (TSB)

Trustee Savings Bank refers to a now defunct type of British financial institution. It is also known by its acronym TSB. These banks began as savings deposit institutions for those who had only meager financial means. The shares of these banks were not stock market exchange traded. Rather they were something like the mutually owned building societies of Great Britain. A key difference between the two types of financial institutions was that the depositors of the TSB's did not have any voting rights or ability to direct the organization's managerial or financial goals and direction.

In consequence for a lack of owner-voting rights, the boards of directors for the Trustee Savings Banks were appointed as volunteer basis trustees. This explains where the name for the TSB's came from in the first place. Reverend Henry Duncan from Ruthwell in Dumfriesshire established Britain's very first TSB in Scotland. He set this up to help out his poorest members of the congregation in 1810. The only reason for the organization lay in serving the local community members.

During the inter-war years a hundred years later, the Trustee Savings Bank model demonstrated that it could effectively compete throughout the retail banking model market with the major commercial banks and building societies throughout the nation. At one point by 1919, these types of financial institutions counted an impressive 100 million British pounds in combined deposits and assets. This amount reached 162 million pounds by 1929 and an incredible 292 million pounds at the outbreak of the Second World War in 1939.

Despite enjoying two centuries of success and growth as independent institutions, the Trustee Savings Banks became combined into one financial institution called the TSB Group plc from the years 1970 to 1985. Their stock traded on the famed London Stock Exchange until 1995 when the group merged with the Lloyds Bank to become the enormous conglomeration Lloyds TSB. At that moment, the new Lloyds TSB combined unit represented the largest bank in the United Kingdom by market share. It was second only to HSBC by market capitalization, as HSBC has absorbed Midland Bank in 1992.

The group which now represented the legacy of the Trustee Savings Banks expanded again in 2009 with the acquisition of the HBOS Halifax Bank of Scotland group. Its name changed again to the Lloyds Banking Group at this point. The TSB name was not lost, as the primary retail banking subsidiaries were Lloyds TSB Bank and Lloyds TSB Scotland. Lloyds again resurrected the TSB name and brand when it divested the 632 branches from Scotland, Gloucester, Cheltenham, and some of the Welsh and English Lloyds TSB bank branches into the TSB Bank plc.

The new operation came into being on September of 2013 and underwent an IPO initial public offering during 2014. The rest of the Lloyds Banking Group changed its name back to Lloyds Bank. This spin off happened because the Lloyd's Banking Group had to be bank rescued by Her Majesty's Government. Thanks to the 43.4% government stake in the group as a result of the Global Financial Crisis, European Union state aid rules required that it spin off a portion of the business.

Trustee Savings Bank plc did not continue for long as an independent entity. It began life in 2013 with a national network of 631 bank branches throughout especially Scotland, and also England and Wales. They counted over 4.6 million customers as well as more than 20 billion British pounds worth of customer deposits and loans. The group had its headquarters in Edinburgh, Scotland.

As the reestablished TSB, the group had a listing on the London Stock Exchange and remained a member of the FTSE 250 index of British based companies until it received and accepted a takeover bid from Spanish-based bank Sabadell. Sabadell made its offer for TSB Bank in March of 2015 and completed the acquisition of the last remaining Trustee Savings Bank on July 8, 2015. TSB Bank still operates as a wholly owned subsidiary of Sabadell, so the TSB brand name remains.

Underwriting

Underwriting refers to a means of determining if a consumer is eligible or not for a particular kind of financial product. These products vary depending on the person's or business' requirements. They might include home mortgages, insurance coverage needs, business mortgages, lines of credit, or financing for venture start up projects. The bank or other financial institution undergoing the underwriting evaluation procedure will look into the odds of the business transaction successfully providing them with a profit in exchange for their offer of financial help.

As banks and insurance firms go through the underwriting process, two different things will occur. The first of these is showing an interest in the project that the borrower is proposing for finance. They demonstrate this by offering the financial aid that the customer is requesting. Next, with a bank or institution underwriting an insurance policy, residential or commercial mortgage, or venture, they are looking to make money on their investment one day in the future. They might either gather these profits at one time in the form of a lump sum at a future date or little by little in monthly payments. In these underwriting activities, compensation is expected, which is commonly paid via finance charges or other fees.

Underwriters contemplate more than simply the amount of risk that an applicant demonstrates. They also consider the potential risk that working with the new customer might bring to other customers of their company. In order to ensure that the bank or firm does not suffer too much harm to keep up with commitments made to already existing clients, they have developed underwriting standards.

Insurance companies heavily rely on underwriting in performing their business. Health insurance is one example of this. Health insurance providers seriously look into the past and present health of a person applying. Sometimes their underwriting will show that they need to exclude various pre-existing conditions for a certain amount of time when they insure the person. Other times, underwriting will reveal a medical history that demonstrates too much risk for the company. In this case, a health insurance company will refuse to provide the requested health insurance coverage. Their goal is to not insure individuals who they believe will need significant medical treatment over time, so that they can provide a solid financial backing for their existing clientele.

In business, underwriting is commonly employed to determine if new ventures should be given financing. An example of this might be a company that has created a new technology that it wishes to sell. These underwriters will consider how marketable the product appears, the applicant's marketing plan, the expense of creating and selling the new items, and also the odds of the company realizing profits on every piece that they sell. Sometimes, underwriters of these business ventures will express an interest in having shares of stock in the start up company as a portion of their payment for services. Other times, they will only require a set interest rate for the dollar amount invested.

Universal Basic Income (UBI)

Universal basic income (UBI) is known by a variety of names in different countries and continents. Among the more popular are basic income, citizen's income, unconditional basic income, basic income guarantee, universal demo grant, and UBI. This represents a type of social security welfare program and safety net. In it, all residents or citizens of a nation periodically receive an amount of money which the government or another public institution gives them unconditionally. They receive this on top of and regardless of any other income they earn from work or investment returns. When the money is given out to any persons who live with less than the government-mandated poverty line, it is also known as partial basic income.

This universal basic income and its distribution systems could be financed by the revenues and turnover of publically owned enterprises. These are many times referred to as a citizen's dividend or a social dividend. Such a strategy is a component of a market socialism model, as opposed to market capitalism in which participants' incomes are based on their abilities, hard work, and opportunities. Taxation is another means of paying for such basic income schemes.

It was Thomas Paine's _Agrarian Justice_ published in 1795 where he wrote about capital grants to be provided at the age of majority that began the debates concerning universal basic income within the United States. Up through the year 1986, the phrase which referred to this basic income concept most commonly was "social dividend." After that year, the universal basic income wording gained universal appeal. There are many well-known proponents of the social and economic philosophy. Among them are Ailsa McKay, Philippe Van Parijs, Hillel Steiner, Andre Gorz, Guy Standing, and Peter Vallentyne.

In the United States, this Universal Basic Income has been discussed on a number of different occasions as a serious idea for public policy. The numbers which have been bandied about for Americans amount to approximately $1,000 per month, which would be sent via check to every American. Among the conservatives who espoused the concept and argued for it to be implemented were legendary Nobel prize-winning economist Milton Friedman and former Republican President Richard Nixon.

The base case for this Universal Basic Income has been most effectively argued and written extensively about by Andy Stern, who was once the Service Employees International Union president and who serves as a Columbia University professor since then. He published a book called *Raising the Floor* in which he argued dramatically and effectively for the UBI.

Stern argues that the concept of a basic guaranteed income has become more necessary for two reasons. On the one hand, the wars on poverty programs have not been so effective nationally. On the other, the rapid advance of technology has led to unparalleled job dislocation and disruption for millions of American workers. This program would deliver an effective floor, or social safety net, to every American.

Critics of the plan in the U.S. have asked how the Federal Government would possibly afford to pay for this proposed program. Stern referenced the 126 existing separate government programs which each already distribute money to American citizens. Some of these might be rolled into the Universal Basic Income program. Besides this, additional taxes would have to be introduced in order to make the proposal a reality. Economists have predicted that implementing such a UBI would require around $3 trillion each year in funding.

Despite the fact that this concept has many critics, it is also possibly the only significant ideology in the early twenty-first century which has supporters on both the right and the left sides of the political, economic, and social spectrum.

The Swiss were given a vote on the UBI issue for their own country in the late spring of 2016, and they soundly rejected it. Interestingly though, the same voters answered an exit poll claiming they expected to see this policy implemented in Switzerland within the next 25 years.

Unsecured Debt

Unsecured debt refers to a kind of loan that does not have any underlying asset which is backing it. This means that if the borrower defaults, the lender has no valuable property to seize against the loan's repayment. Such debt has a wide range of examples. These include credit card bills, utility bills, medical bills, and other forms of credit or loans which a financial institution offered without requiring any backing collateral.

These debts are extremely risky for lending institutions. The creditors will be forced to sue in an effort to collect their principal should the borrowers choose to not pay back the full amount of their obligations. It is not only personal bills which can be unsecured. Unsecured debt also includes business debts. Because the risk of default is considerable for the lenders, they usually charge higher rates of interest. This is a proverbial double edged sword. Since the higher rates make the financial burden heavier for the borrower, it can literally push them into default in an ironic self-fulfilling prophecy.

Borrowers have the ability to eliminate their unsecured debt. They can do this in the bankruptcy courts of the United States. The results will be that their debts are either discharged or restructured (in the case of businesses especially). Such an action will have consequences for the borrowers. They will find it harder to get unsecured loans in the future.

There are some important differences between unsecured debt and secured debt. Debt which is secured is backed up using a valuable asset. This could include the vehicle for which the loan is made, or the real estate for which it is provided. The official name for this is collateral. The legal terms in secured loans permit the lender to simply seize its underlying collateral which guarantees the loan if and when the borrower defaults on the payments. Secured debts cover a range of loans. These include title loans that vehicles secure and real estate or home loans that the property secures.

Naturally borrowers have far more to lose personally when they default on such secured loans than on any unsecured debts. This is because the loss of the borrower proves to be the gain of the lender in the respect of the collateral. Since this kind of debt turns out to be significantly less risky on the part of these lenders, they are happy to provide a more competitive interest rate, especially as measured against the rates on unsecured debt.

When a person does not make good on their pledge to repay on an unsecured debt, creditors will go through a number of steps. They first contact the borrower in an effort to recover payment. In the event that the creditor and borrower are unable to come to agreement on a revised repayment schedule, then the creditor moves on to the next steps in the process.

They will do one of several things. They might report the delinquent borrower to one of the big three credit reporting bureaus. They could also sell the delinquent debt on to a debt collection agency which will aggressively pursue debt collection. Finally, depending on the state in which the borrower resides, the creditor could choose to file a lawsuit in an effort to force repayment of the debt.

There are states such as Florida which do not allow legally forced collections of debt. These places protect the consumers from aggressive debt collection methods such as court ordered debt restitution. In other states, when creditors file debt collection law suits in the federal or state courts, the courts can decide to force the borrowers to pay back their unsecured debts utilizing certain available resources or assets.

Corporations also receive loans which are unsecured debt. When such debt issues are being rated by the bond ratings agencies, they will typically provide that issue with a lower rating. One example surrounds the Meta Financial Group which issued unsecured debt in 2016. The KBRA Kroll Bond Rating Agency determined that this senior unsecured debt deserved an only BBB+ bond rating because it was unsecured. This is relatively low, since junk bond ratings are BB. Highest ratings from this company were AAA ratings.

Meta Financial was fortunate to receive the BBB rating though there was no underlying asset backing the debt. This was due to the company's strong quality of assets, healthy liquidity profile, and positive capital ratios on a risk-weighted basis. Had the issue been instead secured debt, then the bond rating agency likely would have delivered an A or better rating.

Usury

Usury has several meanings. The modern day connotation of the word equates to charging high rates of interest on loans which enrich the lender unreasonably. This is considered to be immoral, unethical, and in many countries illegal.

The original meaning of the word revolved around interest charges of any type for a loan. In historical Christendom, as well as in modern day and historic Islamic society and nations, the practice of charging any amount of interest was called usury. Today an individual who engages in collection of usury is either called a usurer or in English speaking societies a loan shark.

The term usury is often times utilized to decry an immoral abuse of gaining at the expense of other human beings' misfortunes and suffering. It is also utilized in legal contexts to describe the legal governing of interest rates. In moral contexts, the word has equated charging interest on any type of loans with wrong doing and sin.

Usury has been addressed in religious texts dating back to the Vedic Texts from India and the Old Testament of the Bible from Israel. Buddhism, Christianity, and Islam also condemn the practice. At various points in history, great empires and states ranging from the ancient Chinese and Greeks to the ancient Roman Republic and early Roman Empire have made it against the law for people to make loans with interest attached. Eventually the later Roman Empire permitted these types of loans that included closely regulated interests rates. Medieval Christendom followed the leading of the Catholic Church by banning the practice of charging interest at any interest rate, or even for charging fees for using or changing money.

Philosophers and public speakers like Charles Eisenstein have made the case that the economic turning point within the British and later American led empires and world came with the legal rights to exact interest on loaned money. This began officially under the 1545 dated act, "An Act Against Usurie" passed by England's infamous King Henry VIII.

Banking in the era of the Roman Republic and Empire proved to be quite different than modern day banking of the Anglo-American world. In the era of the Principate, the majority of banking endeavors occurred at the instigation of private citizens as opposed to enormous banking houses and firms of the early modern age and today. The typical interest rates annually on these loans ranged from four to twelve percent. A higher interest rate documented from these times came in at either 24 percent or 48 percent. Interest was charged on a monthly basis with the most typical rates being multiples of 12.

Banking at the time was the purvey of the side street smaller shopkeepers which were lower middle urban classes. The severe currency shortages of the third century and beyond caused these lending shops to decline. In time, the wealthy took over the practice by becoming moneylenders to the ever increasingly poor peasants who suffered from higher and higher taxes in the failing days of the Roman Empire. They eventually had to sell themselves as serfs to cover their debts. This is why the Medieval Catholic Church decided that usury was in fact unfair exploitation of human misery and the poor of society.

This prohibition against charging interest began in 325 at the First Council of Nicaea that made it illegal for the clergy to practice usury by charging interest of any kind. Subsequent ecumenical church councils extended this ruling to the rest of the Christian population. It culminated with the Lateran III council that made it a cardinal sin to accept interest payments on loans. Such individuals who defied the church teaching and ruling on this matter were not allowed to receive Church sacraments like communion or marriage or to have a Christian Last Rights and burial.

By 1311, Pope Clement V decreed that charging usury was heresy, abolishing any secular laws that permitted it still. Pope Sixtus V articulated this moral repugnance against the practice of charging interest best with his statement that charging such interest was "detestable to God and man, damned the by the sacred canons, and contrary to Christian charity."

Visa

Visa Inc. proves to be an enormous American-based multinational financial services operation which is headquartered in Foster City, California. The corporation is a successor company to a pioneer organization in the world of all-acceptance credit cards. Its electronic fund processing and transference occurs all over the inhabited world, typically through the unmatched Visa-branded debit cards and credit cards.

Interestingly enough, unlike many of its smaller competitors, Visa does not issue any of its own cards, establish fees or interest rates for consumers or businesses, or even offer credit to anyone. Instead they simply deliver payment products which are Visa branded to financial institutions that then brand their own credit cards. This allows the third party financial institutions and banks to provide debit cards, credit cards, pre-paid credit cards, and cash accessing programs to their own various clients.

Nielson Report issued a 2015 report that followed the credit card industry. They determined that Visa Inc.'s worldwide network, called Visa Net, handled an incredible 100 billion transactions that year. These had a volume for the year of $6.8 trillion.

Visa maintains operations on every inhabited continent. It is accepted on all 6 continents and most inhabited islands of the world. Their impressive volumes of transactions process through Visa Net. They have two separate fortress-like secure facilities that process these global operations and transactions. These are the Operations Center East, found near Ashburn, Virginia; and the Operations Center Central, found in the area of Highlands Ranch, Colorado. Each of these two key data centers for world finance is massively fortified to protect against any combination of terrorism, crime, cyber-crime, and natural disasters. They are able to function independently of one another. The Visa Inc. company is even able to run them from externally placed utilities in an emergency.

Both of the centers are capable of running as many as 30,000 different transactions at the same time. They can process a staggering 100 billion computations per second. Naturally cyber-security and fraud are major issues to these two financial data center of the world. To this effect, each processed transaction is run against 500 independent variables. Among these are 100 different fraud-detection protocols. Examples of these are the individual spending patterns of the customer involved, the location of the merchant running the transaction, and the geographical location of the customer in question. Only after the 500 variables and 100 fraud protocols pass muster will any single transaction be accepted. This is an unparalleled level of financial security in the realm of credit and debit cards.

The name Visa came from the mind of corporate founder Dee Hock. Hock felt that the word Visa could be recognized around the globe instantly in a number of different languages throughout numerous countries. He believed it gave a connotation of universal acceptance as well.

Back on October 11th of 2006, the company Visa declared that it would merge businesses and transform into a publically held company via an initial public offering. For the restructuring to work as an IPO, Visa decided to merge several of its sister outfits Visa USA, Visa International, and Visa Canada into a single company. Meanwhile, they spun off Visa of Western Europe into an individual standalone company. Its member banks own this European operation and also gained a minority stake in the newly-issued shares of Visa Inc.

The IPO deal was so massive that over 35 different investment banks worked on the offering, many of them as underwriters of this huge Initial Public Offering. This IPO became the single biggest Initial Public Offering in the history of the United States when it initially raised $17.9 billion at once. When the underwriters of the IPO decided to exercise overallotment options, they bought another 40.6 million shares in total. This increased the aggregate number of IPO shares to an astonishing 447 million. The final proceeds amount from the IPO then amounted to $19.1 billion. Today Visa trades on the prestigious New York Stock Exchange NYSE with the stock symbol of V.

Other Financial Books by Thomas Herold

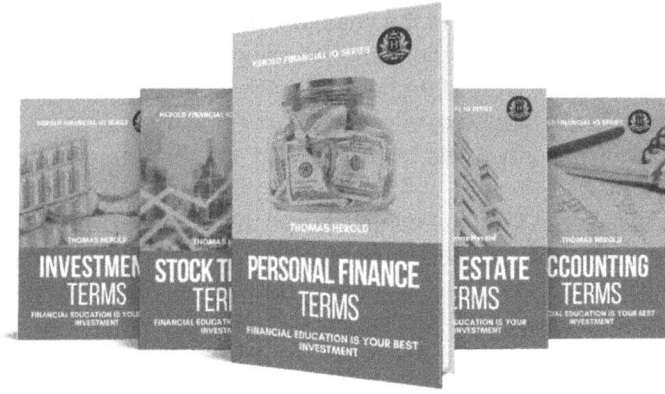

Herold Financial IQ Series
Financial Education Is Your Best Investment

Get Smart with the Financial IQ Series

The Herold Financial IQ series covers all major areas and aspects of the financial world. Starting with Personal Finance, Real Estate and Banking term. Covering Corporate Finance, Investment as well as Economics.

It also includes Retirement, Trading, and Accounting terms. In addition, you'll find Debt, Bankruptcy, Mortgage, Small Business, and Wall Street terminology explained. Not to forget Laws & Regulations as well as important acronyms and abbreviations.

Available on Amazon as Kindle, Paperback and Audio Edition

Go to Amazon.com and search for 'Herold Financial IQ' or copy and paste this link below.

http://bit.ly/herold-financial-iq

High Credit Score Secrets - The Smart Raise And Repair Guide to Excellent Credit

Poor Credit Score Could Cost You Hundreds of Thousands of Dollars
A recent financial statistic revealed that increasing your score from 'fair' to 'good' saves you an average of $86,200* over a lifetime. Imagine what you could do with that extra money?

Improve Your Credit Score in 45-60 Days or Even Less
This practical credit compendium starts off by demonstrating over 50 guaranteed methods of how you can almost immediately boost your credit score. Follow these simple, effective and proven strategies to improve your credit score from as low as 450 points to over 810.

Don't let bad credit hold you back from achieving financial freedom. Your credit score not only influences all your future choices, but it also can save you thousands of dollars.

Available on Amazon as Kindle, Paperback and Audio Edition
Go to Amazon.com and search for 'High Credit Score Secrets' or copy and paste this link below.

http://bit.ly/high-credit

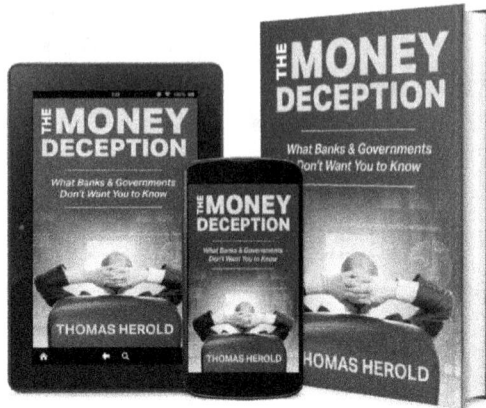

The Money Deception
What Banks & Governments Don't Want You to Know

„It is well enough that people of the nation do not understand our banking and monetary system, for if they did, I believe there would be a revolution before tomorrow morning." - Henry Ford

The Catastrophic Results of Money Manipulation
This money has been souped up by the 1% that now controls 50% of the world's wealth. The fastest and biggest wealth transfer in history is underway. Money evaporates from the middle class, leaving them struggling and without hope for retirement.

What's Happening to Your Money?
Going all the way down into the rabbit hole, it shows you the root of the problem and also lays the foundation for the future. It describes the most likely transition into a new worldwide crypto-based currency, which will become the new basis of our financial system.

Available on Amazon as Kindle, Paperback and Audio Edition
Go to Amazon.com and search for 'Money Deception' or copy and paste this link below.

http://bit.ly/money-deception

Other Books in the Herold Financial IQ Series

99 Financial Terms Every Beginner, Entrepreneur & Business Should Know

Personal Finance Terms

Real Estate Terms

Bank & Banking Terms

Corporate Finance Terms

Investment Terms

Economics Terms

Retirement Terms

Stock Trading Terms

Accounting Terms

Debt & Bankruptcy Terms

Mortgage Terms

Small Business Terms

Wall Street Terms

Laws & Regulations

Financial Acronyms